MRS. FITZHERBERT

MRS. FITZHERBERT

ANITA LESLIE

New York

CHARLES SCRIBNER'S SONS

ERRATUM

The name of the Duchess of Devonshire
referred to in this book should appear
as Georgiana rather than Georgina.

For
SALLY & GERALD
Whose forbears were kind to
Mrs. Fitzherbert

Acknowledgements

The author desires to express her humble thanks to Her Majesty the Queen for a continuation of the privilege accorded by His late Majesty King George VI to Sir Shane Leslie to publish papers preserved at Windsor Castle.

The author also begs to express thanks to the Marquis of Hertford for permission to use letters pertaining to the Seymour family; and to the Duke of Devonshire for permission to publish the statement signed by Georgina, Duchess of Devonshire, and Mrs. Fitzherbert concerning the Prince of Wales' attempted suicide July 8th, 1784; and to Mr. Clifford Musgrave for guidance concerning life in the Royal Pavilion, Brighton.

Above all, the author must acknowledge gratitude to the late Earl of Portarlington, and to her father Sir Shane Leslie, great-grandsons of Minney Seymour, who have laid all the documents they inherited at her disposal. Messrs. Burns, Oates & Washbourne have given leave to use any letters already published.

Biographical Notes

Beauchamp
Viscount (1800–1870). Son of 3rd Marquis of Hertford. (Grandson of 2nd Marquis and the Lady Hertford who turned the Prince against Mrs. Fitzherbert.) Minney's beau, and first cousin once removed. Died unmarried as 4th Marquis.

Creevey
Thomas (1768–1838). Diarist.

Dawson-Damer
Hon. George, Lieutenant-Colonel (1788–1856). M.P. for Tipperary. 3rd son of 1st Earl of Portarlington and Lady Caroline Stuart. Married, 1825, Minney Seymour; three daughters, and one son who became 4th Earl of Portarlington.

Devonshire
Georgina, Duchess of (1757–1806). Famous Whig hostess.

Errington
Henry (–1827). Uncle of Mrs. Fitzherbert, and witness at her marriage to the Prince of Wales.

Fitzclarence
George, Major-General (1794–1842). Created 1st Earl of Munster, 1831. Eldest natural son of William IV and Mrs. Jordan. A.D.C. to Queen Victoria; Governor of Windsor Castle. Married Mary Wyndham, natural daughter of the 1st Earl of Egremont. Committed suicide, 1842.

Fitzherbert
Mrs. (1756–1837), born Maria Smythe, eldest daughter of Walter Smythe of Brambridge and Mary Errington. Married (1) 1775, Edward Weld of Lulworth Castle; (2) 1778, Thomas Fitzherbert of Norbury; (3) 1785, George, Prince of Wales.

9

Fox
Charles James (1749–1806). Whig leader, friend of the Prince of Wales. Married Mrs. Armistead.

Grey
Charles (1764–1845). Eldest son of 1st Earl Grey. A rising young Whig politician in Devonshire House days, loved by the famous Duchess. Prime Minister in the reign of William IV, and carried through Reform Bill, 1832.

Haggerston
Lady (?–1836). Only sister of Mrs. Fitzherbert.

Jerningham
Hon. Edward (1804–1849). 2nd son of 8th Baron Stafford. Lieutenant Dragoon Guards. Married, 1828, Maryanne Smythe.

Jersey
Countess of (1753–1821). Wife of 4th Earl. Protestant mistress of the Prince of Wales.

Hertford
2nd Marquis (1743–1822). Uncle and guardian of Minney Seymour into whose custody she was given after the Seymour case. Married, 1776, Isabella, daughter of 10th and last Viscount Irvine.

Hertford
3rd Marquis (1777–1842). K.G. Only son of 2nd Marquis. Famous roué and art collector—he began the collection of the pictures and furniture now forming the Wallace Collection in Hertford House. Married Maria Fagniani, illegitimate daughter of the Duke of Queensberry.

Pitt
William (the Younger) (1759–1806). Tory Prime Minister at the age of twenty-three. Favoured by George III and regarded as a personal enemy by the Prince of Wales.

Seymour
Minney (1798–1847). Youngest of the seven children of Lord Hugh Seymour and Lady Horatia Waldegrave. Adopted by Mrs. Fitzherbert.

Seymour
Sir George, Admiral. Minney's eldest brother.

Sheridan
Richard Brinsley (1751–1816). Playwright and politician. Friend of the Prince of Wales.

Smythe
Jack. Brother of Mrs. Fitzherbert who died without legitimate children.

Smythe
Maryanne. Adopted daughter of Mrs. Fitzherbert, described by her as a 'niece'. Generally considered a daughter of Jack Smythe.

Smythe
Walter (Wat) (1757–1822). Mrs. Fitzherbert's eldest brother. Married Protestant Louisa Boycott, and had two daughters— Lou and Cou—in whom Mrs. Fitzherbert took a great interest.

.   .   .   .   .

King George III (1738–1820)

Queen Charlotte (1744–1815)
Wife of George III, and mother of fifteen children.

BROTHERS OF GEORGE III

Duke of Gloucester (1743–1805)
Married, 1766, Maria, Dowager Countess Waldegrave, illegitimate daughter of Sir Edward Walpole and Dorothy Clements. Mother of Countess Waldegrave, Countess Euston and Lady Horatia Seymour. The two children of her marriage to the Duke of Gloucester carried royal rank. The daughter died unmarried; the son, known as 'Silly Billy', became 2nd Duke of Gloucester in 1805. Married, 1816, his first cousin, Princess Mary, daughter of George III.

Duke of Cumberland (1745–1790)
Followed the example of his elder brother by marrying in 1771 the Lady Anne Horton. No issue.

SONS OF GEORGE III

Prince of Wales, George (1762–1830)
Eldest son of George III. Married, 1785, Mrs. Fitzherbert. Married, 1795, Princess Caroline of Brunswick. Prince Regent,

1811. Succeeded to the throne, 1820. One daughter, Princess Charlotte, died in childbirth, 1817.

Duke of York, Frederick (1763–1827)
Married the Princess Royal of Prussia; died without issue.

Duke of Clarence [William IV] (1765–1837)
Married Princess Adelaide of Saxe Meiningen, by whom he had no children. His ten illegitimate children by Mrs. Jordan carried the surname of Fitzclarence and the eldest son was created Earl of Munster, Baron Tewkesbury, 1831.

Duke of Kent, Edward (1767–1820)
Married, 1818, Princess Victoria of Saxe-Coburg and had one daughter, born 1819, Princess Victoria; succeeded as Queen, 1837.

Duke of Cumberland, Ernest (1771–1851)
Later King of Hanover.

Duke of Sussex, Augustus Frederick (1773–1843)
Married, 1793, Lady Augusta Murray and had a son, Sir Augustus d'Este, and a daughter, Emma—called Princess Emma in Ireland and Hanover—who married Lord Truro. The marriage of the Duke of Sussex, having been deemed a violation of the Royal Marriage Act, was declared null and void and was dissolved accordingly. The children remained technically of the blood royal in Ireland and Hanover but were illegitimate in England.

Duke of Cambridge, Adolphus (1774–1850)
Married Princess Augusta of Hesse.

Foreword

'Your quest will lead from bonfire to bonfire,' said my father. With these words, he handed over all that he had himself collected in thirty years of browsing through the annotated books and bundles of family letters that pertained to Mrs. Fitzherbert, once the most discussed woman in Europe.

For many years after Mrs. Fitzherbert's death it had been considered unsafe to publish any documents or reminiscences which might reveal the fact of her marriage to the Prince of Wales. When she died in 1837 her few remaining papers had been consigned to Coutts Bank under the seals of the Duke of Wellington, Lord Albemarle and Lord Stourton. A long discreet silence ensued.

Then in 1856 a volume appeared entitled *Memoirs of Mrs. Fitzherbert with an account of her marriage to H.R.H. the Prince of Wales.* It was written by the Hon. Charles Langdale, nephew of Lord Stourton, to whom she had dictated a narrative of her life. Lord Stourton had himself never published Mrs. Fitzherbert's story because his co-trustee, the Duke of Wellington, refused him permission to see the papers deposited in Coutts Bank. Langdale also failed to obtain access to these papers, but he felt compelled to write an outraged defence against Lord Holland when that gentleman published memoirs insinuating that Mrs. Fitzherbert had never taken the Prince's marriage vows seriously. Only 500 copies of Langdale's book were printed, but they contained many stories in Mrs. Fitzherbert's own words.

During the remainder of the century the lady's honour was rigorously upheld. Various contestants argued the legality of her marriage, but none could dispute its religious validity or question the Pope's decision. Where Mrs. Fitzherbert's conscience was concerned, Rome had the final word. According to all the Churches of Christendom she was truly married to the King. And amidst the complexities and changeabilities of his own tortuous brain George always remained constant to this notion. Before, during, and after his marriage to Princess Caroline he firmly believed himself to be the husband of Maria Fitzherbert, miserably forced to commit bigamy in order to clear his debts and produce an heir to the throne.

There may have been children of his marriage to Mrs. Fitzherbert. How well that secret has been kept, how equivocably she answered. Although there could not have been any real danger of a Catholic pretender to England the topic of possible children remained a dangerous one even after Mrs. Fitzherbert's death. Minney Seymour preserved the miniatures of two children *sans nom* who, she whispered, were Mrs. Fitzherbert's. A boy and a girl whose fate cannot definitely be proved. Many papers containing circumstantial evidence were, alas, destroyed by my great-grandmother, Lady Constance Leslie, in a fit of devotion to Queen Victoria who hated the Fitzherbert story, and called her papers, like the Duke of Buccleuch's concerning the marriage of the mother of the Duke of Monmouth, those 'which no loyal subject should wish to possess'.

It seems very possible that Marianne Smythe, the quietly adopted niece of Mrs. Fitzherbert, was her own daughter, but this girl could also have been Jack Smythe's illegitimate daughter (his wife was barren). As for the nebulous son—a yet more dangerous element—what happened to him? Poor little fellow, he must have been hustled out of the way when very tiny. There are few clues—just a miniature and a few whispers echoing on in two English families, while the Jesuits of Georgetown in America keep a picture and a legend.

For seventy years a hush hung over the name of Mrs. Fitzherbert. Not till 1905 did an actual biography dare to appear. This work by W. M. Wilkins is dedicated thus: 'To Lady Constance Leslie, who was the youngest daughter of Mrs. Fitzherbert's adopted daughter Minney Seymour.' Lady Constance's personal copy of this book, filled with marginal notes and comments, give an idea of the affection which Mrs. Fitzherbert evoked in all around her. My great-grandmother was inclined to use books as scrap albums. Wilkins' two volumes, as well as Langdale's heated vindication, are stuffed with Mrs. Fitzherbert's calling cards (the daughter's names added in her own handwriting), curiously worded invitations 'to cards' at the Pavilion and informal letters from the Duke of York. Her own beautifully penned letters are mostly addressed to 'Dearest Minney'. The touch of the old notepaper brings her curiously near, sometimes it is as if my fingers trailing over her ardent slanting writing released her own wistfulness.

Minney Seymour left the Fitzherbert heirlooms divided between her son, Lord Portarlington, and her younger daughters Blanche, and Constance. Constance, my great-grandmother, lived until I was twelve years old. She was a witty old lady and our childish memories were filled with stories of her own Victorian youth that melted back into the Regency days. She could recollect the very words used by her mother to describe a childhood spent in Mrs. Fitzherbert's house in Brighton. To no one did the Prince remain as consistently kind as to this little girl—who he insisted was his own daughter. He never tired of Minney's games. Mrs. Fitzherbert would sit smiling while the child scrambled on the royal knee and evoked a display of that charm which the Prince found as easy to switch on as off. Long after his final break with Mrs. Fitzherbert the Regent continued to write Minney affectionate letters. These fatherly attentions contrasted strangely with his disregard of the Princess Charlotte.

Minney's portrait by Lawrence looks down at me as I write. Her clock given her by George Fitzclarence[1] stands upon the mantelpiece, its wreath of enamel forget-me-nots held by a serpent symbolizing eternity, its face engraved with her name and birthday; a clock carefully devised to be sent her after he had died. Minney's lovely jewellery, given to Mrs. Fitzherbert by the Prince, lies locked below stairs. Minney's precious collection of her adopted mother's letters lie in the attic and she handed the legend of Mrs. Fitzherbert intact to her own children so they might pass it on. Some of us cared enough occasionally to pull out the letters.

[1] Eldest son of William IV by Mrs. Jordan.

It is difficult to write about Mrs. Fitzherbert without becoming her champion. Because she never spoke up in her lifetime she rouses an emotional desire to defend her. Even now, a 150 years after when the insults have lost their sting, one's pen seems to rise of its own volition in indignation. The blemishment of her reputation meant so much to her, and yet she stood her ground and kept her promise never to show those all-important marriage lines until her husband was dead. To appreciate this fortitude one must remember that in those days a woman's reputation meant considerably more than it does now in any strata of society. One of Nelson's captains, intent on defending a brother officer, emphasized his point by stating that an officer's honour 'like that of a woman might be considered ruined if even queried'. Those were the standards to which Mrs. Fitzherbert had been brought up. Nowadays the public shows more interest in high-coloured romance than in marital technicalities. The importance of being an honest woman diminishes in a world where ladies can make and unmake their names with frequency in the divorce courts.

The marriage of the Prince of Wales to Mrs. Fitzherbert has been published in black and white, but the question of children has never been elucidated. My great-grandmother was, alas, a true Victorian; she ransacked her husband's letter-chests, censoring and mutilating with nail scissors improper eighteenth-century Leslie correspondence concerning their eternal bastards, and then, far worse, she got busy on the Fitzherbert papers. Although she carefully docketed and annotated her mother's records of what was an illegal but undoubtedly virtuous alliance she destroyed all reference to Mrs. Fitzherbert's issue. Lady Constance possessed, apart from her mother's papers, a mysterious locked box inscribed 'Duke of Cornwall' (the Prince's Duchy being such). This box had always been in Tilney Street, but it escaped the Duke of Wellington's raid. It contained veiled references to children of the marriage though without information as to their fate. My great-grandmother enjoyed snipping out whatever might have displeased her idol, the 'poor dear Queen'. The Duke of Cornwall's box still resides in a cupboard, and inside it lie a mass of Maria Fitzherbert's letters and papers—all tampered with. Scissors have cut out what one most wishes to know.

In our Irish home where Minney Seymour's daughter spent

16

many a wet afternoon sorting out her inherited papers and trinkets, new generations from the nursery floor were occasionally shown the family treasures. These included the Prince's gifts to Mrs. Fitzherbert, her diamond tiara, ruby cross and the jewelled 'G' for her locket. The inevitable day came when a child after staring at Cosway's picture of Mrs. F. and observing the plump bosom and cheerful, unvamplike countenance framed by a Medusa's wig of curls in turn surmounted by what appears to be a head-dress of cabbage leaves, asked in a puzzled treble voice, 'But *why* did the King love her so?'

Tantalizing question. Why? Old Lady Constance answered: 'When Mrs. Fitzherbert was young, people talked of her as a White Rose. And even when she was old my mother said that her cheeks felt as smooth as petals when you kissed her.'

Suddenly we saw her as she must have been. The loving, shining eyes, the pale clear skin, the inability to dissimulate, the true innocence masking courage and the physical freshness that lasted all her years. Mr. Wilkins describes her with Victorian fervour: 'Her hair was of a pale gold, her eyes hazel-brown, her complexion of the wild rose and hawthorne.' But such might be the colouring of any bore. Maria could not have been the sole woman in England with the gleam of health.

The description handed on by my great-grandmother gives a more exact clue to her lure. A White Rose. Alone among many eager blossoms the White Rose proved inaccessible. And this flower possesses qualities that elude the painter's brush.

There seems to have been no one else like her. George had all England to hunt in, but only Maria cut his heart to the quick. For this one woman, Catholic and virtuous and forbidden, he writhed in torment. Mrs. Fitzherbert married him when they feared for his sanity if she would not give way. Indeed he had to threaten for over a year to open his veins before she consented!

After Mr. Wilkins' book published the much discussed papers which Mrs. Fitzherbert had left in Coutts Bank marked 'Not to be opened for fifty years', little more could be said about the lady until H.M. King George VI, with royal chivalry, allowed my father access to the secret archives at Windsor where he was shown the wedding licence, and allowed to transcribe the immense thirty-five-page proposal letter as well as the Will which the Prince wrote cutting off the Princess of Wales with a shilling and bequeathing his entire possessions to Mrs. Fitzherbert.

The fear of possible long-lost, illegal but not illegitimate, Catholic descendants of Mrs. Fitzherbert wrecking any sort of apple-cart is now as dead as the terror of a Jacobite revival. But for a century it had to be considered.

The chief sources of any life of Mrs. Fitzherbert must always be:

The Fitzherbert Papers at Windsor Castle (Secret Archives).

The Portarlington Papers (left by Minney Seymour to her son the 4th Earl of Portarlington).

The Glaslough Papers (left by Minney Seymour to her youngest daughter Lady Constance Leslie).

The Ragley Papers (Mrs. Fitzherbert's letters to Sir George Seymour her executor and the Prince's correspondence concerning Minney Seymour's adoption).

The Fitzclarence Papers belonging to the present Earl of Munster.

The Chatsworth Papers belonging to the present Duke of Devonshire. (These contain the papers signed by Mrs. Fitzherbert and Georgina, Duchess of Devonshire, describing the mock ceremony of marriage which took place at Carlton House on July 8th, 1784).

There are in all these collections constant references to letters that have been destroyed. The two most interesting correspondences were burnt in her lifetime. After the death of George IV she gave all her royal husband's letters to his executor, the Duke of Wellington, in return for her own. Alas, the Duke immediately set to burning them up in her house in Tilney Street. This was the occasion on which 'after several hours burning' the Duke said to Lord Albemarle, 'I think my Lord we had better hold our hand for a while or we shall set the old woman's chimney on fire.'

'Oh dear, oh dear,' sighed Creevey when he heard, 'that I could not have seen them. They began in 1785 and lasted to 1806, one and twenty years.'

We sigh with him.

An equally fascinating horde went to the flames when the

letters which Mrs. Fitzherbert had written to the Duke of York during the years 1812–27 were returned to her. These she herself spent two years perusing and burning. Then, to further torment posterity, she herself stated these letters gave 'the best private and public history of the country from the close of the American War down to the death of the Duke'.

It was unkind of Mrs. Fitzherbert to leave us quite so little, for to Mrs. Creevey she once confided that she supposed her Life *would* one day be written, but that it would be full of lies, and, as she would be dead, it would not matter.

Here I have chased the truth for her, using fragments that were considered too unimportant to burn or which chance lodged in the safety of royal archives or the tin boxes of country-house attics, and scraping up my own memories of what old Lady Constance related throughout many years in our Irish home.

One cannot but admire Maria Fitzherbert. She suffered much in her time and her tears were so secret. I hope this book reveals, without being 'full of lies', that character which has been distilled for my family by the anecdotes and stories dropped down through a hundred years by Minney Seymour's children—the character of a great lady, uncompromising and of superb integrity, who bore with loyalty the tribulations of a love quite out of the ordinary.

ANITA LESLIE

Castle Leslie
Glaslough

One

SEVERAL versions have appeared concerning Mrs. Fitzherbert's first meeting with the Prince of Wales, for it is at this juncture that any Life of her should open. For years my father searched the Royal Archives and the papers of Chatsworth, Ragley Hall and Castle Leslie without finding a clue. Last year, looking through the chests in his own Irish home, he came on a letter written by his great-grandfather, George Dawson-Damer, who had the sense to record the words of a sweet old lady who sat—all passion spent, the embers fading—in her house in Tilney Street, Park Lane.

'November 14, 1836. Mrs. Fitzherbert told us this evening that the first time she ever saw the Prince was when she was driving with her husband Mr. Fitzherbert. They were in Park Lane when he turned round and said "Look. There is the Prince." The second time was a few days subsequently when she was going with her husband to a Breakfast given by Mrs. Townley at Corney House, Chiswick. As they were turning down the Lane she perceived that the Prince had followed her, and had stopped to look at her.'

The impetuous behaviour of the heir to the throne caused no sensation, for at eighteen he ran after all the beauties, and was having a passionate affair with Mrs. Robinson the actress. Brought up to pray much, and to regard vanity as the harbinger of vexation, Mrs. Fitzherbert laughed off this incident with her husband. Yet perhaps she could not resist enjoying a reminder that at twenty-four years of age she had lost nothing of her looks.

The next meeting occurred on a spring night four years later in very different circumstances. Maria was now a widow in weeds, and in her own words 'unwilling to go out and be seen'. Henry Errington, her uncle, and Lord Sefton, her half-uncle, had urged her to go to the Opera. According to my great-great-grandfather's 1836 note she had agreed

> 'on Lord Sefton consenting to her going in a Cap and Bonnet and a veil. She left the Opera leaning on Henry Errington's arm (the grandfather of the present one) and when at the door, with her veil down waiting for her carriage, the Prince came up to him and said, "Who the Devil is that pretty girl you have on your arm, Henry?" the latter told the prince who she was and then introduced him to Mrs. Fitzherbert.'

As the young widow curtsied before him, the Prince's violent feelings transformed his handsome petulant face. He was un-accustomed to hide emotions before society. Wildly he stared through her veil, trying to make out the delineations of that curiously enchanting face. Their eyes met for the first time—untroubled topaz and fevered grey. Then her carriage drew up and, glad to break the tension, she stepped into it and drove away.

That night, in her house in Park Street, Mrs. Fitzherbert must have tried to quell her own fluster. Alone in her bedroom, when her maid had retired, she surely took a candle to the mirror and stared into it with curiosity, wondering what had so aroused the Prince. She was not actually beautiful although she gave the impression of great beauty. She much disliked the portrait that Gainsborough had painted when she had been married to Mr. Weld. It showed too plainly the strong aquiline nose and deter-mined chin inherited from her father. It could not show the extraordinary freshness, the sweetness which had caused many gentlemen to want to marry her. What could she see in the mirror but hazel eyes and golden hair and an English country complexion?

Maria Smythe belonged to ancient rural England. In its green pastures and in its old unreformed religion she had been gently reared. The daughter of Walter Smythe, second son of Sir John Smythe, Baronet, she had been born in 1756 into Catholic Royalist

22

stock. The Smythes, having sacrificed all for the house of Stuart, received a Baronetcy from Charles II in 1660. For the next hundred years they lived in retirement on their country estates suffering the restrictions imposed on all Roman Catholics, unable to stand for Parliament or to take any part in the government of their country, attending Mass secretly and hardly ever meeting Protestant neighbours.

Maria had been the eldest of six children brought up in Hampshire. The 'Act for the further prevention of the growth of Popery' remained unrepealed throughout her childhood. She saw the doors of the manor chapel locked before Mass, and well she knew her religion must be practised by stealth. Roman Catholics lived 'virtually outlaws in their own country, doomed to a life of secrecy and retirement'. They married among themselves and grew steadily fewer in number on account of the disadvantages attendant on those who clung to the old Faith.

For a few years Maria attended an Ursuline Convent in Paris where many English Catholic girls polished their education. She loved the nuns, and knew happiness within the quiet walls. Once her parents took her out to watch Louis XV dine in public. Seeing the King pull a piece of chicken to pieces with his fingers she burst into laughter. The King turned round and 'sent her a dish of sugar plums by one of his courtiers'.

At sixteen, talking perfect French and with a veneer of Latin elegance, she returned to the country life of Bramwell. In the small secluded world of Catholic gentry she was much talked of and suitors began to call. As her features were always a little heavy for a girl, it must have been her colouring and her animation which lured so many gentlemen to seek her hand. She never seemed to be without a suitor. How can we judge her charm except by the effect it had on the opposite sex?

At the age of eighteen Maria Smythe married a rich childless widower. Mr. Edward Weld of Lulworth Castle, Dorset, was forty-four, head of an aristocratic Catholic family and a great landowner. Although her senior by twenty-six years he made Maria very happy. A contemporary described her at the time (*Journal of Mary Frampton*): 'She was then very beautiful. She dined at Moreton on the day when she was nineteen—perfectly unaffected and unassuming in manner.'

23

To Maria's distress Mr. Weld died after a fall from a horse before they had been married a year. Lulworth Castle and the family fortune then passed to his brother, and Maria moved away to live modestly on a widow's stipend.

Meanwhile at home her four younger brothers began to be a worry to her parents. These boys had grown up in the country, handsome, strong, wild and possessed of an energy for which there was no outlet. Because they were Catholic the Penal Laws excluded them from the Bar, the Army and the Navy as well as from all Government appointments of trust. Not being rich, the Smythes wondered what to do with these exuberant colts, barred from proving their worth in their own land. One of them eventually obtained a commission in the Austrian Army. The others kicked their heels and became subject to challenges and duels.

Three years after Mr. Weld's death Maria married again. She chose the same type as before. Thomas Fitzherbert of Swynnerton in Staffordshire, ten years her senior, was another aged, but wealthy, Catholic squire. His family belonged to the untitled nobility of England which had lived on their estates for seven centuries. He offered the same gracious life she had known when chatelaine of Lulworth Castle, but he enjoyed a wider circle of acquaintances than shy Mr. Weld. He even possessed a few Protestant friends. At Swynnerton, their magnificent country house built in a wooded park, Mr. and Mrs. Thomas Fitzherbert entertained grandly, yet a neighbour, Miss Jervis, daughter of the great Admiral Lord St. Vincent, wrote: 'Mrs. Fitzherbert used to like to come to Meaford, as it was more gay than Swynnerton.' They could sit in the drawing-room at Meaford watching the coaches cross the ford for London, and the ruthless Admiral, who was creating those magnificent fleets which Nelson would some-day handle, became a friend of the young married woman.

Thomas Fitzherbert, twenty-fifth Lord of the Manor—which had been granted to his family in 1125—was among the first Catholic gentlemen to shelve the bitter memories of the Stuart rising of 1745 and openly avow loyalty to England's Hanoverian Kings. In his London house in Park Street Mr. Fitzherbert headed a new generation of Roman Catholics who were ready to take heart at the kindness shown them by George III. Soon the

Fitzherbert town house formed a centre for intelligent discussion which led to pressure being exerted on Parliament until the Roman Catholic Relief Act of 1778 repealed the most obnoxious laws. Maria blossomed forth in this new company, and much enjoyed driving out through the lanes and meadows that lay just beyond Park Street. Her husband gave her contentment, security and companionship. They worried about nothing but growing too fat:

'Mr. Thomas Fitzherbert was a tall and powerful man with a tendency to corpulancy, which he endeavoured to counteract by great abstemiousness in diet and by the most astonishing efforts of bodily activity and violent exercise to which he unfortunately fell a victim. After one of his customary amazing pedestrian feats he was affected with pulmonary disease which became chronic.'

With distress Maria heard her husband coughing his lungs away. She closed Swynnerton and drove off with him to try a winter in the south of France. From the coach window Thomas turned for a last look at his ancestral home. The huge classical house stood high above the park trees—how nearly they had known happiness there.

Maria cosseted her husband across France and took a villa at Nice, but his health seemed broken and in the spring, just as the mimosa began to gild their garden, he died.

For the second time in her twenty-four years Maria found herself a childless widow. Mr. Fitzherbert's brother inherited Swynnerton but Maria received a jointure of £1,000 a year and the house in Park Street with all its furniture and appointments and the horses and carriages; 'also the ponies or Galloways she usually drives in the phaeton'.

Mrs. Fitzherbert did not care to return immediately to England. She remained in Nice for nearly a year, and then visited friends in Paris where she interested herself in English Catholic destitutes.

In 1781 she returned to spend the summer at Brighton. Friends urged her to go back to her London house which lay pleasantly in a garden at the end of Park Street. The young widow had a gregarious nature, but she did not venture back to the capital until 1784 when Lord Sefton (her father's Protestant half-brother and a well-known Whig) begged her to come out with him and Lady Sefton into society which at that time consisted of fifty great families.

At length Maria acquiesed. She had previously enjoyed three London seasons spent with her husband, and even a widow of twenty-seven need not regard life as completely over. In March 1784 the *Morning Herald* announced: 'Mrs. Fitzherbert is arrived in London for the season.'

Lord Sefton begged her to spend as much time as she could in his household, and Lady Sefton introduced her to the important figures in Whig society. Maria revealed a wit that was not unkind and a vivacity that did not tire. Within a fortnight most of the great houses lay open to her. She began to entertain quietly but thought it would be hardly respectful to Thomas's memory to go out much. During the month of May the extraordinary turbulent elections entertained her. Mr. Fox was backed by his friend, the Prince of Wales, who won notoriety by making a personal incursion into the hustings, while the famous sisters, the Duchess of Devonshire and Lady Bessborough, canvassed from their phaetons. For those who liked good talk—and Mrs. Fitzherbert did—there were plenty of happenings to talk about.

Gradually she started to visit private houses with the Seftons and to enjoy meeting the famous. But she had not wanted to go to the Opera. Uncle Sefton had pressed her unduly. How could she have guessed that the evening would terminate as it did?

The Prince's sudden infatuation could easily make her look ridiculous. Perhaps she would be forced to terminate her London season just when she had begun to enjoy herself. Really it was too bad.

And those burning grey eyes! A more frivolous woman might have taken their expression as a compliment, but Maria felt only disconcerted. Not so had Mr. Fitzherbert looked when he came to woo. Nor Mr. Weld before him.

Late on that fateful night after the Opera she turned from the mirror which told so little, only that her hair was gold and her throat white, and taking up the candle walked towards her curtained bed where hung a crucifix.

The mirror must be forgotten. She knew well it was more important to be good than to be beautiful. If she had succumbed to a moment's foolish vanity she asked forgiveness. Retribution must fall uncommon quick, but to her crucifix she would always turn in trouble. Thinking over the prayers the nuns had taught her, she took her rosary of large heavy beads and knelt by her bedside as she had each night since she was a little girl.

Two

EW Princes of Wales have spoken of a happy childhood.
This George, born in 1762, was certainly not among them.
Brought up with singular strictness, he took an early aversion
to a father who offered neither understanding nor sympathy.
George III, obsessed by a sense of duty, had married the ugliest
of all German princesses—instead of his infatuation, the Duke of
Richmond's lovely daughter—and, more rigorous still, he had
remained faithful to her. The boys were all educated according to
his own precepts. While their sole recreation consisted of working
as gardeners under the stern royal eye, a heavy classical curriculum,
kept them eight hours a day at their books. The princesses later
described their brothers being held by the arms and flogged
unmercifully for faults in Latin grammar. The Duke of Sussex
was even flogged for developing asthma attacks!

In such an atmosphere the heir to the throne fretted petu-
lantly, and early turned towards those glittering consolers who
are always waiting for a prince to grow up. The Duchess of
Devonshire recorded in 1782:

'As he only went out in secret, or with the King and
Queen, he form'd very few connections with any other
woman than women of the town. He rode constantly in the
Park of a morning, where from the ladies in their carriages
and on horseback he was considerably ogled. He appear'd
sometimes at the opera and the play where the same *manège*
was continued from the boxes, and where much speculation
was occasioned by the bent of his R.H.'s *lorgnette*.'

Within three years of ignominous whippings in front of his sisters, the Prince of Wales was slinking out at night to meet girls in the bushes around Kew Palace. The first scandal concerning one of his mother's pretty Maids of Honour, Harriet Vernon, has been handed to us by Huish, George's 1831 biographer, in language impossible to emulate.

'On entering on that part of the life of the Prince of Wales, when the passions were first excited, and he may be said to have entered the vestibule of the Temple of Venus, we are fully aware that we are treading on most delicate ground, and that the task is one of difficulty to view from the actual truth, and on the other, not to overstep the bounds prescribed by modesty and decorum. . . .'

On the night when the Prince, disguised in Lord Malden's great coat, first met Harriet, the Duke of York hurried out with the information that the King requested him for a game of chess, 'never perhaps did the Prince of Wales regret his knowledge of the game as at this moment; one second more, and as sweet a rosebud as ever bloomed on its parent stem would have lain defoliaged at his feet; but the barrier had been broken down, although the citadel was not yet gained'. The citadel was topply, however, and soon poor Harriet had sacrificed to him 'all that was most dear to her on earth'. When 'he had enjoyed the kernel the shell was not worth the keeping'.

The biographer then 'throws a veil'; but he hands us an interview between the Queen and her unsuspecting son on the following day that rings very true. Her Majesty started a lengthy discussion on the monotony of the life of a Maid of Honour. 'I don't know,' murmured the Prince, 'she goes to plays, concerts, etc., gratis; she has physicians without fees.' The Queen snapped, 'But you forgot to add that she also flirts with young Princes and goes to meet them by moonlight; and is that also *gratis*?'

The Prince was completely dumbfounded. 'His Majesty requires your presence in the library,' said the Queen. The Prince took the hint and retired.

Needless to add that after a few such hints the Prince of Wales grew anxious for an establishment of his own.

'With every fresh amour his appetite appeared to be sharpened
—like the bee he roamed from flower to flower, sipped the honey
but never visited that flower again,' sighs the eighteen-thirtyish
Mr. Huish. But the seventeen-hundreds took debauchery lightly.
A contemporary exclaims, 'By what analogy was it to be
expected that the generous blood of the heir-apparent was to be
ice-bound, while that of every noble youth in the kingdom might
run riot and flow without reproach.'

Mr. Huish concedes that 'a great number of the bloom-
ing women, who by their beauty adorned the court of his
mother, required little or no persuasion to concede to his
wishes'.

The Prince was spoiled on the one hand, scolded on the other.
He maddened his father and enchanted his mistresses. His tutor,
Archbishop Hurd, when asked for an opinion on the fifteen-year-
old boy, had replied: 'I can hardly tell. He will be either the most
polished gentleman or the most accomplished blackguard in
Europe. Possibly both.' Although carefully training himself for
this double rôle the Prince kept his amours as quiet as possible.
According to Mr. Huish, even if the Prince had been 'sipping the
sweets from many an opening flower—yet it was only some of the
air spirits who hovered about the dark recesses of the gardens of
Kew, or inhabited the sylvan haunts of Richmond's groves, who
could tell of how the lovely rosebuds fell defoliaged, to wither
and die neglected'.

The Prince of Wales was eighteen when he abandoned the
hedges for the footlights and conducted his celebrated love affair
with the actress Mrs. Robinson. All England watched the
romance of Florizel and Perdita. Beautiful Mrs. Robinson
described ardently 'the irresistible sweetness of his smile, the
tenderness of his melodious yet manly voice, the polish and
fascinating ingeniousness of his manners'. But a stern German
monarch demands other traits from an eldest son. 'Irresistible
sweetness and fascinating ingeniousness' cut no ice with King
George III.

His Majesty grew puzzled and angry when he saw the results
of that careful education he had personally superintended.
Instead of showing a noble docility his two elder sons were
already in league against him. They both drank, they both

wenched, they both deceived him. Never, in fact, were there worse advertisements for the system he had devised of intensive study, merciless beatings and dull wholesome recreation.

Poor George III; he meant well and on the whole did so badly. He lost the American colonies and reared a brood of sons guaranteed to plague him and scandalize the nation. Now, just because His Majesty favoured the Tories, his heir clung to the Whigs, and the King's most hated personal enemy—brilliant Charles James Fox—became the Prince of Wales's dearest friend.

Fox, fearless instigator of the new concept that Kings should reign but not actually rule, knew how to enrage the father while delighting the son. He could twist the Prince round his little finger, make him laugh, open his mind, teach him to think liberally and live licentiously in the same lesson.

Roistering, high-gambling, hard-drinking sporting Whigs made great playmates for an over-spanked Prince. Gambling and drinking proved as amusing as seducing maids of honour. Fox knew just how to play his cards. He successfully set his own mistress, Mrs. Armistead, to lure the Prince away from Mrs. Robinson. At twenty His Royal Highness was securely pinioned; physically by Fox's mistress and mentally by Fox's wit.

When the Prince came of age in August 1783, good friend Fox, intent on embarrassing the old King to the utmost, pleaded that George III should give his heir £100,000 a year from the Civil List. The King accused his Ministers of being ready 'to sacrifice the public interests to the wishes of an ill-advised young man'. The Ministers threatened to resign. Eventually His Majesty granted an allowance of £50,000 out of the Civil List, and Parliament granted £30,000 to pay off the Prince's debts and a like sum for a separate establishment.

Luckily the Prince possessed taste to equal his extravagance. The improvement of Carlton House, that lovely little private palace, gave him much joy, but he could not resist the meaner pleasure of further enraging his father by deliberately making an intimate friend of his uncle, the Duke of Cumberland. George III had in the past been deeply injured when his two brothers defied him by marrying commoners. The Duke of Gloucester and the Duke of Cumberland both chose beautiful widows of ordinary blood. To prevent recurrence of such happenings the incensed

King had induced the Tories in 1772 to pass the Royal Marriage Act, making it a felony for members of the royal house to marry under the age of twenty-five without the King's consent.

One evening soon after he came of age the Prince of Wales, sunk in vinous gloom at the end of a long dinner party, turned to the Master of the Rolls and asked what he should do if forced to marry 'some ugly frau'. 'Faith, Sir,' answered Rigby, 'I am not yet drunk enough to give advice to the Prince of Wales about marrying.'

Evidently the matter preyed on the young Prince's mind. He dreaded marriage. Although fond of his own mother—who that very summer was producing her fifteenth child—he could not bear to envisage settling down with a person like her. On the contrary, the Prince admired elegance above all else in women. It was the enchanting Duchess of Devonshire, never his mistress but his best friend, who had taught him to appreciate art and wit and the fleeter joys of life. Georgina, with her red hair and wide mouth and curiously tantalizing smile, was a great lady as well as a great stimulant. She made German royalty seem slightly common as well as appallingly dull. She knew how to live and how to gamble. Devonshire House was the Whigs' base and there she enjoyed pulling strings in the political element. The Prince had cheered her enterprise in canvassing for Charles James Fox that spring. She had even purchased one vote with a kiss fearlessly bestowed on a sulky butcher.

Meanwhile His Royal Highness fought the election as no member of the royal family ever had before. He turned Carlton House into a committee room for the Whigs. Although they sustained a major defeat, Fox won his hotly contested Westminster seat and was then carried in procession to the Prince of Wales's establishment. That night the Prince, clad in blue and buff, the Whig colours, attended a supper party given by the great Whig hostess Mrs. Crewe. When the Prince gave the toast 'True blue and Mrs. Crewe,' the lady nimbly answered, 'True blue and all of you.'

Their Majesties disliked the glittering volatile Duchess of Devonshire but they dared not show it. When Georgina attended their dull drawing-rooms the King and Queen had to remain polite while she, the cynosure of all eyes, filled the dark palace rooms with 'the graces of her deportment, her irresistible manners and the seduction of her society. . . .'

The young Prince called her 'the best-bred woman in England', and avidly consulted her on all matters of taste from Carlton House furniture to the reviving of masquerades. At Devonshire House the headiest talk of a brilliant century shot across Georgina's dinner-table and the young Prince laughed and relaxed and knew ease of spirit among her friends.

When King George finally appealed to his Lord Chancellor for advice on how to break the Heir's friendship with Fox, now aged thirty-four, the best brain and wittiest companion in Europe, the realist reply came, 'Sir, you will never have peace until you clap 'em both into the Tower.'

Such was the scene when Mrs. Fitzherbert ventured into London society.

It was fashionable to be in love with the handsome Prince. He was tall, healthy and active, a graceful horseman and a good shot. Half the ladies of London professed a weakness for him and he responded only too arduously. His new infatuation with a lady of high virtue naturally became a leading topic of conversation. Within a week of the meeting His Royal Highness was sending daily, almost hourly, invitations and intercessions. It was hopeless for Maria Fitzherbert to stay in her 'cap and bonnet'. She must either step into the limelight or fly the country. She sighed at the complications. One night at the Opera had resulted in an emotional eruption which looked as if it must end her venture into society.

To entertain her the Prince, who was among the best dancers in England and had a 'well-shaped leg', devised a series of festivities at Carlton House which she accepted, but she parried all efforts to make her conspicuous. He gave a supper and planned to lead her down on his arm; she saw him advancing and hastily took the arm of Lord Chesterfield.

'The Prince then determined on giving a Ball at which she was to be the Queen—but she declined going to it and the Prince was so annoyed at this determination that, when he found out that she did not intend to be present, he called his carriage and drove to Park Street in search of her. She did not let him in being gone to bed.'

33

The pace proved unbearable. As soon as she went home he would be hammering at her door. The servants, delighted at first, became bewildered and then frightened.

From the evening on which the Prince of Wales secured that introduction on the Opera steps, Maria Fitzherbert knew no peace. If she attended any function His Royal Highness followed like a shadow, forcing opportunities to speak to her, creating jealous interest and arid comment in the small world of London society. He sent word to the Whig hostesses that he would not attend any function unless Mrs. Fitzherbert sat with him. They grimaced but complied. Soon she did not know what to say to her own retainers when the Prince besieged her house in Park Street babbling of a love 'celestial and eternal'.

Mrs. Fitzherbert herself described these weeks: 'The Prince exerted himself to his utmost to please her, and his utmost was very good indeed.' But by July she had become alarmed. She had let him know that there never could be question of her becoming his mistress so to what then could this frenzy lead? The Prince then shouted from the housetops he wanted to marry her. So violent were these protestations that she felt it imperative to break off the friendship—to save her sanity as well as his.

Of course she was flattered as well as embarrassed. She liked him. Indeed she did. Despite the dangers which she sensed when he swore to abjure his crown, Maria Fitzherbert wished she could make him happy.

The twenty-one-year-old Prince was physically attractive, overflowing with vitality and charm. And he played every card he knew, his loneliness, his misunderstoodness, his piteous royal plight, his moral reformation. Few women can resist the intoxication of reforming a rather delightful rake, and in truth the Prince now wished neither to drink or seduce. All he desired, all he talked of, was tranquillity with this one dangerously virtuous woman.

With Maria at his side the Prince believed he could turn into a different person. Her natural tenderness, the absolute sweetness of her look were balm to all the buffetings he had received in childhood. He hungered, he thirsted, he cried to heaven, he was the most infernal bore. Soon the friends who had encouraged him to debauchery found their shoulders wet with tears. They did not like the situation. Only too eager to arrange liaisons for the Prince, none of them wished to be involved in felony over a marriage.

The Duchess of Devonshire returned anxiously from Bath '—— upon coming to town many circumstances had thrown me into an unfortunate intimacy with him and he would not rest till he told me his passion for Mrs. F. and his design to marry her; any remonstrance from me was always followed by threats of killing himself.'

The Duchess eventually agreed to see Mrs. Fitzherbert in her own house; 'she agreed with me in the impossibility of his ideas; and her good sense and resolution seemed to strong that I own I felt secure of her never giving way. . . .'

The climax occurred on the night of July 8th, 1784. Mrs. Fitzherbert was preparing for bed when the surgeon, Keate, Lord Onslow, Lord Southampton and Mr. Edward Bouverie arrived at her house 'in the utmost consternation' to tell her that the Prince had attempted suicide and was in mortal danger. He had stabbed himself with his sword in the breast and was tearing off his bandages. 'Only *her* immediate presence would save him.'

Mistrusting this story she stated in the most peremptory manner 'that nothing should induce her to enter Carlton House at this hour'.

The distraught faces of the supplicants finally reduced her guard and she agreed to go to the Prince on condition that some lady of high character accompanied her. Both parties agreed to ask the Duchess of Devonshire who could be trusted for both brains and integrity. Mrs. Fitzherbert's servants wrapped her in a long cloak and called her coach. The party then drove through the dark streets to Devonshire House and Maria waited nervously while the men went inside to find the Duchess who left a band of guests 'supping and playing'. She listened breathlessly to the story. According to her own account (written January 1797, and now at Chatsworth) Georgina was informed by the four men:

'with frighten'd countenances that the Prince had stab'd himself with his sword; that nothing could be of any use but her going to him, that she was waiting without and would and indeed cd not go unless I wd accompany her; having no-

35

body to consult I consented & travers'd the Court where I found her in her Chariot, and we went to Carlton house where we found the prince in bed, his wound still bleeding. He extorted from her some promise of marriage & we left him; we found Ld Southampton very much frighten'd, and who declar'd his intention of going to the King. Mrs. F. own'd to me her having given this extorted consent which she looked upon as nul, and in consequence we drew up & signed the inclos'd paper, and she went abroad immediately.'

Terrified, Maria Fitzherbert permitted the Prince to slip a borrowed ring on her finger.

The Duchess supported her as they left the room and together the ladies departed from the Prince's ground floor apartment and drove back to Devonshire House where they signed a statement ending 'promises obtain'd in such a manner are entirely void. G. Devonshire, M. Fitzherbert.'

Confident that he must have created a very pretty effect the Prince ceased to claw to his bloodstained bandages and slept happily through what remained of the night. Meanwhile Mrs. Fitzherbert returned to her little home in Park Street and called up the wondering servants. Now there was only one thing for her to do. Tremblingly Maria gave orders to pack her clothes, and spread no word she had gone abroad. Trunks were hastily filled and new horses got ready.

Soon after dawn she was rattling out of London on her way to the coast.

Three

WHEN the Prince learnt that his lady had fled England he threw the pillows and bedclothes about. But within five days he had sufficiently recovered to send a servant to Brighton to rent a house where he could retire to restore his health and devise new stratagems.

The sea air proved anything but settling. As the blunt facts seeped into the Prince's consciousness he felt mounting fury and self-pity. His histrionics in Carlton House had not obtained the desired result. His beloved had flown into exile, and now it was impossible for him to continue the pursuit, for without the King's permission the Heir might not leave England. According to Lord Holland 'he did not conceal his passion or his despair at her leaving England for the Continent'.

By July 17th the Prince had recovered sufficiently to hold a pen for the time it takes to write an eighteen-page letter threatening to end his life in earnest and sending bracelets not as a lover to his mistress, but such as a husband has a right to send and a right to expect his wife to receive. 'You know I never presumed to make you any offer with a view of purchasing your Virtue. I know you too well,' scribbled His Royal Highness. Then tactfully he assured her he had long broken with Lady M. (the fascinating Lady Melbourne, mother of the future Prime Minister). He signed this epistle as 'not only the most affectionate of Lovers but the tenderest of Husbands'.

Accompanied by Lady Anne Barnard—an active friend of the Prince who conveniently kept him posted with news—Mrs. Fitzherbert was taking a rest in Paris. Letter after letter reached her by special courier. The messengers were followed and bribed but the French officials, who at first thought Mrs. Fitzherbert must be an English spy, soon realized what was happening, and the Duke of Orleans, briefed by the Prince and naturally amused, insisted that her correspondence must be treated with respect.

In London the faithful Fitzherbert retainers certainly held their peace for on July 27th, 1784, over a month after she had fled, the *Morning Herald* wrote with innocent inaccuracy:

'A new Constellation has lately made an appearance in the *fashionable* hemisphere, that engages the attention of those hearts which are susceptible to the power of beauty. The widow of the late Mr. Fitzherbert has in her train half our young Nobility; as the lady has not, as yet, discovered a partiality for any of her admirers, they are all animated with hopes of success.'

On the contrary, the first admirer she had met now writhed in the depth of despair. For ten long weeks he remained at Brighton splashing in the sea, planning, scribbling, expostulating. In August King George, aloof at Windsor, tried to insult his son by ignoring his twenty-second birthday. The slight passed unnoticed by a prince otherwise obsessed. But there were no more fêtes at Carlton House, no plans for masquerades or gaming parties, in fact no fun for anyone. Would that death could take him, he wailed to his friends, and the aristocratic, riotous-living radical-minded Whig party with which he had allied himself shook with dismay. Their princely champion might be the end of them.

Charles James Fox, who had so amusingly taught the Heir Apparent advanced political opinions as well as the joys of gambling beyond one's means, suffered acutely. Fox had now married his clever mistress, Mrs. Armistead, and this couple were the Prince's most intimate friends. According to Lord Holland:

'Mrs. Fox, who was living at St. Annes, has repeatedly assured me that he came down thither more than once to converse with her and Mr. Fox on the subject, that he cried by the hour, that he testified to the sincerity and violence of his passion and his despair by the most extravagant expression and actions, rolling on the floor, striking his forehead, tearing his hair, falling into hysterics, and swearing that he would abandon the country, forfeit the crown, sell his jewels and plate, and scrape together a competence to fly with the object of his affections to America.'

The faces of sycophantic courtiers now fell when the Prince's carriage drew up for a visit. China would get broken and the best rugs torn. Besides they were frightened of the King.

Meanwhile the cause of all this emotion went sightseeing in Aix-la-Chapelle. Rather than brood over the mess into which she had fallen Mrs. Fitzherbert decided to enjoy Europe. If the Prince did not see her for a few months he would find a new passion. Innocently she thought it would then be possible to resume a pleasant life in England. Mrs. Fitzherbert carried letters of introduction to the Court of Orange where no one knew of her drama, and so, despite the fact that civil war appeared imminent, she travelled to The Hague.

'In Holland she met with the greatest civilities from the Stadtholder and his family and lived upon terms of intimacy with them, and was received into the friendship of the Princess of Orange, who, at that very time, was the object of negotiation with the Royal Family of England for the Heir Apparent. Frequent inquiries were made about the Prince and the English Court in confidential communication between her and the Princess, it being wholly unknown to the Princess that she was her most dangerous rival.'[1]

Mrs. Fitzherbert, amused and embarrassed, found herself the recipient of questions on what sort of a husband the Prince of Wales would make. Protesting she knew little of the Court life, she replied he should make a very handsome husband indeed. The young Princess of Orange beamed at this news and so started a friendship which was to last through many strange vicissitudes.

As her written statement had attested, Maria attached no importance to that promise extracted under duress in the middle of the night amidst surgeons and bloodstains.

Now with annoyance she read a letter from the Duchess of Devonshire. The Prince had begged Georgina to persuade his beloved to return to England. Mrs. Fitzherbert replied thus:

[1] Dictated to Lord Stourton by Mrs. Fitzherbert.

'My dear Madam,

You may much more easily conceive than my pen is capable of expressing the very unpleasant and cruel situation I feel myself in at this moment, I am a good deal surpris'd at your desiring me to finish this affair one way or the other, you cannot be ignorant, my dear Duchess that from the first moment it was propos'd my sentiments have never varied. Does not the same reasons now subsist and must they not always be the same? I should think I us'd him very ill had I ever endeavoured to deceive him. I have always spoke and acted very openly with him, but still more strongly in my last than I ever did before and I believe that no one can say but that my reasons are just and painted in their true colors that I have neither exaggerated or diminish'd anything. In regard to my coming to England I must beg leave to differ with you in opinion as I cannot see the least good effect it could possibly have. I am perfectly well acquainted with every circumstance and why should I appear to give in to measures I can never consent to. Whatever Mr. F[ox] or his friends say to him they know in their own breasts they cannot approve of and I am confident there is not one of them that will take it upon themselves to say it is a legal proceeding. They may wish to please him and to appear to forward his views which they know can never essentially hurt him, at least that can never bind him to anything. I don't speak with any want of regard or respect of his friends, but they are certainly not my friends. It is very natural for them to say *such and such are the proposals* it is not our affair etc. she is of an age to take care of herself. I must write a line to the —— and as I do not wish to detain your servant I must beg leave to conclude once more imploring your interest with *him* as no one is so likely to succeed as y'self. I remain, Dr Madam, truly and sincerely your very affectionate & obliged humble servant.

M. Fitzherbert.'

Evidently Fox was hinting at some kind of marriage which would calm the Prince but not be a legal proceeding. Maria had no intention of being lassooed.

Having enjoyed the hospitality of the Stadtholder and done

her utmost to encourage the Princess to marry the Heir of England, Mrs. Fitzherbert left Holland in the Royal Barge and spent a year travelling through the most picturesque towns of Europe. In her own words she was endeavouring to 'fight off a situation which threatened to ruin my peace and happiness'.

Mrs. Fitzherbert loved the sun, the mountains, the old churches and villages. Not daring to confide in letters or diaries she amused herself with a Commonplace Book which has survived. Among the phrases she wrote out were:

'Advice is like a jest which every fool is offering another and yet won't take himself.'

'No Law is made for Love,
Love is not in our choice but in our Fate.'

'What's Royalty but power to please oneself?
How wretchedly he rules
That's served by cowards and advised by fools.'

While she wandered through the Alps stopping in inns or renting houses the winter passed into spring, but there was no abatement in the frenzied messages from England. Her discreet behaviour merely whetted the Prince's appetite.

'Courier after courier passed through France carrying the letters of the Prince to her in France and Switzerland. The Duke of Orleans was medium of this correspondence. The speed of the couriers exciting the suspicion of the French Government, three of them were at different times put into prison. They were of course suspected of being concerned in some political plot with the English Lady. But the Duke of Orleans extricated them from these difficulties.'

The King's brother, the Duke of Gloucester, who had married Lady Waldegrave, was travelling on the continent and with his wife called on Mrs. Fitzherbert. After this meeting he wrote to his nephew the Prince: 'I am rejoiced at having had it in my power to show her any attention, especially Sir, as it has met with your approbation.'

As Mrs. Fitzherbert entertained the Duke and Duchess of Gloucester she probably looked at the older woman, once known as England's greatest beauty, and recalled her famous statement to the infatuated Prince—that although too inconsiderable a person to become his wife she was too considerable to become his mistress. The widowed Lady Waldegrave had, in fact, been born illegitimate, but grandly so. Her mother, a beautiful milliner, had never married Sir Edward Walpole only because his father the Prime Minister forbade it. Five exquisite Walpole bastards were brought up like little aristocrats and all the girls married well. In fact this one had married rather too well for comfort, first a rich earl and then a royal duke. Mrs. Fitzherbert knew that the Duchess suffered acutely because the King refused to receive her at Court, but nevertheless she was firmly placed in legal wedlock and her children were royal. *Her* romance had certainly ended safely, but the Royal Marriage Act of 1772 had not then turned such insubordination into felony. Gloucester was not Heir to the Throne and the Dowager Lady Waldegrave had not been a Roman Catholic.

The Gloucesters might treat Mrs. Fitzherbert with sympathy but they could hardly offer advice. They had sailed in less difficult waters. They could but 'show attention' and soothe and dither.

During the spring Mrs. Fitzherbert tried long carriage drives through Lorraine, but she could not shake off the truth. She had to face facts. The Prince was not becoming more reasonable; he was getting worse. Although his friends were terrified at his talk of marriage they also grew very much afraid he might, in hysteria, harm himself. Everyone in England, who knew about the affair, wanted Maria to become his mistress. And this she simply could not do. Perhaps she might have subdued her conventional belief in the importance of womanly virtue; society never raised an eyebrow at *royal* liaisons. But to submit to the Prince meant deliberately disobeying her religion and this Maria Fitzherbert could not bring herself to do. Indeed, she would not have been the first King's mistress who bowed to the altar, but her particular clear-cut English character could not have accepted the compromise. Either she belonged to a man by the laws of her Church or she did not belong at all.

Ruefully the Whig Party realized the impossibility of inveigling her into the position of royal mistress, but certainly great pressure was used. Emissaries hinted that she must hold herself responsible if the Prince did mischief to himself, and at length she was induced to send a written promise 'that she would never marry any other person'.

This promise calmed the Prince for a time, but during April 1785 he again wound himself into a delirium. The King now knew. He and Pitt, the new Prime Minister, conferred in secret over the Prince's determination to marry an English lady abroad. 'I forget her name,' fumed King George, but he would not be allowed to forget it in the future.

The Queen still maintained an affectionate correspondence with her recalcitrant son but she could not improve his relationship with a father who taunted him about Mrs. Fitzherbert. The angry King dared George to leave England without royal permission. When the Prince, with effrontery superb or pathetic, suggested he might lessen heavy debts by 'travelling on the continent', His Majesty slyly seized the opportunity of asking him for a full statement of the debts—hinting, but not promising, that they might be liquidated. His son saw that England had become a cage. Wildly he battered at the bars.

It was April 27th when the Prince of Wales sent for Sir James Harris, Minister at The Hague, and asked if it were possible for him to go there 'in a private character'.

Harris replied uncomfortably:

'I should be very sorry, Sir, to see you in Holland otherwise than in a character which would allow me to receive you in a manner conformable with the respect and affection I bear your Royal Highness; but your coming abroad without your having obtained the King's consent implies that you will come after it has been refused you, and, you may rest assured, in that case I shall receive orders how to act towards you before your arrival; and those orders, let them be ever so much in contradiction to my feelings, I must obey.'

In *The Diaries and Correspondence of James Harris, First Earl of Malmesbury* this long, unsatisfactory conversation is recorded:

'*Prince:* But what am I to do? Am I to be refused the right of every individual? Cannot I travel legally, as a private man, without the King's consent?'

Harris: I think it very immaterial for Your Royal Highness to know whether you can or cannot travel legally without His Majesty's consent; since it is evident that you cannot with any propriety to the public, or satisfaction to yourself, cross the seas without it.

Prince: Why not: I wish to travel on a plan of economy; to be unknown; to live in retirement.

Harris: Without entering into the almost impossibility of Your Royal Highness making so rapid a transition in your ways of life, I confess I see no event would give me so much pain, as an Englishman, as to see a Prince of Wales abroad under such a description. . . .

Prince: I feel what you say; but what can I do? The King proposed to me to lay by £10,000 a year to pay my debts when with the strictest economy, my expenses are twice my income. I am ruined if I stay in England. I disgrace myself as a man.

Harris: Your Royal Highness, give me leave to say, will find no relief in travelling the way you propose. You will be either slighted, or, what is worse, become the object of political intrigue in every coast you pass through. . . .

Prince: But if I avoid all great courts? If I keep to the smaller ones of Germany, can this happen? I may live, unnoticed and unknown.

Harris: Impossible, Sir. The title of the Earl of Chester will be only a mask which covers the Prince of Wales, and, as such, your actions will ever be judged. . . .

Prince: But what can I do, my dear Harris? The King *hates me*. He wants to set me at variance with my brother. I have no hope from him. He won't let even Parliament assist me till I marry.

Harris: But there exists so cordial an affection between Your Royal Highness and the Duke of York, that I should think he might be employed most usefully to reconcile the King to Your Royal Highness. It cannot be a difficult task when undertaken by a brother.

Prince: If he thought it possible, he would come over immediately. He has often expressed his concern at our disunion, and declares he will leave the continent till he can see a prospect of bringing the King to enter into my situation.

Harris: Surely, Sir, the King could not object to any increase of income thought proper to allow Your Royal Highness?

Prince: I believe he would. *He hates me; he always did, from seven years old.'*

Harris, a wily diplomat, coolly smashed the Prince's pipe-dream, but he did try to persuade the angry King to settle a few debts. No pleadings, however, could over-ride the 'cross currents of personal hatred and political intrigue'. The King resented his eldest son, and Prime Minister Pitt refused to help the Prince of Wales in any way unless he would first break with Fox and the Opposition. Perhaps, with reason, Pitt feared that if aided the Prince might spend money on undermining the Tory Party.

The outlook seemed gloomy enough but before a month elapsed a curious change overcame the Prince. When Harris saw him again on May 23rd, the Prince greeted him lightheartedly: 'If you are come, my dear Harris, to dissuade me from travelling, let me anticipate your kind intentions by telling you I have dismissed that idea from my mind. I see all my other friends, as well as yourself, are against it, and I subscribe to their opinion.'

What in heaven's name had come over him now? While full of misgiving at this change of face, Sir James tactfully proceeded to propound plans to ease the financial dilemma.

'I thank you, but it will not do. I tell you the King hates me. He would turn out Pitt for entertaining such an idea; besides, I cannot abandon Charles Fox and my friends.'

Harris replied that Fox and the Duke of Portland had often told him it was a mistake for His Royal Highness to plunge into party problems on their account. 'They have repeatedly declared that a Prince of Wales ought to be of no party.'

The Prince continued to harp bitterly on his father's harshness, and then suddenly produced from his escritoire a bundle of letters which Harris had to admit were 'void of every expression of parental kindness or affection'.

The diplomat ventured a final word: 'May I suggest, Sir, the idea of your marrying? It would, I think, be most agreeable to the King, and, I am certain, most grateful to the nation.'

The Prince then truly exploded. 'I never will marry. My resolution is taken on that subject. I have settled it with Frederick. No. I never will marry.'

'Give me leave to say, Sir, most respectfully, that you cannot have really come to such a resolution; and you *must* marry, Sir. You owe it to the country, to the King; to yourself.'

'I owe nothing to the King. Frederick will marry, and the crown will descend to his children; and as for myself, I do not see how it affects me.'

'Till you are married, Sir, and have children, you have no solid hold on the affections of the people, even while you are Prince of Wales, but if you come to the throne a bachelor, and His Royal Highness the Duke of York is married and has sons to succeed you, your situation, when King, will be more painful than it is at this moment. . . .'

Sir James was puzzled at the time by the Prince's vehemence. He could not know that Mrs. Fitzherbert (who, the Prince's spies informed him, had been plagued of late by marriage proposals from a handsome scoundrel, the Marquis de Bellois) had at last written to say she *might* come home.

All these months the Prince had been seeking consolation and advice from the highly embarrassed Smythe family. Maria's invalid father threw heart attacks at each royal visit. Her brothers, tough youths in their way, were shocked and avoided the tearful Prince, especially Wat Smythe, who deplored the whole entanglement. But His Royal Highness chased after them, determined to plead his case. Most frequently he appealed to Maria's uncle, the sedate, evasive Mr. Henry Errington, that well-bred Catholic gentleman who had, unwitting of all the trouble to follow, introduced his dear niece on the Opera steps. Mr. Errington could not stand the Prince's tearful outbursts and kept retreating to the country. On June 21st, 1785, His Royal Highness wrote to him:

'I yesterday sent a note to your home requesting you would have the goodness to call upon me for a few moments at

Carlton House. But your servants sent me word that you were out of Town and that it was not known when you were expected again in Town but certainly not for a week or ten days to come. The object of the conversation I wish to have with you was *this* to request you would carry a message from me to Mrs. Fitzherbert which is just to mention to her, that as it cannot be less painful and awkward to her than is, I confess to you the footing we are upon in the world and as no one can feel more for her than I, I dare to hope she will not be surprised or offended with me, if when we meet—I bow to her and shake hands with her which will put an end to the difficulty we have both of us so long felt at meeting at a third house . . . etc. I will not trespass longer upon you except to say that I hope to see you when you return to Town and am at all times, dear Errington, very sincerely yours,

G. P.'

The Prince took pleasure in deliberately informing Mrs. Fitzherbert's mother as well as her uncle that he intended to marry her, that in fact he regarded it as a *fait accompli*. In the month of October, after a new outburst of threats to commit suicide, Maria sent a message saying she *might* consent to matrimony. What had changed her mind? The Prince's violence of feeling? The boredom of exile? The flattery of being chased by the man whom all the ladies of London were most bent on chasing? Or something more subtle? Had Maria Fitzherbert, who had only known two elderly husbands, gradually fallen in love?

Naturally her mention of a secret but true marriage sent the Prince into transports of delight. He had now only to arrange where the ceremony should take place.

For eighteen months Mrs. Fitzherbert had been incessantly bombarded. The Prince's most faithful courtier Hunter was for ever turning up with some long dramatic missive. Only one of these survives, but one is enough. Forty-two pages long, it reveals how many quills the Prince could wear out in a single effusion, and the handwriting grows tremulous at each point where emotion overcame him.

After Maria received this she knew she was trapped, and if she loved him perhaps it was joy rather than fear that filled her heart.

47

Four

'I hardly know, *my dearest and only beloved Maria*, how I am to begin this letter to you. Such a train of extraordinary and wonderful events have happened lately, which at first created the greatest apprehensions and alarms in my bosom, and since have tended to the facilitating and entire arrangement of our plan, so that nothing now is wanting but the arrival of my adored Wife in this Country to make me the happiest of Men, that I can hardly persuade myself that I have not been in a dream for these ten days past. . . .'

So BEGAN the Prince's letter to Mrs. Fitzherbert and forty-two pages later it ended:

'. . . . I shall not add another syllable, but leave the decision of this affair to what you may think my merits are respecting you, to the sincerity of my attachment, and to my not having a wish nor a desire in life that does not centre in you, in short I trust the whole of your generosity. Come then, oh come, dearest of Wives, best and most sacred of women, come and for ever crown with bliss, him who will through Life endeavour to convince you by his love and attention of his wishes to be the best of husbands and who will ever remain unto the latest moments of his existence

unalterably Thine

November 3d 1785'

Within six weeks of receiving this letter which swore that only the Duke and Duchess of Cumberland and perhaps the

Devonshires would be present at what the Prince called 'our happy though secret union' Mrs. Fitzherbert returned to England to face her destiny. The Prince had eagerly anticipated their meeting:

'I then shall either meet you in a Hackney Chaise by myself between Rochester and London, or wait till I hear of your arrival in Park Street, to which place I shall fly upon the Wings of Love the moment I know you are come. I think I had better come into the House the backway through the stables and the Garden, you know the way I mean. However you shall not be arrived ten Minutes before I am with you. I will not trust even to your sending. Whichever of these two plans you approve of most either of meeting you on the Road, or waiting till you are arrived, I will follow, as I must see you the moment you arrive, in order to settle where you choose to be married, as we must be married the night you come, before anything is known of your being in England. . . .'

We shall never know which meeting-place she bade him prepare for.

Having asked his amenable brother, Frederick of York, to make things easy by marrying one of those ugly German princesses necessary to Hanoverian succession, the Prince now trembled with excitement over the difficulties of arranging the forbidden ceremony for himself. The first chaplain applied to refused, 'he dare not betray the duty he owes to the Prince by assisting in an affair which might bring such serious consequences to him'. The Prince then sent for Parson Johnes Knight, who arrived at Carlton House without knowing why he had been summoned. The Prince

'began by apologizing for bringing him from Bushey Park, and then in his own persuasive language detailed his long love for Mrs. Fitzherbert, the misery he had endured, the taunts he had received from the King in consequence of its having been suspected that he had in the preceding Summer gone from Brighton to the French Coast to visit her, and he then drew

49

up his shirt and shewed a scar on his side caused as he, the Prince, said by his falling on his sword that he might end his life with his hopeless love—the Prince then spoke of his determination to repeal the Royal Marriage Act the instant he came to the Throne—etc.'

The Rev. Knight feared that if he 'refused the Prince might bribe some clergyman who would later betray all to the Tory Prime Minister Pitt. Also, as Mr. Knight candidly states, 'his tact was so nice that he never failed in the most minute circumstance which he supposed might captivate those whom he for the present hour chose to associate'. The unhappy chaplain acquiesced reluctantly.

Hardly had he walked home, however, than Knight remembered a previous conversation with his friend Lord Luke, in which that gentleman had mentioned the Prince's desire to marry a commoner and 'trusted no clergyman would be found to perform the ceremony'. Shamed, he wrote excusing himself to the Prince who released him from the engagement but never forgave him. In desperation the Prince now turned to Fleet Street Prison, where he found a clergyman named Burt, paid his debts of £500, promised him a Bishopric and obtained his promise to perform the marriage service. It was not necessary to have a Catholic priest for an Anglican ceremony stood valid in the eyes of Rome and all Christendom. According to the old Canon Law the ministers to a marriage were the parties concerned who made the contract, not the officiating clergy.

So all was arranged in deathly secret, except when the Prince forgot and blurted out unwisely. Mrs. Fitzherbert's arrival in London 'was fixed for a particular Tuesday'. H.R.H. had been invited by Sir Ralph Payne to a ball at his house for that day, but the Prince took him by the hand, squeezed it, and said that nothing on earth could induce him to accept any invitation on the day he expected Mrs. Fitzherbert.

What a homecoming she had! The servants in her Park Street house had swept and polished and garnished for their lady. Hardly could they understand the comings and goings and whispers of various members of her family. Nor could they have understood the fears which now kept Charles James Fox and the

Whigs tossing sleepless on their pillows. Using his lucid mind and superb command of language Mr. Fox enumerated the salient points in a letter which it must have been exceedingly difficult for the Prince to ignore.

December 10 1785

'Sir,

I hope your Royal Highness does me the justice to believe, that it is with the utmost reluctance I trouble you with my opinion unasked at any time, much more so upon a subject where it may not be agreeable to your wishes. I am sure that nothing could ever make me take this liberty, but the condescension which you have honoured me with upon so many occasions, and the zealous and grateful attachment that I feel for your Royal Highness, and which makes me run the risk even of displeasing you, for the purpose of doing you a real service.

I was told just before I left town yesterday, that Mrs. Fitzherbert was arrived; and if I had heard only this, I should have felt the most unfeigned joy at an event which I knew would contribute so much to your Royal Highness's satisfaction; but I was told at the same time, that, from a variety of circumstances which had been observed and put together, there was reason to suppose that you were going to take the very desperate step (pardon the expression) of marrying her at this moment. If such an idea be really in your mind, and it be not now too late, for God's sake let me call your attention to some considerations which my attachment to your Royal Highness, and the real concern which I take in whatever relates to your interest, have suggested to me, and which may possibly have the more weight with you, when you perceive that Mrs. Fitzherbert is equally interested in most of them with yourself. In the first place, you are aware that a marriage with a Catholic throws the Prince contracting such Marriage out of the succession of the Crown. Now, what change may have happened in Mrs. Fitzherbert's sentiments upon religious matters I know not; but I do not understand that any public profession of change has been made. Surely, Sir, this is not a matter to be trifled with; and your Royal Highness must excuse the extreme freedom with which I write. If there

51

should be a doubt about her previous conversion, consider the circumstances in which you stand. The King not feeling for you as a father ought, the Duke of York professedly his favourite, and likely to be married agreeably to the King's wishes; the nation full of its old prejudices against Catholics; and justly dreading all disputes about succession;—in all these circumstances your enemies might take such advantage as I shudder to think of; and though your generosity might think no sacrifice too great to be made to a person whom you love so entirely, consider what her reflections must be in such an event, and how impossible it would be for her ever to forgive herself.

I have stated this danger upon the supposition that the Marriage would be a real one; but your Royal Highness knows as well as I, that according to the present law of the country it *cannot*; and I need not point out to your good sense, what a source of uneasiness it must be to you, to her, and above all to the nation, to have it a matter of dispute and discussion, whether the Prince of Wales is or is not married. All speculations on the feelings of the public are uncertain, but I doubt much whether an uncertainty of this kind, by keeping men's minds in perpetual agitation upon a matter of this moment, might not cause a greater ferment than any other possible situation.

If there should be children from the Marriage, I need not say how much the uneasiness as well of yourselves as of the nation must be aggravated. If anything could add to the weight of these considerations, it is the impossibility of remedying the mischiefs I have alluded to; for if your Royal Highness should think proper, when you are twenty-five years old, to notify to Parliament your intention to marry (by which means *alone* a *legal* Marriage can be contracted), in what manner can it be notified? If the previous Marriage is notified or owned will it not be said that you have set at defiance the laws of your country, and that you now come to Parliament for a sanction for what you have already done in contempt of it? If there are children, will it not be said that we must look for future applications to legitimate them, and consequently be liable to disputes for the succession between the eldest son, and the eldest son after the legal Marriage: And will not the entire annulling the whole Marriage be suggested as the most secure way of preventing all such disputes?

If the Marriage is not mentioned to Parliament, but yet is known to have been solemnized, as it certainly will be known if it takes place, these are the consequences: First, that at all events any child born in the interim is immediately illegitimated; and next, that arguments will be drawn from the circumstances of the concealed Marriage against the public one. It will be said, that a woman who had lived with you as your wife, without being so, is not fit to be Queen of England; and thus the very thing that is done for the sake of her reputation will be used against it; and what would make this worse would be, the Marriage being known (though not officially communicated to Parliament), it would be impossible to deny the assertion; whereas, if there was no Marriage, I conclude your intercourse would be carried on, as it ought, in so private a way as to make it wholly inconsistent with decency or propriety for anyone in public to hazard such a suggestion.

If, in consequence of your notification, steps should be taken in Parliament, and an act be passed (which, considering the present state of the power of the King and Ministry, is more than probable) to prevent your Marriage, you will be reduced to the most difficult of all dilemmas with respect to the footing upon which your Marriage is to stand for the future; and your children will be born to pretensions which must make their situation unhappy, if not dangerous. These situations appear to me of all the others the most to be pitied; and the more so because the more indications persons born in such circumstances give of spirit, talents, or anything that is good, the more will they be suspected and oppressed, and the more will they regret the being deprived of what they must naturally think themselves entitled to.

I could mention many other considerations upon this business, if I did not think those I have stated of so much importance, that smaller ones would divert your attention from them rather than add to their weight. That I have written with a freedom which on any other occasion would be unbecoming, I readily confess; and nothing would have induced me to do it, but a deep sense of my duty to a Prince who has honoured me with so much of his confidence, and who would have but an ill return for all his favours and goodness to me, if I were to avoid speaking truth to him, however disagreeable, at so critical a juncture. The sum of my humble advice, nay, of my most earnest entreaty, is this— that your Royal Highness would not think of marrying until you can marry legally. When that time comes, you must judge for yourself; and no doubt you will take into consideration, both what is due to private honour and your public station. In the meanwhile, a mock Marriage (for it can be no other) is neither honourable for any of the parties, nor, with respect to your Royal Highness, even safe. This appears so clear to me, that, if I were Mrs. Fitzherbert's father or brother, I would advise her not by any means to agree to it, and to prefer any species of connection with you to one leading to so much misery and mischief.

It is high time I should finish this very long and, perhaps your Royal Highness will think, ill-timed letter; but such as it is, it is dictated by pure zeal and attachment to your Royal Highness. With respect to Mrs. Fitzherbert, she is a person with whom I have scarcely the honour of being acquainted, but I hear from everybody that her character is irreproachable and her manner most amiable. Your Royal Highness knows too, that I have not in my mind the same objection to inter-marriages with Princes and subjects which many have. But under the present circumstances a Marriage at present appears to me to be the most desperate measure for all parties con-cerned, that their worst enemies could have suggested.'

The Prince glanced through this appreciation of the situation with slight pain. He hated facts, especially such facts as these presented in black and white. It was rather selfish of Fox to become quite so ruffled on future possibilities. Bothered, of course, about his Whig Party, and wondering who would make him Premier. He was a good friend, however, and good friends must be soothed.

The Prince deliberated a careful reply. It was long after

midnight when he finished the letter, blithely re-read each paragraph and without compunction sent it off:

'My dear Charles,
Your letter of last night afforded me more true satisfaction than I can find words to express; as it is an additional proof to me (which I assure you that I did not want) of your having that true regard and affection for me, which it is not only the wish but the ambition of my life to merit. Make yourself easy, my dear friend. Believe me, the world will now soon be convinced, that there not only is, but never was, any grounds for these reports, which of late have been so malevolently circulated. I have not seen you since the apostacy of Eden. I think it ought to have the same effect upon all our friends that it has upon me—I mean the linking us closer to each other; and I believe you will easily believe these to be my sentiments; for you are perfectly well acquainted with my ways of thinking upon these sort of subjects. When I say my ways of thinking, I think I had better say my old maxim, which I ever intend to adhere to—I mean that of swimming or sinking with my friends. I have not time to add much more, except just to say, that I believe I shall meet you at dinner at Bushey on Tuesday; and to desire you to believe me at all times, my dear Charles, most affectionately yours,

George P.

Carlton House
Sunday morning 2 o'clock
December 11th, 1785.

'Make yourself easy,' wrote the Prince, but could any friend of his ever do so again? And the simile of swimming or sinking was a little too vivid when it looked as if he was dragging the Whig Party down. On the Thursday he married Mrs. Fitzherbert.

It was December 15th, 1785. The Cumberlands and the Devonshires evidently got cold feet and were all 'out of town', but Maria found two witnesses of her own religion who were willing to run the risk of committing a felony. Wat Smythe remained 'much against his sister's marriage with the Prince of Wales', but another brother, Jack, and her uncle, Henry Errington, bravely accepted to stand by and witness the certificate of marriage.

It was a cold winter's afternoon. The curtains of her Park Street house were pulled. The candles lit. Outside the wheels of an occasional carriage sounded on the frosted cobbles. In her own small drawing-room, dressed in plain travelling clothes, Mrs. Fitzherbert gave her hand to the heir of England.

Mr. Burt, the clergyman, read out the ceremony. To the time-honoured questions which in the Christian religion alone bind man and wife, their two distinct voices answered 'I will'.

When the service ended the Prince took a quill, penned a marriage certificate in his famous flowery handwriting and handed it to the two witnesses to sign. Jack Smythe and Henry Errington, putting themselves in jeopardy, inscribed their names. Then, having added his own signature, the Prince handed the paper to his wife to sign and keep. He was very pleased with himself. He had battled for a Christian marriage with this lady and had obtained it by threats of suicide. What did it matter to him if this day's work infringed the Royal Marriage Act? No matter either if it defied the Act of Settlement which specified that a Sovereign who married a Roman Catholic forfeited the throne.

What cared George Prince of Wales when Maria Fitzherbert, the woman he wanted, could at last lie in his arms?

Five

THE Royal Marriage Act declared that any marriages without the Royal leave were null and void from the point of view of English law. It did not declare they were not marriages at all and it *could* not declare they were invalid in the eyes of the Christian Church. Children born of such unions would be illegal but not illegitimate.

Mrs. Fitzherbert and the Prince of Wales spent their honeymoon at her own small villa at Richmond.[1] Their carriage broke down on the way at Twickenham and the Prince never forgot his delirious happiness on that late winter evening when they stood by the roadside watching repairs by lamplight. Waiting beside Maria he looked up at the clear vault of the sky. Never again for him were the stars to shine quite so brightly.

At the villa candles flickered welcome in the windows and servants stood respectfully waiting to serve a supper laid for two. They stepped across the threshold together—the large young man of twenty-three and the widow of twenty-eight—and stood warming their hands in front of the fire. Whatever the future meted out at least they would have this—a few days' honeymoon like ordinary people.

By Christmas they had returned to London where society talked of nothing save the rumour of 'certain illegal nuptials'. Before New Year Sir Gilbert Elliott wrote to his wife 'the report is that Mrs. Fitzherbert is to be at Carlton House; that she was married by a Roman Catholic priest, is to have £6,000 a year, and is to be created a Duchess'. Naturally the gossips got it wrong.

---

[1] Probably Ormeley Lodge, an elegant little villa with the Prince of Wales's feathers carved in the brick above the entrance.

No one dared ask Mrs. Fitzherbert outright how she had married the heir to the throne, but the royal dukes, the uncles and brothers of the Prince seemed to wish to treat her as a member of the family. Uncles Cumberland and Gloucester, who had sailed in the same boat, took pains to be pleasant, but they had not married Catholics nor were they in the dangerous position of Heir Apparent.

Gloucester wrote to the Prince concerning his impressions on the continent:

'I felt myself particularly called on some unfortunate occasions to give her every public mark of attention, also trying to make her long exile as bearable as I could. I cannot express how much she made our little society comfortable by her friendly and constant good-humoured behaviour.'

And later:

'I have seen so much of her that I think I can with truth say she has few like her. I am convinced she loves you far beyond herself—I only allow myself to rejoice that the two people I have every reason to love the most, seem to be so happy in each other, and must last because there is so much good temper and good judgement.'

The royal dukes might treat her with regard but Georgina Devonshire, who had been so willing to partake in the early excitements, evinced no wish to accompany the 'Prince's wife' in public.

On February 6th, 1786, her mother, Countess Spencer, wrote feelingly: 'What will you do about going to the Opera with Mrs. Fitzherbert? I wish it could be avoided, for it is certainly very plain that both he and she mean to shew that they are not upon the same footing as they were.'

Indeed not! The Prince's carriage could be seen early every morning at Mrs. Fitzherbert's door waiting to carry him home, and he insisted that she should have place of honour at all functions. If precedence could not be waived in her favour he refused to attend. Lady Charlotte Bury wrote in her diary: 'The

Prince never forgot to go through the form of saying to Mrs. Fitzherbert, with the most respectful bow, "Madam, may I be allowed the honour of seeing you home in my carriage?" ', and Catholic Lady Jerningham noted in a letter of March 1786:

'The Prince is very assiduous in attending her on all public places but she lives at her own house and he at his—Mrs. Fitzherbert has I believe, been married to the Prince. But it is a very hazardous undertaking as there are two Acts of Parliament against the validity of such an alliance: Concerning her being a subject and her being a Catholic. God knows how it will turn out—it may be to the glory of our Belief or it may be to the great dismay and destruction of it.'

While the tongues were wagging and the pens scratching, Maria and George appeared to be living blandly and contentedly together like any respectable man and wife—except that they kept separate establishments. But Carlton House now seemed to the Prince merely the place where he worked and entertained. His *home* was the house where his spouse awaited him.

Their agreement was that the Prince should accord her the honours of his table and escort her publicly while she spoke not a word and never showed the marriage licence. The promise of Maria Smythe would hold fast 'till death us do part'. He knew her word could be trusted just as he knew—and hated the knowledge —that his own could not.

Now, through the spring of 1786, the Prince appeared to be calm and reasonable. Mrs. Fitzherbert showed no ostentatious tastes so he dropped ostentation. For the first time in his life he was happy and his charm increased with happiness.

On March 17th Mrs. Talbot wrote: 'Mrs. Fitzherbert makes a good deal of talk. I make no doubt she is married to the Prince of Wales. He goes by my door every day at the same hour and seems very constant to her at present. It is said she is with child. After a while, she will be a most unhappy woman.' The Duke of Gloucester wrote: 'I think, Sir, by a certain paragraph you do not think it impossible that a son & heir may be upon the stocks already.' But that dangerous fact, if fact it was, has not to this day been divulged.

London found itself puzzled and alarmed but unable to be outraged. Mrs. Fitzherbert seemed to be so respectable and her influence on the Prince most sedative. Nevertheless they lived under the harsh glare of publicity afforded by the caricaturists. Newspapers had just started and cheap coloured prints could be issued by the thousand. For the first time in history the private lives of the English royal family were portrayed by a gutter press to a nation hilarious or indignant in turn. The cruel brilliancy of the eighteenth-century satirists gave appalling publicity to George III's seven riotous sons, and probably no woman in history has been caricatured as often as Mrs. Fitzherbert.

The famous Gillray caricatures which began on March 13th showed first 'The Marriage of Figaro' in which the Prince placed a ring on Mrs. Fitzherbert's finger while over her head floated his three feathers. Burke appeared as the clergyman reading the service from Hoyle's Games. A week later came 'The Royal Toast: Fat, fair and forty' (though she was under thirty). In "'Twas Nobody saw the Lovers Leap' Fox was represented as the Nobody encouraging the Prince to leap with Mrs. Fitzherbert. On April 1st came 'The April Fool or Follies of a Night', depicting the Prince dancing with his lady while Burke played the tune with firearms. These and others far less tender were circulated throughout the kingdom, doing great harm to the Prince and arousing anti-Catholic people to switch allegiance to the Tories.

The Prince insisted that Mrs. Fitzherbert sell her house in Park Street—which perhaps she was glad to do for it had grown almost too full of memories—and take up residence in a large house in Pall Mall nearer to Carlton House. Alas, the Prince's passion for building included the more expensive forms of tearing down and doing up. He spent £50,000 on Mrs. Fitzherbert's establishment and was to be severely rapped on the knuckles by the King when this came out as a 'detail' in his quarter of a million of debts.

In July the Prince and Mrs. Fitzherbert went to Brighton to 'economize'. Here they lived modestly enough in two rented houses, she in a small villa and he in a 'respectable farmhouse' with a view of the sea, rented from his cook, the famous Weltye. In his present state of content the Prince thought it fun to play poor. What a pity that this domestic idyll with picnics and drives across the downs should rock a dynasty!

Even at Versailles Marie-Antoinette was sending for the British Ambassador to ask his advice about allowing the Princesse de Lamballe to go to Brighton. 'I cannot judge the propriety or impropriety of her being in a place with the P. of Wales and Mrs. F ——' wrote the Ambassador to Georgina Devonshire.

'Meanwhile the Prince entertained little and kept no state. The wilder spirits among his friends were absent.'

The wilder spirits were Sir John Lade, an illiterate eccentric, who by brilliant horsemanship and handling of his own coach-and-four won a unique place in Brighton society—where many dashing spirits lived only for driving—and the Barry brothers headed by Lord Barrymore, a crazy talented Irish absentee landlord. These fellows were deemed a bit too rough to be introduced to Mrs. Fitzherbert as yet.

The newly married couple gave carefully chosen parties for each other in their two small houses. For a time the Prince only wished for the company of a few intimates—but what intimates they were!

Yet, of all the scintillating Whigs, Sheridan remained the Prince's dearest friend, perhaps because he never showed disapproval of whatever unutterable steps the Prince might take. In this happy summer of 1785 he was the 'intimate' to travel down the Brighton road to that 'respectable farmhouse', where they sat down at seven to the superb food and wines over which so much personal trouble had invariably been taken. After sunset the candles would be carried in and the three might sit late, glad of no other visitors. One can see them now, Maria with her flawless skin and tranquil ways, always allowing the men to show off, the Prince at his most delightful, and Sheridan who if searching for a dinner partner would be the best choice in history. The decanters went slowly round, conversation sparkled, the moon might come out over the sea and the fresh breezes blew; and in their cottages along the shore the fisherfolk, who yet remained, wondered what new junketings might shake Brighthelmstone that their grandfathers had known as a simple village.

Six

ON JULY 18th, 1786, the Earl of Mornington wrote to the Duke of Rutland from Brighton: 'People talk much of the Prince of Wales' reform, particularly in this spot, which he has chosen as the place of his retreat. . . . Mrs. Fitzherbert is here, and they say with child.'

This rumour was bound soon to arise. To this day it remains but a rumour. If Mrs. Fitzherbert did in truth bear two children to the Prince—as Minney Seymour hinted—then tremendous precautions of secrecy were taken. She must have retired to her own family and allowed the tiny babies to be taken from her at birth. This would have been a great sorrow to her, for, as later events show, she dearly loved children.

During the year 1786 the Prince and his bride divided their time between London and Brighton where they enjoyed the bracing air and comparative peace. The beaux and dandies of London society soon followed them. The bathing chariot had been invented and the thickly apparelled bodies of Britain's aristocracy could be submerged in the salty sea when too much food led to too much pain.

On the Prince's twenty-fourth birthday (August 12th) the Queen wrote to him wistfully:

'A late instance must have convinced you that as personal dislike is or can be lodged in the breast of the best of Kings and Fathers and it would have made every sincere friend of yours happy if, after the proper day of coming to Windsor you could have been persuaded to add that of seeing the King, particularly as he expressed himself to be ready to receive you. Nobody can more anxiously wish than I do the return of the days when all the family were united and when I am sure you were more happy than you are now.'

This letter, like all those he received from his anxious parents, the Prince merely passed on to Mrs. Fitzherbert who slipped them in her papers.

Meanwhile Brighton transformed itself; shops and libraries carried the Three Feathers over their doorways; Rowlandson travelled down to caricature the bathing and horse-racing, and everywhere the people saw the Prince and 'Mrs. Wales' enjoying themselves.

Mary Frampton's diary for 1786 describes Mrs. Fitzherbert calling on her mother in London:

'If ever the Prince loved any woman it was she: and half London, had he thrown his handkerchief, would have flown to pick it up. . . . Mrs. Fitzherbert's very uncomfortable life since her connection with the Prince affords as strong a lesson as was ever given in favour of virtue, for she never desired any benefit from it. . . . Her chariot was without any armorial bearings nor has she ever worn any, since her liveries by accident resembled the Royal ones, the Fitzherberts' livery being red turned up with green and she had gold ornaments.'

The discomfort mentioned must have been mental rather than physical, for Mary Frampton later recollected:

'When Mrs. Fitzherbert was living in Pall Mall within a few doors of Carlton House, we were at one of the Assemblies she gave which was altogether the most splendid I was ever at. Attendants in green and gold, besides the usual livery servants, were stationed in the rooms and up the staircase to announce the company and carry about refreshments. The house was new and beautifully furnished. One room was hung with puckered blue satin from which hangings the now common imitations in paper were taken. A whole-length portrait of the Prince of Wales was conspicuous in one of the drawing-rooms and his bust and that of the Duke of York ornamented the dining-rooms. Her own manners ever remained quiet, civil and unperturbed and in the days of

63

her greatest influence she was never accused of using it improperly.'

Mrs. Fitzherbert's most intimate friends were Lord Hugh and Lady Horatia Seymour, a newly married couple of high standing to whom the Prince had revealed his own secret wedding. Lord Hugh, brother of the powerful Marquis of Hertford, was a naval officer and spent much of his time at sea, although he later entered the Prince's household. His wife, one of the three beautiful Waldegrave sisters painted by Sir Joshua Reynolds, had been bred in an atmosphere of tension over royal marriages for she was a daughter of the Duchess of Gloucester who started the monarch's aversion to non-royal brides. George III simply could not get over the shock of discovering he had an illegitimate beauty as sister-in-law even if she were the Countess Waldegrave. The Royal Marriage Act ensued. Lady Horatia and her sisters found suitable and interesting husbands among the nobility, but their mother, the Duchess, who had been kind to Mrs. Fitzherbert during her exile, could not stop fretting at the King's snubs.

In Hugh Seymour the Prince found a friend of stout integrity. He made him Master of the Robes and Keeper of the Privy Purse, and confided all his troubles. Before going off to battle, Lord Hugh left his sword to the Prince. It was the highest token of affection he could bestow.

Having no children of her own—on view at any rate—it was natural that Mrs. Fitzherbert should show great interest in the children which arrived for Lord Hugh and Lady Horatia. She congratulated them on managing their infants while they congratulated her on keeping the Prince out of trouble.

In her quiet way Maria Fitzherbert proved a clever hostess. Every entertaining figure of the Whig oligarchy graced her table, and although she was not quick in conversation she possessed that lure irresistible to men—she was a good listener. Her serenity and sympathy proved exactly what the fiery, ribald, hard-punching wits of that or any era most desire. Over and again contemporaries remarked on her unaffected manners and amiability. 'A very mild, benignant countenance without much animation', 'certainly very handsome, though too fat', remarked the women. But 'best and most sacred of women', wrote the Prince who could pick and choose throughout Europe. Not really enjoying rivalry in intellectual flights but always ready for understanding, it was the *men* who preferred her society to that of stormier beauties whose tongues could lash like their own.

On Beau Brummel alone did Mrs. Fitzherbert turn a withering eye. 'Brummel had never taken pains to please Mrs. Fitzherbert, who persuaded the Prince that his young associate spoke disrespectfully of him behind his back. . . .'

Brummel once called on Mrs. Fitzherbert in London and found the Prince on her sofa. Annoyed by his arrival the Prince remarked icily when the Beau set down his snuff-box, 'Mr. Brummel, the place for your box is in your pocket and not on the table.'

This snub led a short time later to Brummel calling for '*Mistress* Fitzherbert's carriage'. Later came the Brummel's famous remark, 'Who's your fat friend?' at a masked ball. Later, inevitably, Beau Brummel faced penniless exile and no kind word from the Prince ever reached him in Calais.

Of the Prince's six younger brothers, brought up as German princelings rather than as English gentlemen, the Dukes of York and Clarence became Mrs. Fitzherbert's devoted friends. The others held her in deep respect. She was the sort of wife they all wanted.

But taking note of the discomforts attendant on marriages that contravened their father's special Act, only one dared imitate his elder brother. The Duke of York married obediently and then took up with Mary Anne Clarke, who got him into such trouble through selling Army commissions; the sailor Duke of Clarence lived with his actress Mrs. Jordan and fathered ten illegitimate Fitzclarences, and the Duke of Kent spent twenty-seven years in the arms of his French Canadian Mme St. Laurent. Unwisely, the younger Duke of Sussex placed himself in the same predicament as the Prince of Wales by marrying Lady Augusta Murray.

He suffered far more because he openly avowed the marriage, thus giving King George the monstrous right to cause the union to be legally annulled and his two children declared illegitimate. The Duke of Cumberland became entangled in various unsavoury scandals. Only Cambridge, avoiding both mistresses and debts, stuck to that dull respectability approved by the British public in their royal dukes.

65

Seven

THE first fifteen months of Mrs. Fitzherbert's marriage passed happily enough. The old King had entered an easier political era, he no longer cared so bitterly about Whig affronts to his royal powers, and he had recovered from the shock of losing the American colonies.

Until the spring of 1787 His Majesty did not approach his son on the subject of Mrs. Fitzherbert. The whole nation had heard by now that the Prince of Wales was married to the Roman Catholic lady who entertained for him at the Marine Pavilion, and comic scurrilous lampoons obtained a great sale. At this embarrassing moment the Prince realized that the size of his debts must force him to appeal to Parliament. He had been taught how to spend joyously and with taste. No one ever gave him a lesson in finance. The closing of Carlton House to 'economize' at Brighton made no difference to the large sum he owed. In April 1787 his loyal friends Fox and Sheridan brought the matter of the Prince's debts before the House of Commons. They asked that he should be granted £100,000 per annum and that his standing debts of £29,000 should be paid. Mr. Pitt the enemy, and Chancellor of the Exchequer, rose grimly and referred the matter to the King. George III then asked for 'an explanation of past expenses'—an explanation that never sounds as well as one might wish. The Prince fumbled through his accounts and found it exceedingly difficult to explain away £50,000 spent on an establishment in Pall Mall whose pale blue ruched-silk hangings had been copied by the entire fashionable world as a wall-paper.

The Prince and Mrs. Fitzherbert waited nervously for the outcome of this debate. Although her name would not be mentioned, the fact of a marriage was, for the first time, to be discussed in the House of Commons, Pitt hesitatingly asked for the form in which a motion which involved *Circumstances of such peculiar delicacy* could be brought forward.

It is doubtful if the Prince ever confessed to Maria Fitzherbert exactly what he said to his defender Fox before this fray. But without doubt he led them both up the garden path. He certainly told Fox to say he had not married. And he certainly assured his spouse that he had said no such thing. Both Fox and Maria were to be outraged. Presumably Mrs. Fitzherbert could not expect the Prince to forfeit the throne by *admitting* his marriage. But she thought he would abide by their mutual promise to *say nothing*.

According to the *Dictionary of National Biography*:

'The rumour of this union seriously endangered his chance of obtaining parliamentary assistance in 1787. The leading Whigs headed by the Duke of Portland had declined to injure their Party by espousing his cause. At the meeting at Pelham's the Prince denied that he was married to Mrs. Fitzherbert but Fox alone was eager to support him.'

How often were the Prince's friends to be left floundering in a quagmire when they rallied to help him.

On April 27th the motion to pay the debts was raised. Mr. Rolle, a stout Protestant squire, stood up bluntly asking for assurances concerning 'a question which went immediately to affect our Constitution in Church and State'.

Whigs and Tories slashed in the dark. No one had proof of a marriage, and when Sheridan leapt into the fray Pitt tried to stop the motion. He stated that should it be passed *it would force a discussion of the most painful and unpleasant sort and he should be driven with pain and reluctance to state plainly and distinctly matters of the utmost delicacy*.

This meant the Chancellor of the Exchequer threatened disclosures. They were all skating on thin ice. The Whigs knew that a revelation of their Prince's marriage to a Roman Catholic must cost him the throne. And the Tories did not want to light the bonfire. Better to catch the Prince some other way.

Sheridan entreated the House to consider in what predicament the Prince must stand after these discussions, and he protested that 'innuendoes had been thrown out'.

67

Mr. Pitt continued to wish that no more might be heard of 'a motion so pregnant with mischief', while Sheridan assured the House that 'to every question which should be proposed respecting any part of his Royal Highness' conduct an explicit and satisfactory answer would be given'. These flowery words deceived no one. Nothing concerning the Prince could ever be explicit or satisfactory. But the House was afraid.

The Prince was given three days in which to deliberate. Flustered and fussed he summoned Fox to Carlton House. 'Whatever words he may have used, Fox was given to understand that he had the Prince's solemn word that no marriage had taken place and that he might state this in the Commons'.

Then His Royal Highness hurried to Mrs. Fitzherbert and promised that he had not given Fox leave to say anything at all.

Mr. Sheridan waited on Mrs. Fitzherbert and informed her that some explanation would probably be required by Parliament on the subject of her connection with the Heir Apparent. She stated coldly 'they knew she was like a dog with a log around its neck and they must protect her'. She meant they must say *nothing* just as she *said nothing*.

On April 30th the 'delicate subject' was resumed. Alderman Newham, who had first asked for payment of the Prince's debts, rose and the House listened in tense silence.

'Newham stated that a great deal had been said of the tenderness of the ground upon which he trod: and several Honourable Gentlemen on both sides of the House had, no doubt with the best intentions, entreated him to drop his design. He declared himself totally exempt from those apprehensions with which others were so unaccountably filled. If there was danger in the measure, let those who gave occasion to it tremble at the consequences. As a member of that House he saw no danger, and he would assure them from authority that the Prince saw none; and in proof of the latter assertion, he was authorized to declare that it was by the express desire of His Royal Highness the motion was introduced and that the Prince was ready to meet the *assassin-like attacks which had been made upon his character* and would shrink from no inquiry however minute into every part of his conduct; from a consciousness that his actions had been uniformly regulated by a due regard to the dignity of his high rank and to those principles of honour which characterize the gentleman. Mr. Pitt's explanation on Friday had given him great satisfaction; but something had fallen from Mr. Rolle which he hoped that gentleman would explain. That he should apprehend his intended motion would *involve both Church and State in confusion*, excited his surprise in no small degree: nor could he account for the Honourable Gentleman's apprehensions in any other way than by supposing that a *report as unfounded as it was insidious, which prevailed among the vulgar, had operated upon his mind, a report which he had authority to contradict in the most positive and unequivocal terms.'*

Mr. Rolle insisted that he had not been alone in his fears and that many other gentlemen had been equally alarmed. He was happy to hear from authority that their and his apprehensions were groundless, at least *so far as regarded the report which had circulated so rapidly and was so generally believed*. Mr. Rolle then continued to deprecate the motion to pay the Prince's debts because he felt persuaded that it would be the means of opening a breach between the Sovereign and Heir Apparent. His Royal Highness's necessities had been represented as immediate and pressing, but he had not heard where they originated nor to what cause they were imputed. His royal grandfather never possessed the revenue of the Duchy of Cornwall which alone amounted to £10,000 a year.

As an independent member of the House he was not to be deterred from making every inquiry, etc., etc.

Mr. Fox then rose—his blackbeetle-brows at their most caustic angle, his face rather red. He stated clearly that *the insinuations which had been thrown out against His Royal Highness, whatever quarter they came from, were in the extreme illiberal, unjust and rancorous.*

'Expose to the public eye the whole correspondence relative to the augmentation and I will pledge my life and honour that nothing will appear which is not perfectly consistent with the respective relations of a subject and son.

Thro' the whole, the obedience of the former and the duty and affection of the latter, are eminently distinguishable.'

As to the suggestion of danger to the Church—*it was a report that went far beyond the limits of probability and he had authority to pronounce it an infamous falsehood.*

He accused Pitt of hinting at calumnies 'which never had and common sense could see, never could have happened'. Pitt evasively replied that as he did not understand the observations of the last Right Honourable Speaker he could not possibly answer them.

They were sparring. Every member of the House understood exactly what Fox referred to. So did the English public, when it read the account of this debate next day.

Mr. Rolle, backed by the blunt country gentlemen, the squires of England, stood up and asked to be answered explicitly as to *whether the circumstance to which he had alluded was true or not.*

The vital question had been put at last and fearlessly. The House held its breath.

Then Fox, whose integrity none doubted, rose to deny the marriage, saying *he had the first authority to give it the most positive contradiction.* It not only 'never could have happened legally, but never did happen in any way what-so-ever'.

Sheridan, eager to defend his Prince at all costs, then mocked Mr. Rolle for having been taken in by a report calculated 'to injure a most amiable character and wound the honour and feelings of the Prince'.

'Amiable character' was as near as any gentleman would go to naming Maria Fitzherbert.

Mr. Rolle excused himself coolly. 'As the report was in general circulation' he thought it just as well that he had been the means of drawing forth a flat contradiction to it.

In vain Sheridan pressed Rolle for an apology, but the debate ended on a less vicious note with Sir Edward Astley pleading for some financial help to the Prince. 'It was a humiliating as well as an affecting sight in passing Pall Mall to see his Palace literally in ruins.'

Meanwhile in the scintillating 'ruins' of Carlton House the Prince waited and fidgeted and mopped his brow. How tiresome

70

this all was—how insufferable that he should be forced to make a bald statement. All he desired was elegance and banquets and the company of delicious witty friends and the loving arms of one sweet lady. Why were these questions—these hateful disclosures—necessary? How badly he was being treated.

Then he stiffened with worry. Fox and Sheridan had carried the House cleverly, but whatever happened his dear Maria must not be ruffled. He decided he must break the news of Fox's statement himself. How did he do it? According to Mr. Bodenham:

'Mrs. Fitzherbert was on a visit with the Honourable Mrs. Butler, her friend and relative, and at whose house the Prince frequently met Mrs. Fitzherbert. The Prince called the morning after the denial of the Marriage in the House of Commons by Mr. Fox. He went up to Mrs. Fitzherbert and taking hold of both her hands and caressing her, said: "Only conceive, Maria, what Fox did yesterday. He went down to the House and denied that you and I were man and wife. Did you ever hear of such a thing?" Mrs. Fitzherbert made no reply, but changed countenance and turned pale.'

In vain the Prince tried to explain away his own responsibility. Maria said she would have nothing more to do with him.

'The Prince sent for Mr. Grey, and after much preamble and pacing in a harassed manner about the room exclaimed: "Charles certainly went too far last night. You, my dear Grey, shall explain it"; and then in distinct terms though with prodigious agitation, owned that a ceremony *had* taken place. Mr. Grey observed that Mr. Fox must unquestionably suppose that he had authority for all he said, and that, if there had been any mistake, it could only be rectified by His Royal Highness speaking to Mr. Fox himself, and setting him right. . . . This answer chagrined, disappointed and agitated the Prince exceedingly, and after some exclamations of annoyance he threw himself on a sofa muttering. "Well then, Sheridan must say something".'[1]

[1] Lord Stourton's narrative of the account given him personally by Charles Grey, then a young Whig politician frequenting Devonshire House. Later Prime Minister.

An uncomfortable week followed. While Pitt sent verbal apologies to Carlton House—which were turned away—His Royal Highness deluged Maria with protestations of his own innocence. Heaven knows what Mrs. Fitzherbert could have expected when any subject as desperate as her marriage arose in the House, but she evidently regarded Fox's words as plain treachery and thought she had been publicly degraded.

Lord Stourton says:

> 'She determined to break off all connection with the Prince, and she was only induced to receive him again into her confidence by repeated assurances that Mr. Fox had never been authorized to make the declaration; and the friends of Mrs. Fitzherbert assured her, that, in this discrepancy as to the assertion of Mr. Fox and the Prince, she was bound to accept the word of her husband. She assured me that the public supported her by their conduct on this occasion, for at no period of her life were their visits so numerous at her house as on the day which followed Mr. Fox's memorable speech; and to use her own expression, the knocker of her door was never still during the whole day.'

The great Whig hostesses and the old Catholic families rallied round her. The Archbishop of Canterbury considered this 'very odd. The lady is more received than ever she was and stands more forward.'

Meanwhile Mr. Fox had the misfortune to meet Henry Errington coming out of Brooks' Club. That Catholic gentleman spoke curtly: 'Mr. Fox, I hear you have denied in the House the Prince's marriage to Mrs. Fitzherbert. You have been misinformed. I was present at the marriage.'

Fox froze. He had defended the Prince to the best of his ability and tried to get the debts paid off. He had never intended to lie.

Perhaps he had misunderstood the Prince's vague instructions as to what might be said, perhaps he had half-believed that no marriage had taken place.

Whichever motive had propelled him in the debate he felt bitterly injured now. And from henceforth Mrs. Fitzherbert would be his enemy. Their views had always conflicted. Fox had once written the Prince not to marry her. 'If I were Mrs. Fitzherbert's father or brother, I would advise her not by any means to agree to it, and to prefer *any other species of connection* with you to one leading to so much misery and mischief.' He frankly thought her duty lay in becoming the Prince's mistress—preferably a Protestant mistress. If only her conversion to the Church of England could be proclaimed the Whig Party might consider its own danger lessened.

On May 1st Sir Gilbert Elliot wrote:

'I think yesterday was a very good day for the Prince as the story of Mrs. Fitzherbert was what staggered great numbers and he offers such unreserved satisfaction on every point which has been started against him that the natural desire of every man to relieve him from so unbecoming a situation seems now to have nothing to contradict or restrain it. This conversion leaves Mrs. Fitzherbert in an awkward way: but for my part I feel much better satisfied with her conduct than I did before.'

She had proved herself steadfast. The country could but wonder what her silence concealed.

On May 4th Sheridan again re-entered the lists. According to *Hansard*:

'He concluded with paying a delicate and judicious compliment to the lady to whom it was supposed some later parliamentary allusions had been pointed, affirming that ignorance and vulgar folly alone could have persevered in attempting to detract from a character, upon which truth could fix no just reproach and which was in reality entitled to the truest and most general respect.'

These words actually had no meaning, but in its present temper the House dreaded meaning.

Pulteney wrote on the same day: 'Sheridan attempted very foolishly to repair his statement respecting the marriage by saying

73

that Mrs. Fitzherbert's situation was truly respectable at which everyone smiled.'[1]

But it was not a malicious smile. Sympathy was slipping towards her.

On May 7th Sheridan's wife wrote in a letter:

'In short we are all in high spirits about it. Poor Mrs. Fitzherbert is very much to be pitied and I am glad for the honour of the fine world that they have shewn more good nature and attention to her than perhaps the outrageously virtuous would approve. Everybody has been to visit her since the Debate in the House of Commons and all people seem anxious to countenance and support her. Her behaviour has been perfectly amiable throughout.'

Hardly an apt judgement when it was Mrs. Fitzherbert's virtue which had caused all the trouble. The constant reference to her 'amiability' is to twentieth-century ears unintelligible. If a Prince breaks the law and risks his throne what matter if the lady prove amiable or otherwise? But England in the seventeen-eighties considered this trait as of paramount importance. To be a great lady one *had* to be amiable.

After the notorious debate Fox met the Prince once. His words were recorded by a witness 'I always thought your father was the greatest liar in England; but now I see that you are.' After which Fox avoided royal company. His Royal Highness, hating dispute and feeling slightly guilty, continued to toast Fox as 'the best man in England' when Mrs. Fitzherbert was not present. Still handsome, though inches were spoiling his waistline, the twenty-five-year-old Prince soon persuaded Maria to take him back. Once they were alone together they found it impossible to quarrel. She knew he had no sense of honour but she loved him.

Within three weeks—May 25th, 1787—Sir Gilbert Elliott wrote: 'I met the Prince of Wales as I went past the Queen's House in his phaeton, in which I understood he took Mrs. Fitzherbert to the Epsom Races, and on his return, after a cold dinner, he was at the Duchess of Gordon's ball, where my daughter saw him dance. Mrs. Fitzherbert danced a good deal.' This sounds

[1] Rutland Papers.

74

pleasanter than worrying nervously whilst Parliament wrangled over one's private life. And on the same day General Cunningham wrote of a supper at Sir Sampson Gideon's: 'The Prince sat at table with Mrs. Fitzherbert and all her particular friends near him. His attention to her has been more marked than usual.'

Mrs. Fitzherbert's reticence won the day. She had no need to prove she was an honest woman. The uncomfortable fact was now accepted. The Prince's uncles stood bravely by her, and his brothers, York and Clarence, treated her exactly as if she were the Princess of Wales.

Old Gloucester now wrote her from Florence where he was visiting with his wife (May 24th, 1787):

'Dear Madam,

I take the opportunity of a private hand to desire your acceptance of a Cestus done in oyster-shell. I hope you will think it pretty. Your little friend will enclose a note if she has time, but she has a good many people to visit here and we are just setting out for Geneva. Pray send us by the safest opportunity some account to trust to of the present negotiation. I hope the Prince will be made easy in his affairs. I sincerely hope you are well and happy, for I know you desire it. I remain, dear Madam, your humble servant,

William Henry.'

The royal family realized that a person of integrity had married into their circle. This was the first of many tokens of affection she was to receive. She particularly valued this one—perhaps because of the time at which it arrived.

The next summer passed happily enough. The Prince pronounced himself eager to cut London expenses and let Carlton House fall into ruins. His creative urge was finding a new outlet. He was tired of his Town palace. Might it not be much more fun to rebuild the Marine Pavilion at Brighton?

That summer the *Sussex Weekly Advertiser* opened a social column:

'July 25 1787. His Royal Highness accompanied by the Duke and Duchess of Cumberland and Mrs. Fitzherbert visited the Theatre at Brighton.

August 6. His Royal Highness attended the races with Mrs. Fitzherbert and dined with her at the house of Colonel Pelham.' Etc.

A few people still looked askance at the affair. The Duke of Rutland, Viceroy of Ireland, wrote his Duchess in July: 'If you go to bathe in the sea do not go to Brighton, because you will be under a difficulty about Mrs. Fitzherbert.' But disobediently the Duchess went and the first thing a visiting doctor described in early August was:

'The Duchess of Rutland was by far the fairest of the fair. Mrs. Fitzherbert did not dance the first set but the second she danced with Isaac Corry and after dancing she sat down with her partner and in a few minutes the Prince and the Duke of Cumberland came and sat beside her. The Prince expressed affection in his looks and the Duke esteem. She discovers strong sensibility and considerable dignity in her countenance and deportment.'

On August 9th the *Morning Post* remarked: 'Mrs. Fitzherbert looks more elegant than ever. One could hardly help exclaiming with the Army of Mahomet II, when he showed them Irene: "Such a woman is worth a Kingdom." '

Meanwhile Fox retired abroad. He had reason enough to sulk; he had been scurrilously misled. Eventually the Prince sent for him, but Mrs. Fitzherbert reiterated her refusal ever to speak to him again. 'She was, however, obliged sometimes to see him, and was much urged by the Prince to a reconciliation. But though of a forgiving disposition upon other occasions, she was inflexible on this point, as it was the only means left her to protect her reputation.'[1]

At this time Fox sent a message that he would make her a Duchess if he got into power. She refused and it was then he played his last card. Within earshot of Mrs. Fitzherbert, Fox introduced a brilliant unscrupulous actress, Mrs. Crouch, to the Prince of Wales. His Royal Highness was easier to capture for a night than hold for a week. On this occasion he appeared to be much taken by the lady.

[1] She related this to George Dawson-Damer.

76

Mrs. Fitzherbert found herself in an emotional dilemma. She could neither remonstrate as a wife nor upbraid as a mistress.

But Fox had not chosen cleverly enough. Mrs. Crouch made a gallant try but her influence did not last three days. Fox's strategy only served to annoy Mrs. Fitzherbert. Poor Mrs. Crouch died in Brighton, where in the Church of St. Nicholas a tactful memorial states she could 'gladden Life by the Charms of her Conversation and refine it by her Manners'.

Eight

THE Prince's debts were paid and his income augmented. Throughout 1788 he appeared to be quite happy playing house with Mrs. Fitzherbert. This proved rather an expensive game—decorating her reception-rooms in Pall Mall and re-designing the new residence at Brighton—but what fun it was! Apart from his building mania the Prince had started to collect seriously. He trained his taste, starting with horses, silver, food and wine; later he became a connoisseur of pictures and furniture. His clothes were always magnificent and, like his personality, quite different to those worn by anyone else.

At this moment his architectural bent remained conventional. His new Marine Pavilion built by Henry Holland, the architect of Drury Lane Theatre, was of classical design. The Prince had not yet acquired exotic taste.

Both in Brighton and London Mrs. Fitzherbert accompanied her husband on official occasions. There was, however, a stir when, in February 1788, she appeared at the trial of Warren Hastings. When the Prince led her into Westminster Hall, Queen Charlotte rose and withdrew. Macaulay has described the throng which sat listening to Burke's and Sheridan's bitter orations against the man who had saved India for the British Empire:

'There appeared the voluptuous charms of her to whom the heir of the throne had in secret plighted his faith. There too was she, the beautiful mother of a beautiful race, the Saint Cecilia whose delicate features lighted up by love and music, art has rescued from the common decay [a reference to Mrs. Sheridan as painted by Sir Joshua Reynolds], and there the

78

ladies whose lips more persuasive than those of Fox himself, had carried the Westminster election against palace and treasury, shone around Georgina, Duchess of Devonshire.'

Of course cartoons and caricatures of the 'Wales household' continued to pour forth. Gillray's pencil produced his famous skit 'Wife or No Wife or a Trip to the Continent', which depicted the Prince placing a ring on his bride's finger while Burke read the service and Fox gave her away; then came 'The Morning after Marriage or a Scene on the Continent'; and the 'Fall of Phaeton' in which the Prince upset Mrs. Fitzherbert from a phaeton under the eyes of the King and Queen, an incident which, to England's huge delight, had actually occurred when the Prince was showing off his high-spirited horses in the Park.

Meanwhile the demented Lord George Gordon, who had ignited the anti-Catholic riots some eight years before, took the liberty of calling on Mrs. Fitzherbert to demand her proper title. Her brother, Mr. Wat Smythe, returned the visit, demanding a duel if he called again. (The Smythe brothers previously bored or disapproving found themselves much occupied these days.)

Lord George then wrote to Pitt: 'I think it my duty to inform you as Prime Minister with this circumstance, that you may be apprised of, and communicate to the House of Commons the overbearing disposition of the Papists.'

This fell flat so he tried to produce an affidavit he could force upon the lady but was disallowed by the Attorney-General. 'After Lord George had equally attacked the moral character of the French Queen and the Empress of Russia, the Court was compelled to interfere and the Attorney-General observed, 'You are a disgrace to the name of Briton.'[1]

While the Smythe brothers coped with these skirmishes and threatened wholesale horse-whippings, the Prince and Mrs. Fitzherbert retreated to Brighton where she now met some of the wilder characters.

'September 15. The Prince of Wales, the Duke of Gloucester and Mrs. Fitzherbert were present at the theatre on three occasions to see Lord Barrymore perform.'

[1] *Gentleman's Magazine*, Vol. 57.

Then suddenly King George went off his head. The immediate cause of this attack was furious disappointment at the Duke of York for abandoning him for the Prince of Wales. Unable to bear the pain of this 'betrayal' he lay crying out while madness rushed into his mind 'Frederick is my favourite, my friend. Yes, Frederick is my friend.' But the heartless second son remained drinking at the Pavilion or gambling at Brooks' Club. Soon it would all be over. No scandal leaked into the papers however.

'October 27. The Prince was so alarmed by the accounts he received of the King's indisposition that he immediately set off from Brighton for Kew. The King being on Wednesday much better, the Prince returned on Thursday morning to Brighton. Last Friday a deer was turned out on the Steine for the diversion of the Prince and Mrs. Fitzherbert who were present in their respective carriages.'

'November 10. His Majesty's alarming indisposition occasioned the Prince and Mrs. Fitzherbert with their suite to leave Brighton at least a fortnight earlier than they otherwise intend to have gone from that place of pleasure and gaiety!'

So wrote the social columns. Behind the scenes turmoil prevailed. The old King had always tried hard to do the right, not the amusing, thing. Long, long ago in his clumsy emotional youth he had himself fallen in love—terribly, painfully in love—with the fifteen-year-old daughter of the Duke of Richmond, but he accepted the advice of his elders and promised Lord Bute he would 'keep my thoughts even from the dear object of my love, grieve in silence and never trouble you more with this unhappy tale', if Bute said No. And No had been the answer.

After the torture of this adolescent romance George III appeared to take a masochistic pride in fidelity to the ugly German princess selected for him. The strain of so many years of high-minded morality and sense of kingly responsibility—in a world which tended to mock both—had in the end unhinged his mind. In truth George III had faced worries of large dimensions. The Declaration of Independence of the American Colonies had not infuriated him so much as his defeat by John Wilkes who cleverly played the derision of the London mob against their unsubtle, slow-witted, well-meaning monarch. Curtailment of the Power of the Crown seemed more dreadful to him than loss of a continent. Then Rockingham and Burke had brought in their dangerous—the King thought treasonable—radical ideas and their Economical Reform Bill (1783) which pruned the royal household of its more extravagant sinecures. Fox had become the real power in a coalition government and devoted his energies to curbing the royal power. George III believed it the end of kingship if he could not appoint his own ministers without advice. He wrote to the Prince of Wales on the possibility of abdication, 'the resigning of my Crown, my dear Son to you, quitting this my native country for ever and returning to the dominions of my forefathers'. But he had not done so. Instead he reigned on, watching his heir bait him with Mr. Fox. His six other sons turned strangely against him, too, and his daughters miserably called their apartments a 'nunnery'. At least none of his brood could marry unless he consented—he had curtailed their activities there. But why did they not *love* him? Could his family not understand that he also had known anguish? But he had let his heart die. Why would they not do the same? He had tried so hard—so hard. Now the burden wore him down too heavily. And into the clouds he fled, away from painful thoughts, away from duty nobly borne, away from reality.

The doctors thought he would die and the Prince waited up for two nights, wearing full decorations. The King's death would have been wonderfully convenient. He could then make Mrs. Fitzherbert a duchess with special precedence and push the Whigs to repeal the Royal Marriage Act, or simpler still give himself legal permission to marry his own wife. What a pity her Catholicism must prevent him setting her on the throne as Queen. However, one might make some sort of arrangement. Sheridan would explain to the Commons. Not Fox this time—no, Fox had muffed it somehow and been very rude. Fox would be Prime Minister of course, but Sheridan would do the *explaining*.

In December the Prince posted to Windsor with Admiral Jack Payne who, with Lord Hugh Seymour, was his closest confidant. Mrs. Fitzherbert herself left Brighton with the Sheridans and drove back to her London house to await events.

The King's illness precipitated a political crisis. Fox was

81

recalled from exile to take a violent part in the battle which immediately arose between the Whigs and Tories concerning the appointment of a Regent. Pitt and the Queen fought adamantly to impose as many restrictions as possible on the Prince of Wales —who was loyally supported by his six brothers. The Tories were particularly anxious the Regent should not be given the power to create peers—they were terrified of the titles he might bestow on Mrs. Fitzherbert. Once more her status was hotly debated in the House of Commons; without her name actually being mentioned, except by Lord Belgrave as 'a very amiable and respectable character'.

Fox, refusing to be embroiled a second time, left London. As Lady Eleanor Butler noted (February 5th, 1789): 'Mr. Fox is at Bath in order to avoid the disputes which Mr. Rolle's impertinent question will occasion. It is said Mrs. Fitzherbert is determined to assert her claim.'

Mr. Rolle stood up in the House to declare that he only 'gave his consent to appointing the Prince of Wales as Regent upon the ground that he was not married to Mrs. Fitzherbert either in law or equity' and when a clause in the Regency Bill was introduced annulling the powers of the Regent, if he either ceased to live in England or married a Catholic, Rolle moved an amendment excluding from the Regency 'any person proved to be married either in law or in fact to a Papist'.

Pitt declared the amendment unnecessary, but he praised Mr. Rolle. Then Dundas stood up and said that Fox's denial of a marriage two sessions before was enough for him. He regretted Fox's absence on this occasion, but was so sure of his sincerity that he was confident he would have come to the House even at the risk of his life if anything had occurred to alter his opinion.

Fox may have writhed when he heard these words, which put him into an unbearable situation. But Grey, who *did* know about the marriage, felt able to stand up and denounce the marriage rumour as 'false, libellous and calumnious'.

Everyone was getting tired of the matter. The Attorney-General assured the House that 'rumours could not be made a ground for that House to legislate upon' and that he 'knew not how to agitate a subject of such delicacy. He therefore wished at all times to close the door upon such discussions.'

That was that.

No sooner were the arrangements made for a Regent than the King recovered. It was small comfort to His Royal Highness that Ireland had voted him Regent without restrictions. In England it was 'partly the fear of the Prince's Papist wife, who had so great an ascendancy over him, that inspired the great towns and country districts to pour addresses in upon Pitt at this juncture, assuring him of their support'.

If George III had died the Tories would, however, have been ousted. Then some genius among the Whigs could surely have devised a method of turning Maria Fitzherbert from a millstone into an asset.

In February of 1789 *The Times* published several scurrilous notices concerning Maria Fitzherbert. Her brothers, ever glad for an excuse to fight duels, hurried to the editor with challenges. Two days late the paper announced:

'Whether this kind of bravado conduct in Mr. Smythe will have any influence upon the spirited truths sent to *The Times* for publication either respecting Mrs. Fitzherbert or any other public character, its future conduct will show.' Whether influenced or not by threats of horse-whips and pistols *The Times* grew more respectful henceforth. George Selwyn noted 'The Duke of Portland now sups every night with His Royal Highness and his brother at Mrs. Fitzherbert's.' In May the.Duke of York fought a duel with Colonel Lennox, whereof Edmund Burke wrote at length to Mrs. Fitzherbert:

'This affair has occupied the public attention for a fortnight or three weeks past. It has filled the Newspapers: and yet the King has, either known nothing or seemed to care nothing, about a business, which, as a father, a Supreme Magistrate, or a commander of an Army or as a person of a Character compounded of all three, ought to have been an object of his vigilant attention.'

But George III, though partially recovered, could not bear to apply his worn-out mind to the painful subject of his sons.

The exasperated Prince again began to drink heavily, especially if his wife was not present, and Lady Eleanor Butler noted (June 18th, 1789): 'The Prince was drunk at the Birthday.

(June 4th). He could not behave decently at either of the Ambassadors' galas because Mrs. Fitzherbert was not invited.'

Maria tried to temper his excesses and withstood his insufferable practical jokes with good humour. While the French King and Queen slipped from their thrones the Heir of England sported with Lord Barrymore. He induced this gentleman to ride his horse to the top floor of Mrs. Fitzherbert's house. The horse 'could not be induced to make the return journey and two blacksmiths were at last called in to get it down by main force, their reward being a bowl of punch at the Castle'.

These larks doubled up the Prince with laughter, but he was *not* amused when Barrymore, dressed in the cook-maid's clothes, sang 'Ma Chère Amie' under Maria's bedroom window at three in the morning.

Mrs. Fitzherbert must have spent many bored evenings waiting for his return. 'He was young and impetuous and boisterous in his character and very much addicted to the pleasures of the table. It was the fashion in those days to drink very hard, and Mrs. Fitzherbert never retired to rest until her royal spouse came home.' When she heard him and his staggering companions on the stairway she would, according to the Duke of York who usually accompanied his brother, hide behind the furniture. On finding the drawing-room empty the Prince usually indulged in another ghastly repetitive joke. He would draw his sword and search the room as if looking for thieves until he found her.

But she stood it—as many another English wife had to stand it—and according to Lady Hester Stanhope:

> 'Mrs. Fitzherbert had a great deal of tact in concealing the Prince's faults. She would say: Don't send your letter to such a person: he is careless and will lose it. Or when he was talking foolish things she would tell him: You are drunk tonight, do hold your tongue.'

Sir Osbert Sitwell comments: 'If this was constituted tact perhaps it was as well that she never indulged in plain speaking.' But somehow she controlled him. It could not have been easy, for nothing maddens a man more than to be scolded for drunkenness by the woman whose couch he shares. At least he drank *less* with her than with anyone else—the attraction of opposites held good.

Nine

THE French Revolution with its disruptive violence and shattering of tradition caused more chatter than fear in English drawing-rooms. French and English parliamentary procedure could not be compared, and the strata of society had assumed entirely different forms. The English Revolution was over and had left the people with a well-founded horror of civil war. However hard the lives of the poor might be they did not reckon that cutting off a king's head would bring more meat to their tables. The French Revolution was considered in very poor taste and fleeing aristocrats received much sympathy in England. Several parties of refugees arrived on the Brighton beaches. Mrs. Fitzherbert opened her house to them, and her tiny oratory was packed for daily Mass. When a flock of exhausted Benedictine nuns landed at Shoreham nearby Mrs. Fitzherbert collected money and drove out to meet them. She found among the sisters a former school friend, Catherine Dillon, whom she had not seen since her Paris Convent. How widely had their paths diverged. Under Mrs. Fitzherbert's protection the sisters were driven to Brighton and lodged in the Ship Inn where the Prince was waiting to show how endearing he could be. He bowed the ladies into the parlour and indicated that they should sit while he stood by the fire discussing their future plans. He thought Holland might provide refuge, but meanwhile they must proceed to London to open a school under his patronage. The poor sisters sat bewitched by this magnanimous and handsome protector. Whatever the Prince of Wales did in the future, to them he would remain Europe's First Gentleman. Eventually the sisters settled near Rugby where to this day the convent sings the *Domine Salvum fac* in gratitude to the English royal family. How the Prince enjoyed 'doing good' and how kind he could be when the reward was Maria's approving smile!

An even more dramatic arrival on Brighton beach was that of the beautiful young Duchesse de Noailles disguised as a cabin-boy. The local Press got busy (August 29th, 1792):

> 'The Duchess was received on coming on shore by His Highness the Prince of Wales with Mrs. Fitzherbert and Miss Isabella Pigot. The Prince with his usual affability escorted the Fair Fugitive to Earl Clermont's, where tea was provided for the Prince and twenty of his friends. . . . The Prince with that humanity and gallantry which so invariably distinguished him, paid every attention to this amiable stranger. She this day rode out with Mrs. Fitzherbert.'

The young Duchesse stayed in Mrs. Fitzherbert's house, borrowing her embroidered brocade gowns. In the small oratory she gave thanks for survival and wept for France. Within a week she appeared to have forgotten her dire adventures (September 10th, 1792):

> 'Mrs. Fitzherbert, the Duchesse de Noailles and many other ladies of distinction were present at the cricket match, and dined in a marquee. The Prince's band of music attended and played during the whole time the ladies were at dinner. In the evening Mrs. Fitzherbert, the Duchesse, Lady Clermont and Miss Pigot walked round the ground, seemingly the better to gratify the spectators with the sight of a French lady.'

Which was the civilized nation *now*? Guillotine on one side of the Channel. Cricket on the other.

Miss Isabella Pigot, an admiral's unmarried daughter, had procured one of the few jobs open to gentlewomen. Settling down in the house of kind Mrs. Fitzherbert she busied herself writing notes to the Prince, of which many survive:

> 'If you will have the goodness to hint to me what hour you would like to have Mrs. Fitzherbert return home, as I am

86

persuaded from her manner and conversation she will with the greatest pleasure be punctual.'

'Mrs. Fitzherbert is just gone to Lady Harrington's and is to call me again. Therefore pray don't attempt to come here but rely on it I will meet you at home by one o'clock.'

'Mrs. Fitzherbert is dressing and begs you will have the goodness to allow me to say for her that she shall be very happy to attend you to Brighton tomorrow.'

Miss Pigot revelled in her own importance when the Prince went to her for advice:

'I have told her what I have done and showed her your answer which from a mind so harrassed as yours nothing can be objected to on it. For God's sake calm your spirits and feel more happy. Have a little confidence in her and rely on it she will do everything that is right by you, but she says her spirits are so damped and her nerves so bad, she must go out to endeavour to soothe her mind by change of scene and country but begs me to say she shall be at home again by a little after twelve and very happy to see you. Pray dear Prince come, be kind and good-humoured which your own good heart and disposition will ever incline you I am sure to, and believe me you have much joy and happiness still in store for you. Don't ever exact too much but be assured you will in a very short time carry your point in every desire and wish of your heart, and mutual allowances and little indulgences must be expected and good will granted from two people in whatever situation they are destined to live together.'

During the winter months Miss Pigot paid country visits and lived on stories of her career as a go-between.

'Belle Pigot,' says Lady Forester, 'was a most singular person. She was very intimate with George IV and knew all the court gossip. She made regular rounds of visits in the Autumn and Winter to the great Houses in Staffordshire and

Shropshire and remained in each House long enough to pay all her expenses. Everyone was delighted to have her. She was so amusing with her royal gossip. One day not being able to get post-horses, seeing a return Hearse drive up to the Inn, she went on by it.'

She would. Royal tittle-tattle must not grow stale. The urge to divulge hot gossip drove her relentlessly over the winter roads, and when she sat bolt upright on a chair in front of the fireplace, all the guests of the mansion, bored with local tales of fox-hunting and polling-booths remained riveted around her— fans ceased to flutter, snuff-boxes lay forgotten. To be *in* on the secrets of the Prince and Mrs. Fitzherbert? What fortune for an indefatigable spinster.

But, according to the diary of Lord Robert Seymour, the actual gathering of this material may not have been as amusing as the subsequent recital:

'The Prince of Wales, Mrs. Fitzherbert, the Duke and Duchess of Cumberland and Miss Pigot went on a party to Windsor during the absence of the Royal Family from Windsor and going to see a cold bath Miss Pigot expressed a great wish to bathe in this hot weather. The Duke of Cumberland very imprudently pushed her in and the Duchess of Cumberland having the presence of mind to throw out the rope saved her. Mrs. Fitzherbert went into convulsive fits and the Duchess fainted away. They afterwards pushed in one of the Prince's attendants.'

Hanoverian high jinks.

The Prince had enjoyed racing, but an unfortunate scandal concerning the Prince's jockey served at this time to drive His Royal Highness from the Turf. The charges of pulling a horse in one race and letting him win next day were never proved, but the Prince angrily refused to give any explanation or try to exonerate his jockey. He simply closed the subject by pensioning the man and selling off his racehorses. The royal colours were never again seen at Newmarket, and the Jockey Club argues the case to this day.

Hundreds of contemporary letters mention the Prince and Mrs. Fitzherbert together, usually with the Dukes of Clarence and York, at various balls and dinners. The Sussex weekly newspapers chronicled their doings with cheeky comment:

'April 16. 1792. His Royal Highness the Prince of Wales, Mrs. Fitzherbert and many of the nobility graced the Steine. How much better this than to waste property and reputation with the Jockey Club at Newmarket.'

'May 28. On Saturday last the Prince of Wales and Mrs. Fitzherbert were present at a grand field-day given in honour of the Duke and Duchess of York.'

'September 3. The Prince's fête took place last Monday. The Prince and Mrs. Fitzherbert looked on for a considerable time with great good humour.' Etc. etc.

They visited the theatre together, patronized sports and entertained publicly as man and wife. Meanwhile, not only the royal dukes, but the King and Queen had to realize how discerning and unavaricious a person had entered their orbit. By nature a peace-maker, Mrs. Fitzherbert tried to soothe the tension between father and son. Accustomed to affectionate family relationships she was shocked at the Prince's hatred of his father. Although the Queen feared her son's entanglement and was even ready to use the notorious Lady Jersey to detach her son from a Catholic, she did send a message of gratitude to Mrs. Fitzherbert concerning her good influence on the Prince. Once she received her secretly.

So the years went by; nine years of domestic bliss marred only by bewilderment at increasing debts. His Royal Highness's building mania outpaced his purse. As he grew older, stouter, more liverish and self-indulged, the Prince tired of conventional forms of architecture and yearned to rebuild every house he owned. His artistic senses, as often occurs when a man becomes physically unhealthy, grew sharpened and more original. Now the classical tranquillity of the Marine Pavilion bored him. He had encased the original farmhouse in a Greek temple. Now why not

89

encase the temple in a Russian cathedral or Indian palace? Turkish minarets and Chinese pagodas might be added. The Prince toyed happily with thoughts of pinnacles, spires, and domes. And within, instead of the plain marble halls and stately pillars of the waning eighteenth century, why not dazzle and shock? Walls coloured like peacocks' tails and eastern sunsets. . . .

But even very small domes cost money and the Prince's creditors were already clamouring for £375,000. The wily old King proved adamant. His son's debts would be paid the day he married a German princess. And the Queen, with a mother's frantic intuition, saw that another woman might at this juncture be used as the thin end of the wedge. Lady Jersey—brilliant, hard and heartless, an experienced grandmother-vamp—might well succeed in evoking that atmosphere of coddling and debauch needed by a faded stallion. Her Ladyship was despatched to Brighton to discuss with the Prince the enlargement of his establishment and her own position in it.

Guessing at the intrigues afoot and determined not to be caught in any humiliating imbroglio with another woman, Mrs. Fitzherbert for the summer of 1794 rented the beautiful and already historic house called Marble Hill at Richmond. Here she could entertain the royal dukes and nobility who spent much of their time along the banks of the Thames. Marble Hill, a most perfect little Palladian mansion, had been built and superbly decorated for Lady Suffolk, mistress of George II, a hundred years before. When she sat alone in the ornate and perfectly proportioned rooms, when she stepped up the carved mahogany staircase by candlelight or perhaps when she leaned from her bedroom window at night to look over to the river, Maria Fitzherbert may have thought of the building's creator, sweet Henrietta, who knew how to manage things so cleverly. She persuaded George II to spend £12,000 on Marble Hill, and then made Pope and Swift help her lay out the garden and choose wines for her cellar. George II had reached deep into his pocket to construct this gem. He never dreamed that some day his great-great-grandson would instal a dangerously virtuous lady there.

During the month of June, while the Prince remained at Brighton savouring the news of Howe's great Atlantic battle against the French, Mrs. Fitzherbert passed warm days in the

90

shade of the huge old trees, supervising the garden or boating gently on the wide river. Each evening, if not giving a dinner party herself, she drove out in her carriage to the houses of the Dukes of York or Clarence. Meanwhile the Prince's usual go-between, Miss Pigot, was kept busy scribbling her informative little notes to the Pavilion.

Lady Jersey launched her attack very suddenly indeed. Exactly what her tactics were we cannot know, but her seductively maternal approach produced surprising results with the fattening Prince.

One morning Mrs. Fitzherbert came in from a morning beneath the humming lime-trees of Marble Hill, and was giving instructions for her evening drive to Bushey to dine with the Duke of Clarence, when a letter arrived from Brighton written in the usual vein:

'June 23 1794
    My dearest Love. I have just received a letter from my Sister by the coach this evening, desiring me to come to Windsor, which though exceptionally inconvenient to me at this moment, in particular, owing to my being to give my annual Regimental dinner on Wednesday, I mean to comply with and to set out tomorrow morning early, having put off my dinner with all my Company to Friday. I therefore mean to pass Wednesday in London and return home here on Thursday. I have just been dining at the General's, where we have had a very pleasant and very jolly party. Adieu, my dear love, excuse haste.

                                        Ever thine, G. P.'

She left the letter on her dressing-table and that evening drove to the Duke of Clarence's where the company expected the Prince might join them at dinner. Maria was actually sitting down at the Duke's table when a note was handed to her. In it the Prince stated he never intended to see her again.

The 'dearest love' of that morning turned white. The Duke of Clarence himself shaking at this sudden turn of events escorted her to the front door, but she preferred to travel home alone in her carriage.

She had never trusted her Prince; indeed that was not possible when he could not trust himself, but she had loved him, and their marriage had lasted happily for nearly nine years.

Slowly and stiffly she climbed the famed mahogany staircase of Marble Hill. The servants wondered what illness affected their lady. On her table the morning's letter lay where she had left it. She lit candles to re-read the familiar writing and then endorsed it thus: 'This letter I received the morning of the day the Prince sent me word he would never enter my house. Lady Jersey.' Her brief bitter comment lies still among the Fitzherbert papers.

Ten

HAVING behaved in this odious fashion, the Prince soon wished he hadn't. But for a time Lady Jersey manipulated the strings cleverly. While seeking to oust Mrs. Fitzherbert from the Prince's affections she dropped frequent hints that if he married a German princess under her guidance, his £375,000 of debts would be paid and life would become a bed of roses. His Royal Highness listened for a week, but the ultimate realization that he had lost his Maria proved too painful to bear.

Within a month Lady Stafford was writing to Lord Granville:

'July 18th

I understand that the misunderstanding between the Prince and Mrs. Fitzherbert is made up. The story is too long to write, but after he had been persuaded by a certain lady to give up and to write according to that idea to Mrs. Fitzherbert, he found he could not live without her and sent messengers of Peace in numbers.'[1]

Lord Hugh Seymour and Admiral Jack Payne returned from sea after fighting 'the Glorious First of June' to learn of the Prince's desertion. Lord Hugh, who had won renown while commanding the *Leviathan*, protested bluntly to the Prince. He refused to conceal his disgust that any man should 'forfeit his honour' by dismissing a woman 'whose only means of defence was to break her word'. Admiral Payne, a more pliable character, listened to the Prince's excuses and tried to improve bitter feelings. As usual the Prince thought he could evoke Maria's

[1] Granville Papers.

sympathy by pretending to be ill. Soon Payne was sent buzzing to Marble Hill. Some of his high-strung notes to the Prince survive:

'July 29 1794
I feel the strongest necessity of remaining here as long as I can get Mrs. Fitzherbert to stay, who would have left this place for Margate this morning, but has now consented to stay till tomorrow evening and to go to London. Her mind is very much disturbed at the thought of your being ill, but be assured, my dear Prince, that her dread of writing herself to you again, in my mind seems to arise more from the persuasion of the impossibility of your being happy in future than any resentment of what is past and the more violence you betray will more strongly confirm this opinion. I have got her to promise to write to you but more at present is impossible to do and that has been avoiding all past causes of complaint and considering only that which in future comfort and tranquillity might arise and I am persuaded that if I had revived all past transactions and attempted to talk over again what has so often embittered the peace of you both, Mrs. Fitzherbert would not have remained here an hour.'

'July 30 1794
I am not sorry I stayed till Mrs. Fitzherbert's departure as I did not get her into a state of mind tranquil enough to write a letter till 2 o'clock in the morning of her leaving this and which I put in the post here to avoid any changes that might prevent its being sent. . . .' Etc.

Mrs. Fitzherbert stolidly refused to write the Prince any letters because she feared the likelihood of their falling into the hands of Lady Jersey. Her Prince was so weak—so tragically weak and forgetful.

Meanwhile the King's advisers were busy. On July 15th Lord Mornington, elder brother of the future Duke of Wellington, wrote from Brighton:

'I heard last night that the Treaty of Separation and

94

Provision is on foot (if not already concluded) between His Royal Highness and the late Princess Fitz. I think you ought to marry His Royal Highness to some *frau* immediately; I am told he is very well disposed to take such a wife, as it may be His Majesty's pleasure to provide for him.'

Throughout August Lady Jersey continued her intrigue, and even while sending Admiral Payne to beg for Mrs. Fitzherbert's forgiveness, the Prince let himself reel towards another marriage. On August 21st he veered again and wrote Payne:

'I have at last taken my resolution and all I can say is that I shall ever be happy to contribute anything that lays in my power to render Mrs. Fitzherbert's situation as comfortable as possible and to testify every sort of attention and kindness to her and that too in the manner that can be most pleasing to her feelings *mais tout est fini.*'

Three days later King George III had the pleasure of informing Pitt (August 24th, 1794):

'I have this morning seen the Prince of Wales who has acquainted me with his having broken off all connection with Mrs. Fitzherbert and his desire of entering into a more creditable line of life by marrying; expressing at the same time the wish that my niece, the Princess of Brunswick, may be the person.'

There had in fact been two German Princesses to choose from, both first cousins. The Queen's niece Louise of Mecklenburg, an attractive, cultured young lady much desired by Her Majesty as daughter-in-law, and the King's niece, the hearty, simple, jolly, tactless Caroline of Brunswick favoured by His Majesty and Lady Jersey—whose scouts assured her that no rival need be feared in this inelegant Princess.

In November 1794 the diplomatic James Harris, now Earl of Malmesbury, who had manfully shouldered the responsibility of persuading the Prince not to abscond to the Continent in the wake of Mrs. Fitzherbert ten years before, was ordered to

Brunswick to ask the Duke for the hand of his eldest daughter. In early December the marriage by proxy took place.

Mrs. Fitzherbert retired quietly. After nine years of moods and lies and hysterics perhaps she found it a relief to live as a widow again. If she had borne children this peaceful interlude may have given her the chance to see them and to discover a more human existence with her own family.

Uncle Henry Errington insisted that she continue to accept her usual £3,000 a year. This was 'honourable alimony'. Indeed the Prince's faults did not include meanness and he never ceased to fuss over her financial arrangements. He minded not being able to pay her the £10,000 a year promised as a marriage settlement. In late December before Princess Caroline started for England, the Prince asked the Lord Chancellor to obtain the King's promise to continue Mrs. Fitzherbert's pension if he should die before his father. The answer came in the affirmative:

'His Majesty was pleased to receive this communication in the most gracious manner, observing at the same time that in the natural order of things the occasion was not likely to present itself, but that Your Royal Highness had no reason to entertain any uneasiness on this account.'

At the same time the Prince wrote to Henry Dundas asking him to request the King to continue her pension in case of 'any happenings which might terminate my life'. To this letter he added a P.S. 'I hope you will excuse this scrawl as I really know hardly what I write.'

The Prince's friends worried over his state of mind. They already had a King who lapsed into occasional madness, and it would be the final blow if the Prince of Wales followed suit. Several of his entourage deliberately showed they would not tolerate his behaviour to Mrs. Fitzherbert and this hurt him mightily.

He could bear to be cast aside by his former lady-love Lady Melbourne, but when his own dearest friends Lord Hugh and Lady Horatia Seymour showed cold disapproval, the Prince raged with ill-feeling. So they cared more for Maria than for poor lonely him. The Seymours were both strong characters and while

96

Lord Hugh commanded his ship, Horatia had spent much time with Mrs. Fitzherbert. Their stand was natural if courageous. The first Seymour children, four little boys known as 'the Jolly Boats', had become dear to Maria, and the Seymour letters are full of references to 'Mrs. Fitz'. In a way Maria must have been fascinated by the career of Horatia's mother, the 'beautiful Waldegrave', who had been the last English commoner to manage a royal marriage. When Lord Hugh was sent back from the Fleet with news that the French Royalists in Toulon had joined the English he wrote excitedly to his wife: 'I am tired to death having travelled thirteen days and nights, without having been more than fourteen hours in bed. . . . I will desire the two beds at Mrs. Keppel's to be ready tomorrow for yourself and Mrs. Fitzherbert in case of her coming to town.'

After the 'Glorious First of June', in which Lord Hugh's ship the *Leviathan* had engaged a more powerful enemy ship *La Revolutionnaire* single-handed, Lord Howe spoke warmly of his 'good judgement and determined courage in the battle'. Lord Hugh received a medal and the thanks of the House of Parliament.

The pleasure of receiving these honours was somewhat spoilt by his breach with the Prince. It seemed, however, that the Seymours were well able to live without royal favour—not so easy in those days when only patronage could procure jobs for a large family—yet it was the Prince who minded the breach. He had relied on Lord Hugh's clean-cut friendship. Now in pique he decided to demote him from the Privy Purse to mere Lord of the Bedchamber—a post of unfortunate name in the circumstances.

Lord Darnley, writing to inform Lord Hugh of the change, hoped he would not quit the Prince's service, as His Royal Highness so needed sincere friends 'to prevent him committing fresh follies'.

Admiral Payne continued to trot to Mrs. Fitzherbert with messages but for the next year she hid away, preferring solitude to solicitude. She could not bring herself to believe the Prince's betrothal arrangements would materialize, and several months passed. It was not considered necessary for the Heir actually to meet his prospective bride. The Duke of York, who had seen

97

Caroline eight years before, spoke well of her and that sufficed. Rumour had it that even the King grew uneasy as the marriage day approached and told the Queen he would himself be ready to accept the responsibility of breaking off what might prove a disastrous match. But official preparations continued.

However she used her newly granted freedom this winter must have been a bitter one for Mrs. Fitzherbert in her lovely, lonely house. Now regrets became inevitable. No mind could be strong enough to withstand the intrusion of the past. *If* nine years before she had accepted exile; *if* she had entered a convent, as many Catholics complained she should have done; *if* she had replied roughly to the Prince, jeered at his threats to take his life, broken his love by breaking his conceit: should she have done any of these things and at what point? But whatever now appeared to be right and wise, nothing could erase the last nine years. Pacing by the bleak river, Maria forced herself to realize that the future can only be forged out of past actions.

Eleven

FROM DECEMBER 29th, 1794, the day on which Caroline of Brunswick set out from her father's palace, until April 2nd, 1795, when the Princess reached Gravesend, James Harris, the Earl of Malmesbury, endeavoured to tutor her in the manners becoming to a future English Queen. He found it hard going.

The suave diplomat who had handled the Prince during those frenzied days when His Royal Highness clamoured to follow Mrs. Fitzherbert to the continent, regarded Caroline's easy-going ways and light-hearted banter with grave misgiving. During the months the Princess spent at the Court of Hanover, waiting for France's wars to allow her safe passage to the North Sea, Lord Malmesbury reiterated advice and hints. No ambassador relishes the task of telling a headstrong princess how to behave. Not that she took his rebukes unkindly. Hearty, twenty-seven-year-old Caroline listened with good nature and often tried to follow his counsel. But she could not change herself into an entirely different person.

With horror, Malmesbury observed that the Princess could seldom be bothered to wash or change her clothes, and the Prince of Wales, despite his own gross appetites, was as fastidious over women as over furniture. He liked pale honey-coloured mahogany of delicate design, exquisitely ornamented, perfect in detail; and he liked ladies to match.

Lord Malmesbury had the embarrassing task of telling Caroline's lady-in-waiting that the Prince would expect a *cleaner* wife. His diary records 'Madame Busche executes her commission well, and the Princess comes out the next day well washed all over.'

Caroline was warm-hearted, robust, free in her talk and

accustomed to intimate badinage with Court ladies. She had never been schooled in decorum, and her instinct did not guide her to the correct tone. Now, with a pathetically happy lack of modesty, she looked forward to sharing the bed of this Prince so handsomely depicted in miniatures. She expected affection and intended to make a good show of her marriage even if the Queen were set against her. But even her courage was not always becoming. When Lord Malmesbury thought proper to inform Her Highness that infidelity on the part of a Queen Consort was high treason in England and punishable with death she gave a guffaw of laughter.

Ominous fears crept into Malmesbury's experienced breast. But would it have mattered greatly if she *had* been different? The rôle of Princess of Wales was at this juncture one in which no ordinary mortal could hope to forge success.

Poor Caroline—she had heard about Mrs. Fitzherbert but not the true story—was met at Greenwich by Lady Jersey whom she recognized as the Prince's mistress. Her heart must have sunk a little for, owing to a deliberate error on Lady Jersey's part, she had to wait an hour for her carriage. Then to her amazement the bride-to-be was criticized on her dress by that hard-hearted whore whom a Prince, who preened himself on taste, had thrust into his future wife's household.

Caroline brought out the worst in the Prince even before she met him. Lady Jersey found her match in Lord Malmesbury, however. When she asked to be allowed to sit forward in the coach to London he answered, 'that as she must have known that riding backward in a coach disagreed with her, she ought never to have accepted the situation of a Lady of the Bedchamber who never ought to sit forward; and that if she really was likely to be sick, I would put Mrs. Ashton into the coach with the Princess. . . . This, of course, settled the business.'

The Prince saw his betrothed for the first time that afternoon at St. James's. Smelling strongly of liquor he walked up to the lady, a stranger in his land, and stared coldly. She attempted to kneel at his feet as etiquette decreed, he caught and raised her, looked again and without speaking, turned round and retired to a distant corner of the room where he called out to Lord Malmesbury, 'Harris, I am not well; pray get me a glass of brandy.'

'Sir,' replied the Earl, who never lost his head, 'had you not better have a glass of water?'

'No,' answered the Prince with an angry oath, 'I will go directly to the Queen.' The bridegroom strode away.

Caroline had been warned she would be unpopular with Queen Charlotte, who wished her own niece in her place, but the insult of this welcome stung her martial Brunswick spirit. The Princess's eyes did not fill with tears. On the contrary her chin went high.

When Malmesbury walked back to her side no diplomatic oiling could soothe her. 'My God,' the Princess said in French. 'Is the Prince always like that? I find him very fat and not nearly so handsome as his portrait.'

Malmesbury, having ineffectually excused the Prince as being flurried at this first interview, sighed with relief when a messenger summoned him away to the King who wished to hear all about the bride. With hums and haws and many omissions the ambassador attempted a description.

That night Caroline dined with the royal family, and throwing Malmesbury's advice to the winds let herself go in 'flippant, rattling, affecting raillery and wit' with not a few shafts directed at the furious Lady Jersey and the stony-faced Prince. She could hardly have created a worse impression. But the Queen still refused to take the responsibility of advising her son to break off the engagement. She merely took him aside and said, 'You know, George, it is for you to say whether you can marry the Princess or not.'

During the next few days George could not goad himself into action. He merely sought solace in the bottle and in listening to Lady Jersey—who began to wonder if maybe she had not picked *too* unattractive a rival. Uneasily the old King entrusted the bridegroom to his favourite brother Clarence who watched anxiously, wondering what dear George might do in the brief freedom remaining to him.

Meanwhile in all the London clubs money was being wagered that the Prince's marriage would not come off. If Caroline could have heard the jokes of the town she might have set a precedent for outraged princesses by returning nose in air to Brunswick. But she thought of her soldier father, and how proud he had been when his daughter was chosen as suitable consort for an English king. She made up her mind to see it through.

Twelve

APRIL 8th, 1795. The Prince of Wales' wedding day. His debts were being paid—but out of income, he remarked sourly. His bride had been embraced and detested. Westminster Abbey stood ready and the city of London was decorated for the occasion. According to that nosy little *Sussex Weekly Advertiser*: 'The House of Mrs. Fitzherbert in Pall Mall was among those illuminated in honour of the Prince's nuptials. The lady herself was at her villa. . . .'

How was Maria taking it? Rude caricatures depicted her and Caroline boxing for the three feathers of Wales. More curiosity simmered around the cast-off wife than around the new Princess. During this entire week she tried to shut herself away, except from the adoring royal dukes who still called daily bringing little bits of news, determined not to lose her friendship.

There was nothing for Mrs. Fitzherbert to do. Absolutely nothing. So she did it with dignity. 'Mrs. Fitzherbert uttered no cry and made no complaint. She closed her doors to her friends and went into retirement as though she were widowed, thus escaping the sympathy of those who wished her well and the curious gaze of the vulgar.'

Of course the Prince had to stage a dramatic incident. Two days before the marriage, looking out from her window at Richmond, Maria saw a horse cantering back and forth through the trees. The well-known figure had come to show himself alone and pathetic once more. He had betrayed her but he could not drag himself away. Back and forth over the green fields that surrounded her house the Prince of Wales rode and hoped that she watched for him. But no hand waved from the windows of

Marble Hill. Dusk descended and then darkness. Slumped with self-pity the horseman rode away.

Having brought the future Princess of Wales from Brunswick and been present at her nerve-freezing presentation, Lord Malmesbury begged to be excused further duties and had retired. Now the good-natured, worried Duke of Clarence had to face the unpleasant job of following his unpredictable brother. Years later Clarence confided that the only time his elder brother

'had ever spoken to him on the nature of his union with Mrs. Fitzherbert was on the evening of his Marriage to Princess Caroline when George III desired him not to quit the Prince and he drove with him to Carlton House to dress for the Ceremony. After dinner as they passed through the garden, the Prince of Wales said, "William, tell Mrs. Fitzherbert she is the only woman I shall ever love".'[1]

The marriage of the Prince of Wales took place in the Chapel Royal. Two unmarried dukes supported him at the ceremony, and these avowed he had full need of all the support they could give, for he arrived so drunk they could hardly keep him from falling to the ground.

Caroline, gorgeously dressed in white satin sparkling with diamonds, waited by the altar. She chatted with the Duke of Clarence who, knowing all he did, must have watched her with pity. He had promised to call on Mrs. Fitzherbert next day and tell her all. How could he describe this eager unmannered girl?

The ceremony continued without a hitch, although at one stage the Prince suddenly rose from his knees as if he were going to fly for his life. The King went over and commanded him to continue kneeling. He obeyed meekly so perhaps he was just feeling sick. Then the Archbishop of Canterbury, who ought to have previously satisfied his conscience concerning the Prince's right to be married in church, added to the atmosphere of tension by laying down the book and gazing long and earnestly at the King and Prince of Wales after the passage concerning 'any person knowing of a lawful impediment'. During the silence that ensued, the embarrassed congregation hardly dared look at each

[1] MS. Note by Sir George Seymour. Ragley Papers.

103

other. The Prince had tears streaming down his cheeks, the King appeared wooden. Lord Hugh Seymour, by duty forced to attend the ceremony, stared coldly at his weeping master. But no protesting voice arose and the Archbishop continued the service, though reluctantly it seemed.

After the wedding the Queen held a Drawing Room and then a family supper party took place at Buckingham House. In the evening, while bells rang joyously and England cheered the royal couple, George drove his bride to Carlton House into which he had piled so much beautiful furniture and where he had made such dramatic scenes.

The illuminations had drawn out London's citizens. The streets were thronged with drunken crowds gaping, feasting and shouting. Their Prince, still blubbing with self-pity, took a final pull at the brandy bottle and made for Caroline's apartments. She told the story, probably accurately, to Lady Bury. For weeks it seemed unbelievable to her that a child could result from the drunken embraces of this husband who, in her own words, passed the night 'sleeping under the grate where he fell and where I left him'.

Thirteen

M RS. FITZHERBERT had given up her house in Pall
Mall when the Prince wrote her dismissal. Now she
bought a smaller house in Tilney Street overlooking
Hyde Park which was to remain her London home for nearly
forty years.

Two days after the marriage the Prince accompanied Caroline
to Windsor for a short visit. Then he took her to Kempshott in
Hampshire, a hunting-box where he had often stayed with Mrs.
Fitzherbert who had laid out the garden and decorated the
drawing-rooms. He could remind himself of her at every turn.
The peculiar taste of this arrangement was guaranteed to ruffle
the sensibilities of both wives and had probably been instigated
by Lady Jersey, the only lady-in-waiting permitted to the Princess
at this juncture.

Caroline was no prude. Occasionally she tried to tease the
Prince about his mistresses, but he took this in very poor part.
Her tentative jests fell flat, her attempts at cameraderie struck
him as odious.

In June 1795 debates in Parliament over payment of the Heir's
debts were resumed and the Duke of Clarence openly stated that
'it was a matter of public notoriety that, when the Prince of
Wales' marriage was agreed upon, there was a stipulation that he
should in the event of that union be exonerated from his debts'.

Caroline realized for the first time the bitter truth. The Prince
had married against his will, loathing first the idea of her and then
the sight of her. He had married because he needed money from
the nation. That night in the grate was the price he had to pay for
solvency.

The crow-like habit of reviling the weakest member drew friends away from Caroline. No one wanted to risk being on the wrong side. The Princess of Wales was easy to criticize, but no heart with a shred of kindness could dislike her. She was a decent German woman with ordinary feelings and lusty humour but no tact, and many small faults and eccentricities. She dressed badly, and could not manipulate the hysterical moods of her insulting spouse, and she did not know how to parry the dagger thrusts of Lady Jersey. She was outraged and unsubtle, but her courage and dignity in the abominable predicament in which she found herself aroused admiration in the English nation apart from the Court and must do so still. Historians have harped on Malmesbury's complaint that she did not wash, but that was *before* he told her Lady-in-Waiting. Presumably the next few months entailed daily scrubbing. Any prince who was a man would have regarded with tolerant amusement this high-spirited tomboy, ordered her to the bath-tub and taught her to curb her tongue.

When, at the end of June, Caroline realized with amazement that she was pregnant, she demanded the dismissal of Lady Jersey and appealed directly to the King who remonstrated with his son. Lady Jersey retired to plan revenge, and the Prince drove his wife to Brighton where she pronounced herself delighted with the sea air. They attended a field day at the camp together.

During August and September the Prince left his royal wife in the Pavilion and tried to see Mrs. Fitzherbert. He could not bear the suspicion that her silence might be due to contempt rather than grief.

Eventually some kind friend divulged the whole Fitzherbert story to the Princess. She felt no enmity. It was not this she minded. If only she could have had an occasional kind word. . . .

On January 7th, 1796, a daughter was born to Caroline at Carlton House. The nation rejoiced for now the succession was secure even if no other child arrived. Like Mrs. Fitzherbert the Princess of Wales was extremely fond of children, and this baby gave her comfort, though she knew that by law of the land the upbringing would not be left in her hands and she told a friend, 'This I shudder at very greatly.'

The Prince ought to have been grateful for the prompt arrival of an heir, but his little daughter only seemed to arouse more sadistic impulses. On January 10th, 1796, three days after the baby's arrival, he wrote that unbelievable pompous Will, which lies now in the Windsor Archives, leaving all he possessed to Mrs. Fitzherbert. He did not show it to her for three years, so it must have been devised more to appease his feelings than to lure her back. As always when unhappy, he had been eating and drinking far too much and a bilious fever fell on him after Christmas. He thought he was going to die.

The Will, which in its entirety would cover ten closely printed pages, arouses amazement and in its most pious passages absolute nausea. It begins thus:

'To Thee O ever merciful and Almighty God do I in these my last moments with the truest fervour and devotion and with all humility address myself to unveil my whole soul, and before my eyes are for ever closed, to speak that truth and to render that justice to others as well as to myself before my Creator as well as before the whole World, without which when brought before Thy great Tribunal I could never expect that mercy and justice to which all Christians are taught to look forward and in which faith as a true professor of the Christian Religion I have lived and now die.

By this, my last Will and Testament, I now bequeath, give and settle at my death all my worldly property of every description, determination and sort, personal and other, as shall be described, to my *Maria Fitzherbert*, my wife, the wife of my heart and soul. Although by the laws of this Country she *could not avail herself publicly of that name, still such she is in the eyes of Heaven, was, is and ever will be such in mine. And for the truth of which assertion I appeal to that Gracious God* Who I have here invoked to witness this my last disposition of my property, together with such explanations and declaration as are necessary for me to make, to enable me to quit this Life with a *clear conscience* and even without a sigh, except at the thought of leaving *Her* (and perhaps too without first receiving the blessing of her forgiveness) *who is my True and real Wife, and who is dearer to me, even millions of times dearer to me than*

107

life I am now going to resign. [The Prince often fancied himself on the verge of death.]

As much has been said in the World relative to our separation, I take it upon myself now to declare *that She (My Maria Fitzherbert)* has been most infamously traduced; that Her person, *Her Heart and her mind are, and ever have been from the first moment I knew her down to the present moment, as spotless, as unblemished, and as perfectly pure as anything can be that is human and mortal. Had it not been for the most infamous and basest of Calumnies, my too credulous and susceptible Heart, and which knew no other feeling in Life but for Her, could never have been brought, even for a single instant, to harbour a thought of separating from such Worth: nor was such a separation (O my God, as thou well knowest) voluntarily sought by me.*

But as entering further upon this point would involve others whom I pray to Heaven to forgive, and to lead to more than I am now able to write, I shall bury this part in oblivion.

As to Her (*I must also in justice to myself, so far say*), I am *most confident that had not similar base vile and scandalous wretches calumniated Me to Her and represented me in lights and in a manner,* I here ever in the presence of my Creator I have never deserved she *never could, or would, have persevered with such apparent cruelty and obduracy so foreign to the generous feelings of her Soul, in rejecting so great a length of time, every explanation, every submission, every step my tortured Heart frequently tried, and was most ready and anxious, to make, and which finally drove me to despair.*

I now therefore George Augustus Frederick Prince of Wales, Duke of Cornwall etc. etc. etc. do by this my Last Will and Testament leave, all my property, all my personalities of whatever kind or sort *to my Maria Fitzherbert,* who is my Wife in the eyes of God, and who is, and ever will be, such in mine. . . .

I likewise will and leave to Her the whole of the furniture of Carlton House, as it is all bought with my own Money together with all the Bronze ornamented chimney pieces, all the Hangings, Chairs, Tables ornamented and inlaid Tables, bronzed Tables, Cabinets and Consoles, girandoles, Clocks whether of Bronze or of other material. . . .'

In rambling language that appealed often to Heaven, the Prince went on to bequeath as well 'an immense Sum of money due to me from the Crown and from the Nation on the Arrears of the Duchy of Cornwall' and to hope all this 'just tribute' would evoke Maria's blessing on him. Having called her in several paragraphs 'my only true and real Wife' he then turned to his parents, asking their forgiveness for unintentional errors and left the management of his newly born daughter to the King and after his death to the Queen and his sisters Augusta and Mary and to the Duke of Clarence:

'This I have been so far induced to be explicit upon, meaning that the Mother of the Child, called the Princess of Wales, should in *no way either be concerned to the education or care of the Child or have possession of her person* for though I forgive the falsehood and treachery of her conduct towards me, still the convincing and repeated proofs of her entire want of judgement and of feeling, make me deem it incumbent etc. etc. to prevent the Child's falling into such improper and bad Hands as Hers.'

The Prince was in forgiving mood, he scattered his forgiveness like manna on all who had crossed his path.

More amiable are his references to Miss Pigot on whom he settled five hundred pounds annually for life because she had been 'so uniformly kind and attentive in her conduct both to *my Maria Fitzherbert* as well as to me'. And he speaks kindly of his domestics whom he asks his brothers to look after, especially 'my old and faithful Servant Santague, who from the time I was nine years of age has attended me with a Parent's care. . . .'

In point of fact the Prince was adored by his servants and showed them consideration at a time when most menials were appallingly treated.

The Will draws to its close with three pages of esoteric intentions concerning Mrs. Fitzherbert. Having stated his wish to be buried with as little pomp as possible, that the miniature of 'my beloved wife' should be buried with him 'and placed right upon my Heart' he further desires, that when she in turn dies, her coffin should be placed next to his 'and if she has no objection, that the two inward sides of the two Coffins should be taken out and the two Coffins soldered together'.

He then insists on her pension and promises grandly, as if with the Almighty's consent, 'Round thee, shall my soul forever hover, thy guardian angel, for as I never ceased to adore Thee whilst living, so shall I ever be watchful over Thee and protect Thee against every evil.'

The Will ends:

'Carlton House. January 12, 1796.

The whole of this Paper is written, signed and sealed by my own hand, so help me God.

George R.'

What Lady Jersey was doing during the scribbling of this Will it is hard to imagine. She must have blotted her copybook badly somewhere. The Prince had conveniently forgotten her existence.

Fourteen

THROUGHOUT the early spring of 1796 the Prince planned lures for Mrs. Fitzherbert. He wanted her back as his wedded, waiting wife to go home to every evening. He thought he could not live were her bedroom door not open to him. But this time Maria remained adamant. She saw the Prince in society occasionally but never alone. She was presented to the Princess. The eyes of the two wives met—an occurrence frequent enough in modern society but unique in the eighteenth century. She continued to accept her pension. That was all.

On April 30th, when the Prince had been married just over a year, he wrote Caroline a letter of dismissal as churlish as that he had sent Maria when he thought he no longer wanted her. Coldly informing the Princess of Wales that he wished for a separation, he promised to refrain from claiming marital rights even in the event of his daughter's death.

Probably he hoped this promise on his part would make it easier for a Catholic lady to regard him again as her husband. But Mrs. Fitzherbert could not return to his fold as if nothing had happened. She was shocked at his cruelty to Princess Caroline, and for three years she refused to meet him except as a polite, if not particularly grateful, subject. Miss Pigot and Admiral Payne bombarded her in vain with messages, notes, suggestions, explanations. She received them amicably but with resolve. The Princess of Wales's husband could not order her to bed.

His Royal Highness then wound himself into a dramatic frenzy such as he had tormented her with before. Early in 1799, worn down by threats, all heard fifteen years previously, she gave, and then withdrew, a promise to one of the royal dukes that she would be reconciled. Her momentary weakness elicited an hysterical torrent from the Prince, who was staying at Windsor Castle. This time he used the dangerous threat that if she refused to return to him he would openly declare their marriage. For all *he* cared, her brother and uncle could be punished for felony. If he abandoned the throne she must consider it all her fault.[1]

One summer night the Prince, shaking from head to foot, woke his younger brother the Duke of Cumberland, who had recently returned to England and whose nerves were therefore fresh, and pressed a letter into his hand with the order to deliver it immediately to Mrs. Fitzherbert. (Throughout the years there does not seem to have been a week when one of the royal brothers was not hurrying off to Mrs. Fitzherbert.) The Prince was weeping with hope and remorse and he insisted this missive must be 'delivered into her own hand only'. Cumberland obediently sent for horses and galloped off; Mrs. Fitzherbert was roused at dawn to receive him and read pages before she even had a cup of tea:

'Save me, save me, on my knees I conjure you, from myself. What. After a *solemn promise given, pledged to my brother* to be mine again, is there truth, is there honour in this world, and is it not inherent in you, Oh my friend, my friend Payne what will you say? Was it only to *trifle* with my *feelings that my hopes were to be raised, that fortune, prospects the only ones of life and happiness to me were to be held out to me, because the agonies I had already suffered were not sufficient: if you wish my life you shall have it, if you break your sacred promise recollect I am freed from all ties of attachment to this World as there is no reliance no more faith existing, I have then no fears left, nothing but honour in a world in which I have experienced nothing but misery and deceit . . . etc. reiterate your promise or recollect you sign yourself my doom.*

Wednesday morn. 4 o'clock. It is now two hours since I wrote the above, I have calmed myself and examined my heart, tis *honest and pure*, my tears are dried up. But my *resolution*

[1] Already the Prince had spoken indiscreetly of this intention. The Glenbervie Diaries reveal, March 31st, 1799, 'Is it that there is a foundation for what is generally whispered, viz. that the Prince of Wales is going to declare his marriage with Mrs. Fitzherbert? But what will be proposed for the Princess and her child? Shall we have the old case of Henry VIII renewed and the tables turned on the Protestants?'

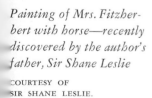

*Mrs. Fitzherbert from the
painting by Cosway*

*Painting of Mrs. Fitzher-
bert with horse—recently
discovered by the author's
father, Sir Shane Leslie*

COURTESY OF
SIR SHANE LESLIE.

Mrs. Fitzherbert—from a painting by Hoppner

George, Prince of Wales—from a painting by Hoppner

Morning Promenade upon the Cliff, Brighton.

This caricature of the Brighton social set was published in 1806. By James Gillray.
COURTESY OF PRINTS DIVISION, THE NEW YORK PUBLIC LIBRARY.

One of the many caricatures of the time attacking Mrs. Fitzherbert. This one, published 1786, shows beetle-browed Charles James Fox holding Mrs. Fitzherbert's left hand. By James Gillray. COURTESY OF PRINTS DIVISION, THE NEW YORK PUBLIC LIBRARY.

WIFE & no WIFE — or — A trip to the Continent.

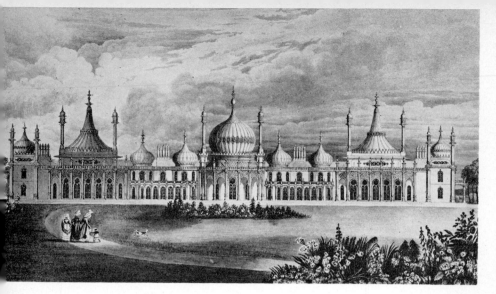

terior of Royal Pavilion at Brighton. From "Views of the Royal Pavilion" by John Nash.
RTESY ART DIVISION, THE NEW YORK PUBLIC LIBRARY.

e Music Room of the Royal Pavilion at Brighton. From "Views of the Royal Pavilion"
John Nash. COURTESY ART DIVISION, THE NEW YORK PUBLIC LIBRARY.

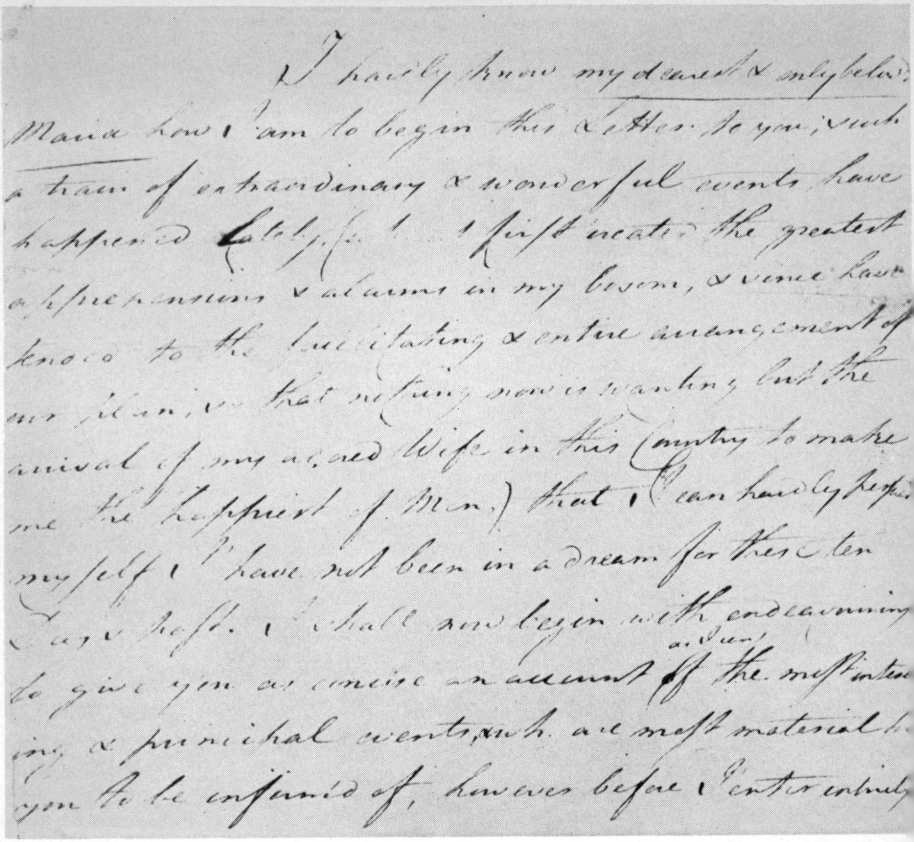

I hardly know my dearest & only belov'd Maria how I am to begin this Letter to you, such a train of extraordinary & wonderful events have happened lately, (w.ch at first created the greatest apprehensions & alarms in my bosom, & since have tended to the facilitating & entire arrangement of our plan, so that nothing now is wanting but the arrival of my adored Wife in this Country to make me the happiest of Men,) that I can hardly persuade myself I have not been in a dream for these ten days past. I shall now begin with endeavouring to give you as concise an account as I can of the most interesting & principal events, w.ch are most material for you to be informed of, however before I enter entirely

First page of the Prince's 42-page love letter to Mrs. Fitzherbert written before she returned to marry him in 1785. REPRODUCED BY GRACIOUS PERMISSION OF HER MAJESTY THE QUEEN. WINDSOR ARCHIVES.

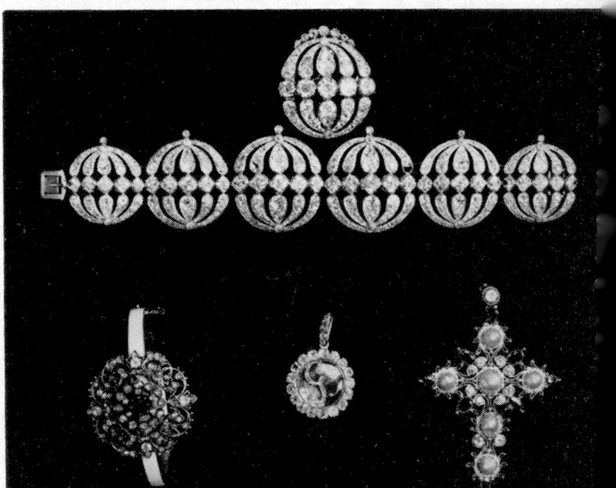

Some of the jewelry presented to Mrs. Fitzherbert by the Prince. The locket containing the diamond "G" was almost her first present.

The house in Tilney Street

UPPER RIGHT: *Swynnerton Hall*

RIGHT: *Marble Hill House*

Steyne House

DRAWINGS BY SHELDON LESLIE

Minney Seymour—from the painting
by Sir Thomas Lawrence

George Dawson Damer, husband to
Minney Seymour

Mrs. Fitzherbert by Cosway

is fixed. This letter precedes me, and my brother will deliver it into *your own hands himself, he knows* nothing of the contents.'

The Prince went on to threaten that if she did not consent to returning to his arms he would disclose their marriage and put her brother and uncle into danger.

'The wretched experience of the last five years have made life only desirable in one shape to me, and that is in you. I am wrapped up in you entirely; after seventeen years of a husband nothing can alter me, shake me or change me, alike yours in life or in death. . . .

And now God bless you my Maria, my only life, my only love.

Thine unalterably thine. George P.

Windsor Castle. June 11-12, 1799.'

'Think not that Payne or any advice whatever, will make me change my purpose, or *forswear my oath, thank God my witnesses are living,* your Uncle and your Brother besides Harris who I shall call upon, as having been *informed by me of every minutest circumstance of our marriage.* Oh my heart, my heart but I am composed and calm whatever your answer may be . . . etc.'

Despite his vaunted 'brilliant classical education', this Prince of Wales must, as a letter writer, be granted top marks as a soporific bore.

Mrs. Fitzherbert was disturbed, however. Not by his hints of suicide and doom, which she had heard before, but by the trouble he might cause those humble 'living witnesses'.

For some time past the royal family had been privately asking her to consider a reconciliation. The Queen had actually written Mrs. Fitzherbert in her own hand because she feared for her son's health. After his rupture with Lady Jersey the Prince had been, or pretended to be, extremely ill. He enjoyed a fever and bleated to his sisters that he was sure he would die if Mrs. Fitzherbert did not return to him. The Prince had well mastered the art of obtaining his own way by threat of nervous breakdowns. He could almost be said to have invented them.

Although calm and contented Mrs. Fitzherbert found the increasing strain intolerable. Must she go through it all over again? Happily for her mind's sake she had somewhere to turn for guidance. She appealed to her own Church to tell her what to do.

In the summer of 1799 Mrs. Fitzherbert informed the Prince that she had dispatched a petition to the Pope asking where her duty lay. If His Holiness said she should return as his wife she would do so. If not she would leave England for ever. The responsibility was off her shoulders.

It was the sort of clean-cut decision to abide by the rules that the Prince admired—and was himself incapable of. She allowed him to drive over from Kempshott for dinner while she stayed with Henry Errington. His Royal Highness seemed cowed, and agreed to attempt no further meeting until an answer had arrived from the Pope.

Meanwhile Mr. Nassau, one of the chaplains of Warwick Street Chapel in London, had been selected to travel to Rome.

'Mr. Nassau had his audience of the Pope on the eighth of July: His Holiness received him with great condescension and good-nature, bade him sit down and harkened to the narrative of his business with familiar attention. The conversation held in Latin and closed with the Pope's directing him to state the case in writing. . . .'[1]

While awaiting the answer Maria retreated to Wales. The Prince remained as good as his word and did not pester her, though he sent a copy of the infamous Will. An undated letter from him reads: 'As to the Paper I have put into your hands, it was with no view of distressing your feelings etc.' The Prince simply wished her to be acquainted with the contents. The relief he had felt in writing it four years before had, he said, restored him to life. 'Think not, my Angel, that there is one unkind expression about you contained in the whole of it. . . . How I have ever loved and adored you etc.'

Mrs. Fitzherbert made a quiet circuit. Few people knew where she travelled. Only the Seymours were kept informed. In the autumn a letter arrived from Lady Horatia Seymour to say

[1] Ragley Papers.

she was in some distress at having to leave five of her seven children and go to Madeira for her health. Mrs. Fitzherbert hurried from Bath to Portsmouth and asked if she might look after the youngest, a year-old baby called little Mary or Minney. Lady Horatia and her husband allowed her to take charge of the child, but with some misgivings when they realized Mrs. Fitzherbert might rejoin the Prince. The Seymours were Protestant—*very* Protestant! They thought that the Princess of Wales should be considered and that this was a matter for the conscience rather than the Pope. Horatia's sister, Lady Euston, wrote that the distracted consumptive mother grew ill each time Mrs. Fitzherbert tried to discuss the possibility of resuming a marital state with the Prince. 'And she once or twice said, I know, she would not have the courage to be reconciled to him if Hugh and I remained in England, but left to herself there is no answering for what she may do.'

Lord Hugh, who had stood bravely by Maria and been dismissed from the Prince's household because of his clear-cut opinions, deplored any idea of her resuming the connection. He thought the Prince had behaved appallingly to both wives, and that resumption of the marriage bond would create an impossible situation for poor Caroline. Lord Hugh loved Mrs. Fitzherbert and wished her well. He had given his youngest child to her charge. Firmly he hoped and prayed for her good sense now.

Fifteen

ON JANUARY 1st, 1800, to mark the turn of the century the Prince produced one of his more balanced epistles for 'Mine own own own', and before March they were once more united. The Brief from Rome declared that Mrs. Fitzherbert must regard herself as the only true wife of the Prince of Wales. For a time the Prince became exceedingly pro-Catholic. In fact he once said Catholicism was 'the only religion for a gentleman'. This attitude was perhaps natural when the Pope's opinion happened to exactly coincide with his own.

Mrs. Fitzherbert did not inform her friends of Rome's sanction. Many strait-laced Catholics were distressed when they observed her in the Prince's company. Lady Jerningham wrote (March 17th, 1800):

> 'The affairs of Mrs. Fitzherbert and the Prince become very incomprehensible. It is a fact that he meets her whenever he can and a conversation ensues which takes them out of the company. On Saturday, Lady Kenmare tells me, that Mrs. Fitzherbert, Mrs. Butler and the Prince were in a high box all night in conversation, the Princess at the Opera and also Lady Jersey. I comprehend it no longer for I had thought Mrs. Fitzherbert a woman of principle.'

To quell surmise Mrs. Fitzherbert assented to giving a large breakfast for the Prince on June 16th. All London society trooped to this formal afternoon reception with dancing. Several of her guests have described Mrs. Fitzherbert sitting beside the Prince, watching the dancers, with an air of immovable virtue, but they did not know her feelings. Years later she told Lord Stourton: 'She hardly knew how she could summon resolution to pass that severe ordeal, but she thanked God she had the courage to do so. The next eight years were, she said, the happiest of her connection with the Prince.'

It had all been so long-drawn-out and complicated. After fifteen years people grew tired of debating the affair. Now if the baby Princess could remain *incontestably* the legal heir to England's throne what did it really matter if the Prince had gone back to his former wife? As long as the lady demanded nothing except respect and there was no danger of a Catholic pretender, might it not be better to agree with the Prince's wishes? Gossipy letter-writers kept busy. On July 7th Lady Jerningham described a breakfast given by the Duchess of Devonshire:

'We found the Duchess sitting with Mrs. Fitzherbert by an urn. . . . The Prince was *en polisson*, a brown dress, round hat and a brown wig. He stood almost the whole time by his band with Dr. Burney ordering different pieces of music. Lady Jersey was casting round the spot where he stood with her daughters. The Prince was quite annoyed with her and eyed her askance, but she is resolved to plague him.'

An odd little MS note by Sir George Seymour in the Ragley Papers says that Maria had received one other opinion apart from the Pope's:

'On her saying that she wished to God she had a friend on whose judgement she could confide to advise her, Admiral Jack Payne encouraged his faithful servant Jephson to give his opinion, saying he knows the circumstances. Jephson said impassively, if Mrs. Fitzherbert consent to return, she will rue it all her life.'

The old servant was mistaken. Mrs. Fitzherbert's youth had ended, she was now forty-four and the next decade would prove far happier for her than the last.

In March 1801 Lady Horatia Seymour returned to England, leaving her husband commanding the Fleet from Jamaica. She reached London in a very weak condition and took a house where her children could visit her. Mrs. Fitzherbert brought the three-year-old Minney over every day and the Prince several times called to condole with the invalid. At this time Lord Hugh wrote his wife a long letter forgiving the Prince for demoting him:

'I have placed that circumstance to the score of his natural want of steadiness. I am however glad he shows you attention as it proves that he is sensible of having done wrong before. Mrs. F. only does me justice when she says that I was her true friend, and it is as true that she was driven to be glad when I was gone, but she can call me her comforter on that occasion, for she, poor soul, did not dare consult me, and I saw so clearly what was going on, that tho' I heartily wished her removed from the intrigues which were intended to effect what her character disapproved that I could not bring myself to *entamer* the subject which I then knew made her wretched— loving her as I do and have long done, it is impossible that I should not enter into her feelings. . . . I have open'd all the letters addressed to my Dearest, which have arrived since the 28th March, that day of wretchedness for us both, but I have not discovered any from P [the Prince] whose handwriting I only recollect to . . . seen as a P.S. to a letter of Mrs. Fitzherbert which you received before you left Jamaica.'

The Prince was angling to regain the respect of the Hugh Seymours through Maria, but the Admiral was never to speak to his royal master again.

When she grew weaker, Lady Horatia's sisters Lady Euston and Lady Waldegrave moved her to Clifton for better air. She died shortly afterwards on July 12th, 1801. Her husband died two months later in Jamaica. Mercifully he never received the letter containing news of two deaths, that of his adored wife and that of an eight-year-old son cared for by his grandmother, the Duchess of Gloucester.

Suddenly there were six Seymour orphans in the world. Of these, the eldest son George was a midshipman in the Navy, which he had entered at the age of ten. The youngest, three-year-old Minney, had hardly seen her parents. Mrs. Fitzherbert, who had long dreaded the day she might have to return this adorable cherub, wept for Horatia and Hugh but tightened her hold on the child. She immediately pleaded with the Seymour uncles and Waldegrave aunts to leave Minney with her for another year, if not permanently. They consented, though reluctantly.

Mrs. Fitzherbert now divided her time between Tilney Street, and her new house at Brighton. Unless the Prince was ill, in which case she remained to nurse him, she insisted on always occupying a separate residence. In 1801, while wings and façades were added to the Marine Pavilion, a residence in the Egyptian style was built on the Steyne for Maria. The local historian writes:

'The improvement which His Royal Highness has made and is still projecting and the elegant house which Porden, an architect of uncommon merit, is raising for Mrs. Fitzherbert will, I trust, check the listless torpor, and selfless apathy which has too long prevailed at Brighton, and reflect a certain taste and liberality on the sordid natives of this lawless waste.'

The 'sordid natives' certainly remained agog at the minarets and domes, and the smart set of London drove their carriages down for sea air in increasing numbers. The curious could often see the Prince breakfasting with Mrs. Fitzherbert on the veranda of her house and the élite might receive invitations to dine in the Pavilion where she presided.

Social scribblers voice a certain irritation against the Prince and his Lady, not on account of their puzzling marital state but because they had put on weight. The world likes thin lovers. A Brighton buck wrote cheekily to Miss Berry (February 18th, 1803): 'My neighbours here go on most lovingly. The affection seems to grow with their growth and fatten with their fat.'

Later on Lady Bessborough commented:

'I do not know what to do with the Prince and Princess of Wales. Hetty [Lady Hester Stanhope] tells me the Princess is ready to do anything that can please him and if he dislikes her interviews with his Father will go away to avoid them, if she could only have the satisfaction of knowing that it would please him. Just after hearing this I found the Prince's *Fat Friend* was all anxiety to send a message to the Princess, if she could find anybody to take it. . . .'

Mrs. Fitzherbert believed that if Caroline disclosed what she talked about when alone with the King it might alleviate the Prince's distrust and dislike. But no one knew how to convey these hints. As a peacemaker here Mrs. Fitzherbert certainly held a very delicate position. The Prince felt sure that Caroline was intriguing with his father against him. Only Mrs. Fitzherbert could see how to improve matters, but with so many critical eyes upon her she dared not try.

Criticize her the Court always would, but their mockery grew flat with the years. She alone held the Prince's heart—she who had never sought it. The Hon. Mrs. Calvert describes in her Journals a party she gave in May 1804.

'The King being pronounced well, I invited His Royal Highness and he came. He and Mrs. Fitzherbert were the last people in the house and I was much surprised at their going away in the same carriage, but that, I found afterwards, they always did.'

Mrs. Calvert attended the Pavilion where she becomes caustic at finding that Mrs. Fitzherbert did the honours of the house.

'She is now I believe about fifty, very fat but with a charming countenance, her features are beautiful, except her mouth which is ugly, having a set of not good false teeth but her person is too fat and she makes a great display of a very white but not prettily formed bosom, which I often long to throw a handkerchief over.'

As this Irish beauty's cattiness was inaccurate regarding age and teeth it probably exaggerated the bosom also. The proof of the pudding lies in the eating and Maria was surrounded by adoring men all her life. Lady Hester Stanhope said that Mrs. Fitzherbert remained into old age 'physically delicious'.

So there he was, the outrageous, amusing, detestable Prince, during the first decade of the new century. Mature and triumphant, with all he had most wanted. If he had lost his own good looks and good heart he owned Maria, and the vision of a sultan's palace to entertain her in. The wits called his lady 'fair, fat and forty', while Sir Sidney Smith dropped his unsurpassable remark on the Pavilion, 'Looks as if St. Paul's had gone down to Brighton and pupped.'

Sixteen

D URING these years, while the Prince divested himself of the Princess of Wales and Lady Jersey and wooed Maria for the second time, England fought the greatest sea battles of all time. Mrs. Fitzherbert knew many of the captains and admirals who raised their country to world supremacy. It is our tragedy that her letters during the intermittent wars with France have not survived. Especially must we regret her twenty-year-long correspondence with the Duke of York. She herself said these letters would have made the best private history of England. Her old friend, Admiral Sir John Jervis, had become Earl St. Vincent after the victory of that name. When he returned home he talked to Mrs. Fitzherbert about the genius of that young Captain Nelson to whom he had allowed such freedom of action that Nelson had dared sail out of the line and, said Jervis generously, win the battle for him. All that there was to hear concerning the tremendous events of the times came fast to her ears, all the political secrets she knew, all the excitements were discussed at her dinners. The rise of the French revolutionary armies, Napoleon's plan to invade England, the new broadside-guns, Pitt's resignation over Catholic emancipation, the seething destiny of Europe must have been the subject of general conversation. However much disapproval the Prince then evoked, he remained surrounded by the most interesting and amusing of his subjects, and Sheridan often came to alleviate with his wit the dissolute humour of hard-driving, hard-drinking, joke-playing friends.

The summer of 1803 must have been as stirring as 1940 and infinitely gayer. All through July and August England prepared to meet foreign invasion. Spies reported French ports crammed with flat-bottomed barges designed to carry troops, but the peer-less British Fleet kept France's warships in harbour. While Sir John Moore trained his Light Brigade in new tactics the entire nation rose up to join the Volunteers, a vast guerilla force intended to harry Napoleon's troops *after* they had landed. Naturally the Prince of Wales clamoured to be given a command. 'Nervous and agitated' Georgina described him when dining at Devonshire House. While the faithful Duchess attempted consolation in vain, the Prince admitted inability to command an army but swore he could collect the right generals 'to command and direct him'. Then, to the Prime Minister's intense anxiety, he rushed down to Brighton and presented himself as leader to the local Volunteers. Mrs. Fitzherbert did her utmost to calm him, but the Prince's vanity had been deeply stabbed. As a romantic with martial inclin-ations, he *longed* to lead armies. What better theatre for a Prince! He saw himself in the rôle too perfectly. It was torture to be frustrated by that monstrous father.

The King grew still more insane at this period, but the Cabinet were reluctant to admit it, even when His Majesty took to locking himself up in a room with a favourite housemaid or haranguing imaginary generals. Madness in the old monarch seemed less dangerous than the whims of an Heir Apparent em-broiled with a Catholic, and His Majesty remained popular with the nation. People referred to him as Princess Caroline's father did, as 'that decent man'.

In the October, when the invasion really appeared imminent, King George, lucid for a brief spell, reviewed the London Trained Bands in Hyde Park in front of two hundred thousand people. These Bands were entrusted with the defence of London. If the capital fell Englishmen intended to fight village by village, field by field across the entire country. But despite the expectation of enemy landing life continued gaily, perhaps more gaily than before.

Eighteen-hundred-and-three passed. When the new spring came, the wrought-up watching nation realized that Boney wasn't going to try. Mothers and wives felt relief but most young men regretted it. Such a welcome had been prepared! With sadness the smart militia uniforms had to be laid away in cedar.

Meanwhile the Prince still made his London political headquarters at Devonshire House. If crises became uncomfortable, or the King too aggravating, his fast horses galloped him away down the Brighton road. As Sir Osbert Sitwell says: 'In the years between 1788 and 1823 Brighton was, no doubt, the gayest, most fashionable place not only in England, but in all Europe.'

Social activities began at dawn when frail ladies immersed in the icy sea by various famous 'dippers' could be watched through telescopes by enterprising rakes! The late morning was devoted to visits to the smart libraries or promenades on the grassy Steyne, where belles and dandies flaunted the latest fashions and the Prince's horsey friends showed-off 'tooling' their four- or six-in-hands. In the afternoon came tea-parties, card-playing and dancing, and then dinners lasting four or five hours. Balls were frequent both in private homes and by public subscription.

In the centre of this glittering social whirl the Prince and Mrs. Fitzherbert lived exactly as they wished. Mrs. Fitzherbert never aspired to lead the fashion. She was interested in people and their doings, not in clothes. Her silken gowns with puff sleeves and her enormous feathered hats were merely the conventional turn-out of a gentlewoman. No arms whatsoever showed on her coach, those of Mr. Fitzherbert had been removed (in any case they bore an embarrassing likeness to those of His Royal Highness) and she avoided ostentation. When she strolled on the Steyne she would be escorted by her brother or uncle Errington, or by the Prince, who punctiliously insisted on conducting her in public as if she were Princess of Wales. The chimney-pot hats of the gallants were raised as she passed and the ladies watched covertly, wondering at her secret. By what art had she for so long enslaved the Heir to the Throne? How, when she had apparently lost him, did she get him back again? Why should this one guileless, middle-aged woman with her placid smile hold the most flamboyant prince of Europe? The truth was too simple. Maria had never tried. Whatever the feminine sneers at that 'over-plump white bosom', there alone did George of England find he could lay his head in peace.

Mrs. Fitzherbert liked integrity, kindness and coziness. As friends she picked brave, honourable men and simple affectionate women. Her pretty, rather silly sister, Lady Haggerston, frequently came to stay and organized idiotic little pastoral parties for the Prince. Lord Berkeley's son described one of these when Lady

124

Haggerston hired some cows and dressed as a milkmaid. The Prince enjoyed a syllabub made with cream so Lady Haggerston tripped out 'silver pail in one hand and an ornamental stool in the other' to milk one of her cows in front of the Prince. With ribbons flying from her hat and 'the smallest little apron tied below her laced stomacher' she curtsied and then, 'her tucked-up gown showing her neat ankle as well as her coloured stockings, she placed her stool & pail conveniently for use'. It was not until she had sat down to start work that the embarrassing fact dawned on her—this cow was a rather cross bullock. 'Covered with confusion' she hurried back to her sham dairy and the Prince without allowing a muscle in his face to flicker made a few tactful remarks about the weather and wandered off in search no doubt of less complicated refreshment.

Although Mrs. Fitzherbert never spent a night in the Pavilion, except when the Prince was ill, she dined there and sat as his wife doing the honours of his table. The outer-world of ladies buzzed with envy.

Mr. Creevey described his first invitation:

'Mrs. Fitzherbert whom I had never been in a room with before, sat on one side of the Prince, and the Duke of Clarence on the other. In the course of the evening the Prince took me up to the card-table where Mrs. Fitzherbert was playing.'

Later Mrs. Creevey became a close friend and often dined at the Pavilion where it was the Prince's custom to invite one other lady as companion for Mrs. Fitzherbert—if not Mrs. Creevey this might be Lady Downshire or Lady Clare or Lady Berkeley. There were usually fourteen men or more; the habit of sitting down equal numbers had not yet arisen.

The cooking was, of course, superb. Each of the nine courses had to be washed down by a special wine. And amusing conversation must have been needed to wash down the meal, for it lasted four or five hours each night. Between ten and eleven a fresh batch of guests arrived for the musical part of the evening. The Prince expressed delight if anyone could sing or play, and he showed the utmost consideration to shy girls who had to be led blushing to the piano. He never showed any predilection towards

125

making his subjects feel foolish. Guests who detested music must have suffered sorely, however, for in summer the Prince's German band played outside on the lawn and in winter the musicians sat in an adjoining room more or less drowning conversation.

Mrs. Fitzherbert enjoyed whist, and would immediately make up a table and play happily against the noise, but the Prince never touched cards and spent these informal evenings talking casually to an occasional pet guest, or more often merely listening to his band, beating time and sending directions. That excellent tenor voice with which he had as a young man serenaded the fair sex had lasted true throughout periods of debauch. Sometimes still he sang a favourite melody with his violins. Then Maria Fitzherbert lost intentness on her game and as she paused for a moment with cards forgotten in her hand, the other players would see a softness light her face. Thus he had sung to her as a young man. How could she not love him?

Occasionally there would be dancing or even sports. Mrs. Creevey brought her daughters to the Pavilion after dinner on October 29th, 1805. They waited until after eleven o'clock for the Prince to arrive from the dining-room.

'I instantly saw that he had got more wine than usual,' wrote Mrs. Creevey, 'and it was still more evident that the German Baron [a kind of *metteur en scène* who devised Storms of Thunder, Lightning & Rain] was extremely drunk. The Prince came up and sat by me—introduced Mr. Mahon to me & talked a great deal about Mrs. Fitzherbert. . . . Afterwards the Prince led all the party to see him shoot with an airgun at a target placed at the end of the room. He did it very skilfully, & wanted all the ladies to attempt it. The girls & I excused ourselves on account of our short sight; but Lady Downshire hit a fiddler in the dining-room, Miss Johnstone a door, and Bloomfield a ceiling. . . . At last a waltz was played by the band and the Prince offered to waltz with Miss Johnstone, but very quietly, and once round the table made him giddy, so of course it was proper for his partner to be giddy too; but he cruelly only thought of supporting himself. . . .'

Mrs. Fitzherbert wisely stuck to her whist.

A few nights later the Baron launched his *Phantasmagoria*, and Mrs. Fitzherbert joked on the advantages he might take of Miss Johnstone in the dark but only Sheridan created an uproar, sitting on the lap of a hysterical Russian countess when the lights were extinguished.

On another evening which must have been far from gay, the Prince tried to stage a reconciliation between Sheridan and Warren Hastings. Creevey professed himself horrified at this unusual tactlessness. All knew that eighteen years before 'Sheridan's parliamentary fame had been built upon his celebrated speech against Hastings'. The meeting proved a fiasco. Sheridan attempted cordiality but no words could make amends for such bitter injustice. An icy atmosphere blew through the Pavilion's hothouse rooms as Sheridan stretched out his hand, 'attempting to cajole old Hastings, begging him to believe that any part he had ever taken against him was purely political and that no one had a greater respect for him than himself, etc. etc., upon which old Hastings said with gravity that it would be a great consolation to him in his declining days if Mr. Sheridan would make that sentence more public'.

The Prince quickly spotted the hopelessness of a reconciliation. Perhaps when he became Regent he could make amends, for the moment it was better to concentrate on the musical programme and wine arrangements where he really did know what he was about.

Through all their years together Mrs. Fitzherbert had tried to restrain the Prince from drinking himself ill, not an easy task when certain cronies paid a visit. The wild horseplay of Sir John Lade and the successive Lord Barrymores to a certain extent curbed the actual intake of alcohol. A more difficult visitor was the old Duke of Norfolk, who made it his custom to drive over from Arundel every year for two nights 'to pay his respects'. The Duke was famous even in that age for the amount he could drink. To everyone's admiration he always remained apparently sober until the moment he stiffened into unconsciousness, when four specially trained footmen carried him away.

The Duke liked routine. The numerous mothers of his illegitimate children all had to be paid at the same bank on the same day while he watched through a glass partition. Sir Osbert Sitwell evokes the scene: 'Blue eyes, Jewish noses, gipsy skins and woolly black hair were seen to be grafted on to the unmistakable Howard features of the infants borne along in their mothers' arms, or of stalwart children now obliged to wheel their mother in a chair.'

The Prince could not emulate Norfolk's heroic capacity for port. When, after one dinner, surgeons had to be called from London, Mrs. Fitzherbert feared her prince might not survive another paying of respects.

Creevey noted the Duke's following visit when 'Mrs. Fitzherbert who was always the Prince's best friend, was very much afraid of his being again made ill & she persuaded the Prince to adopt different stratagems to avoid drinking with the Duke. I dined there on both days & letters were brought in each day after dinner to the Prince, which he affected to consider of great importance and so went out to answer them while the Duke of Clarence went on drinking with the Duke of Norfolk. . . .'

Mrs. Creevey, in pages always amusing, occasionally inaccurate and generally indiscreet, sketches a winter scene:

'My head is very bad, I suppose with the heat of the Pavilion last night. We were there before Mrs. Fitzherbert came & it almost made her faint, but she put on no airs to be interesting & soon recovered and I had a great deal of comfortable prose with her. . . .

The Prince only allowed two of the gentlemen who had dined with them to join her afterwards lest they disturb her. Before she came, he was talking of the fineness of the day and said, But I was not out, I went to Mrs. Fitzherbert's at one o'clock and stayed talking with her till past 6 which was certainly very *unfashionable*. Now was he not at that moment thinking of her as his lawful wife? For in no other sense could he call it *unfashionable*.'

Of course he was thinking of her as his lawful wife and this was a slip of the tongue. Full of curiosity and gossip, the Creeveys professed themselves appalled by the political intrigues of the Devonshires. Mrs. Creevey tried to ferret out Maria's views (November 8th, 1805):

'It is quite impossible to keep clear of Devonshire House and there her opinions are *all* precisely mine & yours and what is better, she says they are *now* the Prince's: that he knows everything—above all, how money is made by promises, unauthorized by him, in the event of his having power; that he knows how his character is involved in various transactions of that House & that he only goes to it from motives of compassion and old friendship when he is persecuted to do so. In short, he tells Mrs. Fitzherbert all he sees and hears, shews her all the Duchess's letters & notes and she says she knows the Duchess hates her. . . .'

Georgina had always resented the Prince's obsession with Mrs. Fitzherbert, but she had not much time left for hating. She was extremely ill from gallstones, while the knowledge that she must once more confess her colossal gambling debts to the Duke, lowered her extraordinary vitality.

Poor Georgina, she had always tried to find the right moment to divulge her losses. Once she had waited for the birth of a son, but then somehow she had not confessed completely. Later in 1792 came a less propitious moment for revelation. By then the warm-hearted Duchess was with child by young Charles Grey, the future Prime Minister. The Duke banished her for two years to Italy from where she wrote delightfully inconsequential letters to Mr. Coutts her banker. Now, as the sands of her ardent life were running out, the debts seemed, to her bewilderment, to exceed £100,000—an odd little sum to explain away to even the most docile husband.

Dying but ever game, she continued to write letters to Fox and Sheridan and the Prince who still sought her advice on many subjects, including that of a suitable governess for the Princess Charlotte.

To the last, Georgina had to keep her finger on the political pulse. Her mind remained alive despite constant pain, and the Prince mourned for her sufferings. In a letter to her mother she describes his consideration for her and their mutual doctor when the Prince certainly had discomforts of his own.

'I will not allow myself to dwell yet on my gratitude to

129

God for having spared me. The Prince was so kind that, tho'
extremely ill with a diarrhoea he forbid Sir Walter's being told
of it lest he should take him from me. He continues very ill, I
hear, having had 10 motions after a stoppage of 4 days. . . .'

Even a Hanoverian digestion must in time succumb to nightly
nine-course dinners with '116 dishes and a multitude of wines'.

In January 1806 Pitt, the King's friend and the Prince's
enemy, died. The Ministry of all the Talents was then formed with
Lord Grenville as Prime Minister and Charles James Fox at the
Foreign Office. How Devonshire House rejoiced! Georgina
wrote to her son, 'The more you know of Mr. Fox's character
the more you will admire the great features of his mind, the vast
comprehension that takes in any subject, united to a candour &
benevolence that renders him as amiable as he is great.'

In February she gave a brilliant assembly and supper for the
new Ministers. It looked as if the Prince might be in for a particularly interesting time, with his friends on the crest of a new political
wave. But a month later the phenomenal Duchess died and the
Prince saluted her going, 'There we have lost the most amiable &
best-loved woman in England', he said. Before the year elapsed
Fox, who had waited so long to reach power, was also dead.

Seventeen

HILE political storms shook Tories and Whigs and the great sea battles with France were fought and the uneasy Peace of Amiens bloomed and broke, a new generation was growing up. The two women whom the Prince of Wales had named wife were both by nature extremely fond of children. Caroline of Brunswick visited her little Charlotte, England's heir, as often as permitted. And in Mrs. Fitzherbert's house lived the enchanting child, Minney Seymour. The Princess of Wales, as she saw steadily less of her own daughter, took to adopting a number of healthy little boys and girls, orphans or from homes of the very poor. Her home, Montague House, Greenwich Park, seems to have rather resembled a happy kennel for stray puppies. She obtained great consolation from these cheerful youngsters— as observers remark, not minding their running noses or sore faces. The Prince, eager to believe gossip, then started that *indelicate* proceeding in the House of Lords known as 'the Delicate Investigation' which aimed at discovering if one of the boys was, in fact, her own.

Mrs. Fitzherbert may or may not have borne children to the Prince, but however that matter stood she had now come to love little Minney Seymour as if she were her own child, and the Prince, who showed no affection for his legal daughter, focussed an inordinate adoration on this small miss. Every day, whether in London or at Brighton, His Royal Highness liked to enjoy his *play hour*. Mrs. Fitzherbert's drawing-room had to be transformed for these frolics—bamboo furniture proving extraordinarily topply—and pert Minney, all dressed up, would scamper in to sit on Prinney's knee, to slide and play ride-a-cock-horse. Political frustration, his father's tantrums, Napoleon Bonaparte and Nelson's battles were then shelved in the back of the Prince's mind while he indulged in that careless rapture never permitted to himself as a little boy. No one romped in the nursery curriculum laid down by George III.

When in 1802, Minney then being four years old, her uncles Lord Hertford and Lord Euston began to worry over the propriety of allowing her to remain in charge of a Roman Catholic, the Prince hurled himself into the fray. His Royal Highness wrote excitedly to Lord Euston on his feelings towards 'my favourite Minney, who I have the pleasure to tell you is in most perfect health, improves daily and is the most delightful Child in the World'. He then made a long and detailed Proposal which started:

'The Prince of Wales being fully convinced that the welfare & happiness of the Child, are essentially dependent on her continuance under the care of Mrs. Fitzherbert; and it appearing by the evidence before the Master, that she cannot be removed without injury to her hurt and peril of her life; he feels it an indispensable part of the parental duty he so solemnly engaged to her dying mother to fulfil, to protect her to the utmost of his power, in her present happy situation, and therefore nothing short of a stipulation, that she shall remain there unmolested until she shall be of an age to choose for herself, will satisfy his mind.'

In sentences of such and greater length he states his immediate intention of adding £10,000 to the funds already in trust for Minney, his hope that she may be brought up as a 'bosom friend' of the Princess Charlotte, his firm intention of educating her under his own eye as a member of the Church of England, and his determination to resist any efforts to take her away from him and Mrs. Fitzherbert.

Lord Euston and Lord Henry Seymour, the executors, viewed coldly the Prince's pledge to supervise 'the purity of her morals' and refused the proposal, £10,000 and all. So the Prince sent Admiral Payne off with a 'Second Proposal'. This also was brushed aside.

Mrs. Fitzherbert, whose starved maternal instincts had blossomed so late, lived in continual tears and terror. And the Prince of Wales having never seen her in such a state, and himself doting on this child, harangued his lawyers. They shivered slightly on hearing the Prince swear he would *stop at nothing* to win the child. Everyone knew he excelled at that game.

Now a shadow fell over the gay existence which he and Mrs. Fitzherbert had evolved at Brighton. The fear of losing Minney spoiled everything. To celebrate Maria's return to his side the Prince had started to expand the Pavilion and to redecorate the interior in Chinese style. Hand-painted Chinese papers of blue, grey and yellow were chosen for the drawing-room while the Private Apartments blossomed white and green. Porcelain vases, lacquer or bamboo furniture accumulated. It had been such fun to plan it with her. And now this cruel threat ruined their peace of mind. All the dinners and suppers the Prince gave at the Pavilion could not divert them, when the person they wanted most might be snatched away.

There was nothing for it but a lawsuit, a most unusual legal battle fought out finally in the House of Lords with the Prince of Wales and the Royal Dukes pleading on one side and the relatives of Lord Hugh and Lady Horatia on the other. It took three years to build up the case, which attracted tremendous publicity and eventually resulted in some very curious human reactions.

While the Seymours were struggling to remove Minney from Mrs. Fitzherbert, the King and Queen were fighting against the Prince to obtain possession of Princess Charlotte. He did not care for his daughter, but hate for her mother drove him to claim her. Mrs. Calvert, the catty Irish beauty, gave her personal views on Mrs. Fitzherbert's dilemma:

'She has a sweet little girl who lives with her. . . . She is about five years old. Lord Hugh's family and also Lady Horatia's have objected to her living with Mrs. Fitzherbert for many reasons. They very naturally consider the Prince's mistress (for what else can one call her, he having a wife?) not the most respectable protectress—besides she is a Roman Catholic. But she has carried her point & keeps her, promising faithfully to educate her in the Protestant religion and I understand she has a clergyman of that persuasion to come to her, three or four times a week. The Prince and Mrs. Fitzherbert are passionately fond of this little creature, whom they

133

always call Minney. She calls Mrs. Fitzherbert "Mama" and the Prince "Prinney" and I hear at the time that her family wanted to get her from Mrs. Fitzherbert, she often clung with her little arms round the Prince saying, "Prinney, won't you fight for me: You won't let them take me from you!" The Prince, I hear, had engaged to give her ten thousand pounds.'

Fight for her he did when the time came, with no holds barred. Mrs. Fitzherbert had a certain case, for the Will appointing Lord Euston and Lord Henry guardians had been made before Minney was born. The defence was that 'whatever amiable qualities she might possess, the Religion she professed excluded her from the right to retain the custody of a Protestant child'. During the next year or so she appealed to various courts and pathetically produced evidence from Bishops that Minney could recite the Protestant catechism. But judgements were invariably given against her.

In January 1805 Lady Horatia's sister, Lady Euston, wrote to Minney's midshipman brother George:

'We are still in suspense about little Mary though I hope that it will be decided in a few days. It is impossible to express all the anxiety that it has caused me, as everything has been tried that could possibly be thought of to defeat our object. I have never had any doubt of our success, but being obliged to act with such an appearance of harshness towards Mrs. Fitzherbert is extremely painful to my feelings. At the same time I am supported by the consciousness that I am acting in the manner which would most please your dear Father and Mother if they could witness all that is passing, and though I may & must feel for Mrs. Fitzherbert I must not allow such feelings to interfere with my duty to any of the children of the two people I ever had the most reason to love in this world.'

One evening in early November 1805 a messenger from the channel port arrived at the Pavilion with urgent news. The Prince went straight to Mrs. Fitzherbert and told her of the Battle of Trafalgar which had been fought on October 21st and of Nelson's death. She knew the details before any other woman in England. A day later she wrote to her friend Mrs. Creevey:

'Nov. 6 1805
Dear Madam, the Prince has this moment received an account from the Admiralty of the death of poor Lord Nelson, which has affected him extremely. I think you may wish to know the news which upon any other occasion might be called a glorious victory—twenty out of three and thirty of the enemy's fleet being entirely destroyed—no English ship being taken or sunk—Captains Duff and Cook both killed and the French Admiral Villeneuve taken prisoner. Poor Lord Nelson received his death by a shot of musket from the enemy's ship upon his shoulder and expired two hours after, but not till the ship struck and afterwards sunk, which he had the consolation of hearing, as well as his complete victory before he died. Excuse this hurried scrawl. I am so nervous I scarcely can hold my pen.'

Two days later Mrs. Creevey recorded a visit to Mrs. Fitzherbert:

'They found her alone and she was excellent—gave me an account of the Prince's grief about Lord Nelson and then entered into the domestic failings of the latter in a way infinitely creditable to her and skilful. She was all for Lady Nelson and against Lady Hamilton, who, she said (hero as he was), overpowered him & took possession of him quite by force. But she ended in a natural good way by saying: "Poor creature. I am sorry for her now, for I suppose she is in grief."'

Nelson's death affected people in different ways. Young George Seymour, who had been at sea worrying over his little sister, now wondered if he would receive the promotion the great Admiral had promised him. Lady Euston wrote him (November 17th, 1805):

'To have been distinguished by him at your age must be a most gratifying remembrance to you and can never be forgot and I trust that Lord Nelson even in his Grave will still serve his Country.'

What could she have meant? That Nelson must whisper to his

captains in future battles? Or dispatch an angel to the Admiralty to nudge the officer in charge of Master Seymour's promotion?
    Aunt Euston continued:

> 'I am much pleased with what you say about your poor little Sister Mary. I trust that the decision of the House of Lords will be favourable and obtained soon after the opening of the Sessions.'

In June 1806 the Prince of Wales brought the Seymour case before the peers. Lady Euston had written *her* account of the Prince's last visit to Minney's mother for the Attorney-General:

> 'He talked of his own daughter, of little Mary, of Lord Hugh, chiefly addressing his conversation to me & almost without waiting for an answer. Lady Horatia did not speak to him at all, and as she sat with her head turned towards me, she once or twice in a low voice expressed a degree of vexation at his volubility—and she grew more and more faint and I, thinking to put an end to the visit, moved two or three times to take my leave but she detained me. At last she whispered to me: I believe you had better go for I see I shall never get rid of him while you stay. I then left them & before I got home I saw him pass in his Curricle so I knew he could not have stayed long after I was gone. In the evening when I saw her, she said: That she was not sorry that she had seen him, for that after I was gone he had mentioned Lord Hugh and all her children in a very affectionate manner, which she knew would please Hugh as he was certainly more attached to the Prince than he now liked to acknowledge and that his protection might certainly be some time or other of use to her sons.'

This was not quite the version the Prince gave. *He* said that Lady Horatia had been delighted to talk with him, and had pressed her daughter into his care asking him to take an oath & solemnly swear to be 'the father & protector through life of the dear child'. The idea of *him* tiring anyone was quite ridiculous. Invalids revived in his presence.
    Minney's aunt could not know that, hoping to find the peers more amenable than the court judges, His Royal Highness was

dropping some extraordinary hints. He had sworn himself ready to do anything, say anything, to obtain this child. Only George Prince of Wales who went in for 'delicate subjects' could have devised this new line of reasoning. To the consternation of the Seymour family His Royal Highness now whispered that *he* was Minney's father. The stern Protestant uncles and aunts, the legal guardians with all their patter about consciences and respectability, froze in their tracks. No one quite believed it. But the Prince was absolutely sure. How could a child as enchanting as Minney have been sired except by himself? To have cuckolded his stern friend, the gallant Lord Hugh while he was away at sea fighting England's battles, now seemed in retrospect a most desirable act. The more he thought about fathering Minney the surer grew the Prince that he *had* done so.

And who could contradict him? Poor Lady Horatia whom he had exasperated and exhausted could not arise to defend her honour.

Eighty or ninety of the peers he canvassed listened with interest if not with credulity—and promised to stand on his side. So did the royal dukes, except Gloucester, who was a half-brother of Lady Horatia.

More important still, the Prince called upon Lord Hertford, head of the Seymour family, and made a private arrangement. Dazed and embarrassed by the length to which the Prince was ready to go, Lord Hertford gave assurances that if Minney were given to his custody he would leave her with Mrs. Fitzherbert. Lady Hertford went still further. To alleviate the tension she promised Maria that under no circumstances would she allow her husband to weaken even if sore pressed by all the Seymour family. Mrs. Fitzherbert wept with gratitude, and the Prince felt sufficiently secure to write the Duke of Norfolk, safely won over with best vintage port: 'June 3rd, 1806: I have seen Lord Hertford, who will call upon you in the course of the day, or, at any rate, before the business is brought before the Committee.'

Sir Samuel Romilly who appeared for the Seymours has described the final day of the trial (June 14th, 1806).

'I replied in the House of Lords in the appeal respecting the guardianship of Miss Seymour. The order of the Lord

137

Chancellor was reversed and Lord and Lady Hertford were by the House appointed the guardians. Several peers voted against this but there was no division. I counted between eighty & ninety peers who were present. The Prince, who was as anxious that Mrs. Fitzherbert should continue to have the care of the child as he could have been if the child had been his own, and who knew that Lord and Lady Hertford would not remove her, had earnestly entreated all his friends to attend.'

Romilly went on to deplore the Prince's action and to state that 'to canvass votes for a judicial decision is that which cannot be too strongly reprobated'.

But who cared about this when little Minney's future had to be secured? By fair means or foul the Prince meant to get her. When Lord Hertford offered to take the guardianship upon himself the Committee immediately agreed to the proposal and gave him 'unfettered power of action'.

The Prince's friends and brothers rejoiced. They knew a private arrangement had been made. The Duke of Kent promptly wrote to congratulate Mrs. Fitzherbert.

'Accept then the assurance of my best wishes on this, as well as on every occasion in which your happiness is concerned and believe me it is no small gratification to me to reflect that I have had the opportunity of proving by my conduct that in saying this I am far from meaning empty professions. Pray give my love to your *little Angel*.'

Concerning Minney's other aunt Lady Waldegrave who had struggled with Lady Euston to claim the child, Mrs. Fitzherbert wrote:

'Came to town on purpose, wrote to all the Press to support her, turned out the people she had let her house to in Berkeley Square and fixed herself in it, telling everybody my poor Child was to go to reside with her on Saturday evening. What a horrid creature she is! Thank God she has been disappointed.'

Lady Euston, not knowing of Hertford's promise to the Prince, wrote hurriedly to her nephew George:

'After having indulged the House of Lords with four days pleading upon the subject of your poor little Sister, Lord Hertford yesterday proposed himself as her guardian and was accepted as such. . . . What Lord Hertford's plans are we of course do not know. . . . Since I wrote the above I have been told that the Bishop of St. Asaph did propose Mrs. Fitzherbert as Guardian! but as he likewise is said to have talked of spirits coming from *the shades of Pluto,* we are certainly at liberty to doubt, not only whether he is a Protestant Bishop, but also whether he is a Christian.'

Her triumph was short-lived. By July 1st she knew Lord Hertford intended leaving seven-year-old Minney with Mrs. Fitzherbert and she wrote again to George:

'The prospect for your poor little Sister's moral and religious education is a melancholy one, and I am sorry to say from all I hear that the great object of those she now lives with is to fill her mind with ideas of her superiority over her Sister, but I am happy to say that dear Racey's good sense is superior to her Age and she sees the folly of such conduct and only pities her Sister for having such nonsense put into her head. . . . Mrs. Fitzherbert must feel she will be answerable to us all for any misconduct of your poor little Sister and has in fact (to indulge her own inclinations) run the risk of being called to a very severe account if this child fails in any moral or religious duty. . . . Nothing can justify Lord Hertford's conduct, etc. etc.'

Rules were laid down. Only the most Protestant of Protestant governesses might approach Minney. Mrs. Fitzherbert, thankful to have obtained surety, was ready to toe the line meticulously. She became terrified on receiving an outburst from Lady Euston who had *heard* that the French governess might be Roman Catholic! No. No indeed! Mrs. Fitzherbert's guileless endeavours to win Seymour approval showed up rather too obviously when Minney's elder sister Racey came over for the day.

'Racey has seen poor little Mary two or three times, but they are not comfortable together, for I suppose that in order that it may be repeated to us, there is such a display of education that when Racey visits Mary nothing else is thought of, but to show how much she has learned, is learning or is to learn, that Racey can only laugh at the parade.'

Poor Mrs. Fitzherbert tried too hard. The pitiless aunt observing her fears did not spare sarcasm over these assiduous endeavours.

The Prince, of course, remained in raptures. He had won—as he always did when he expended enough tears, cajolery and threats. His little home beside the Pavilion would continue. The three of them could live on happily together, teasing and laughing. As long as the governesses remained *very* Protestant and Minney never inadvertently romped in Mrs. Fitzherbert's private Oratory they were safe. Who could wreck this domestic Utopia?

Who indeed!

Lady Hertford had graciously accepted showers of thanks, but Mrs. Fitzherbert still asked for some method of showing her gratitude. There was nothing in the world she would not do to repay so immense a favour. Lady Hertford possessed a strong character. It had been *her* assurance that she and her husband would leave Minney with Mrs. Fitzherbert which had pulled them confidently through the dreadful weeks before the trial. Over and over again Mrs. Fitzherbert wept tears of thankfulness when she called. There was nothing she would not do for her . . . absolutely nothing!

Lady Hertford smiled coolly. Obviously Mrs. Fitzherbert was besotted by the child, her relief at gaining control of Minney blotted out any senses she might have had. Why should she guess that her benefactor—no beauty herself, rather grim-looking in fact—found it somewhat dull to be Marchioness of Hertford? My lady had decided that more amusing powers might be obtained by playing the rôle of Protestant inamorata to a Prince of Wales.

Eighteen

THE price which Mrs. Fitzherbert must pay for little Minney was not immediately plain. Lady Hertford allowed Maria and the Prince to simmer for a time in utmost content. Her shrewd eye watched the ménage carefully, but she could afford to wait before insinuating herself more deeply in the Prince's confidence, and she knew well that however she behaved towards Minney's adopted mother no complaints could be made. The cards all lay in her pocket.

Within three weeks of the happy ending of the Seymour case, Prinney and Mrs. Fitz were enjoying themselves at Brighton. Lady Jerningham describes the scene:

'Races were being held and a great number of gentlemen are arrived to pay court to the Prince who protects these Races. He was on the course on the Box of his barouche. Mrs. Fitzherbert in another carriage-and-four with her brothers and other gentlemen—the two Barouches standing by each other and the Prince frequently in conversation with her from his Box.'

This carefree scene took place in the very week that the Committee of Lords concluded 'the Delicate Investigation' into the conduct of Caroline of Brunswick and acquitted her of all charges of immorality. (Never has a Prince of Wales kept the House so busy.)

Meanwhile the name of little Miss Seymour started to creep into the records of Pavilion festivities. Around her seventh or eighth birthday there is a description of a Ball given by the Prince:

'Mr. Sheridan, who arrived here the day before, was of the Royal Party. On the night following it being the natal day of the little interesting protégée of Mrs. Fitzherbert, Miss Seymour, this young lady gave a Ball and supper to a party of juvenile nobility at the Pavilion.'

All the summer of 1806 proved a happy one for Maria, but when the Prince's forty-fifth birthday occurred on August 12th, Mrs. Fitzherbert suffered a chill and it was her sister Lady Haggerston who accompanied Minney to the celebration:

'This being the natal day of the heir apparent the morning was ushered in by the ringing of bells and the flag was hoisted on the tower of the Church. Two oxen *pro bono publico* are roasting whole on the Level. At half-past twelve the Prince of Wales, habited as a Field Marshal, a star at his breast accompanied by his royal brother and mounted on a grey charger, splendidly caparisoned, left the Pavilion for the Downs where the following Regiments were drawn up in line. . . . The Royal brothers were all in regimentals with stars at their breasts. The Duke of Sussex wore his Highland uniform. . . . Lady Haggerston and Miss Seymour, the Lord Chancellor, Lord Headfort, Mr. Sheridan and Mr. Smythe were in the Prince's landau. Mrs. Fitzherbert was detained at home by indisposition.'

Mrs. Fitzherbert's Brighton house, built in the Egyptian style, had, perhaps happily, blown down in a gale. Now the Prince ordered his architect, William Porden, to build her a French villa, a little further from the Pavilion, on the western side of the Steyne.[1] While the Prince toyed with the idea of completely rebuilding the Pavilion as an Indian Palace to match his domed stables, countless graceful houses with bow windows and fluted columns were being constructed for the ever-increasing numbers of aristocracy and gentry who, to be fashionable, now had to spend half their year at Brighton.

Delay had been caused in the building of the fantastic Pavilion stables owing to Napoleon's blockage of the Baltic ports which,

[1] This house with its small oratory is now occupied by the Y.M.C.A.

among other inconveniences, made it impossible to obtain timber of sufficient length to support the dome of the exercising school. This engineering feat of Porden's measured eighty feet across. At last it could be finished, and while the Prince's wife moved into her villa the Prince's horses munched beneath the biggest dome in England encrusted with lotus leaves.

The new church on the Steyne now became fashionable. From it the Royal Standard was flown to denote the Prince's occupation of the Pavilion and unctuously the Press recorded: 'the example which the Nobility set here to the lower order of people by attending divine worship on a Sunday is productive of the most salutary effect and the most decorous solemnity prevails throughout the town'. The nobility set other examples as well, less salutary, but on the whole too expensive to be copied by the 'lower orders'.

Meanwhile Lady Hertford played her game very, very carefully. She knew that being Protestant her domination of the blowsy headstrong middle-aged Prince must become popular. Throughout 1807 and 1808 she steadily pressed herself forward, gaining his confidence and, when in London, trying to lure him away from Tilney Street to her own magnificent mansion, Hertford House (now the Wallace Collection in Manchester Square).

Obediently her husband and son, both arbiters of taste, persuaded the Prince to busy himself buying up those exquisite pieces of eighteenth-century French furniture which, owing to the Revolution, were coming on the market. (As a result the Royal collection is to this day unsurpassable.) Discussion of furniture is very safe ground. Such activities appeared blameless if expensive, and her ladyship's nose could be carried primly in the air while society watched every move.

In June 1807 Mrs. Calvert was agog at a grand Assembly at Mrs. Fitzherbert's for 'all the fine world, the Prince of Wales, Duke of York, Dukes of Clarence, Cambridge & Kent were all there, dressed in full uniform'. But a month later, in July 1807, the sky had clouded. 'Last night we went to a ball at Lady Hertford's. I think poor Mrs. Fitzherbert much deserted by him now. He has taken it into his head to fall desperately in love with Lady Hertford . . . without exception the most forbidding, haughty, unpleasant-looking woman I ever saw.'

143

By August all Brighton knew of the Prince's changing affections. 'The Prince & Mrs. Fitzherbert are expected here either today or tomorrow. It is reported the King & Queen are to come to the Pavilion after the races. The Prince going to Cheltenham to be near his beloved Lady Hertford. Alas poor Mrs. Fitzherbert!' When Mrs. Calvert visited Maria: 'She seemed extremely glad to see us and took us all over her house which is a very pretty one. I think the Prince looks dismally.' However, His Royal Highness continued to arrange parties for Minney at the Pavilion. He hired a conjurer to amuse her and her friends and on November 23rd, her ninth birthday, the local paper recorded: 'The Prince arrived here in order we understand to celebrate the birthday of the Hon. Miss Seymour the interesting protégée of Mrs. Fitzherbert.'

Warnings concerning the political danger of being associated with a Roman Catholic had long been showered on the Prince, and Lady Hertford gravely added her advice. Now Lord Carlisle wrote: 'Though I do not only believe, but *know* how innocent Mrs. Fitzherbert is of all that may be imputed to her on that head, yet I solemnly declare I consider her situation as becoming more perilous.'

At this period public opinion became so anti-Catholic that Mrs. Fitzherbert grew frightened and destroyed the Papal Brief authorizing her to live with the Prince, and although she could not bear to burn her marriage certificate she scissored out the names of the two witnesses, her uncle and brother, who could be had for felony.

According to the editor of the Romilly Papers, Mrs. Fitzherbert's decision to employ the good graces of Lady Hertford in the Seymour case

'was attended with consequences of considerable importance. It occasioned a great intimacy between the Prince and Lady Hertford which ended with her entirely supplanting Mrs. Fitzherbert in the Prince's favour; and it produced that hostility towards the Catholics, which the Prince manifested when he became Regent, and his determination to place his confidence in those Tory Ministers, whom he had always before considered as his personal enemies.'

144

When in London, His Royal Highness continued to visit Tilney Street where, ignoring the cool looks of the lady he had twice bullied into accepting him as husband, he still enjoyed the smiles of Minney Seymour. One of Minney's small friends, later Lord Albemarle, has described the children's parties:

'By my little hostess I had the honor of being presented to the Prince. No sooner was His Royal Highness seated in his armchair than my young companion would jump up on one of his knees to which she seemed to claim a prescriptive right. Straightway would arise an animated talk between Prinney and Minney as they respectively called each other.'[1]

Minney remained in ignorance of the strained relationship developing between beloved 'Mama' and doting 'Prinney'. On her tenth birthday (November 23rd, 1808), the Brighton newspaper announced: 'In the evening a grand Ball in celebration of the Hon. Miss Seymour was given to a number of the young nobility and gentry at the Pavilion. The Prince honoured the ball-room with his presence.'

Meanwhile Mrs. Fitzherbert suffered acutely from the prim yet sadistic insistence of Lady Hertford that she must continue to visit the Pavilion, acting as a sort of unwilling chaperone. Now the great dangerous love affair was over. Completely over. Yet the Prince would not allow Maria to retire quietly as a wife no longer infatuating but respected.

Lady Euston, grown reconciled to Minney's adoption, wrote not unkindly to her nephew George:

'I know not what Mrs. Fitzherbert does in all these con-fusions and reconciliations as the World says it is all owing to Lady Hertford's influence that the Prince is put in a way to become a Good Boy. . . . Mrs. Fitzherbert looks remarkably well but she appears in public in an odd situation, having few

[1] Long long after when Albemarle had become the last officer survivor of the Battle of Waterloo he wrote to Minney's youngest daughter, Lady Constance Leslie: 'Christmas Day 1888: Your letter called me back from the tenth to the first decade of my life. I almost fancied myself issuing from the nursery at 6 Tilney Street, for a walk in Hyde Park hand in hand with your beautiful Mother, each of us carrying one penny to bestow upon our two respective old blind women who sat begging at the edge of what was then called "the basin".'

145

people to converse with, and the Prince often not speaking to her at all and at other times she appears indignant with him when he does.'

What was the hold that Lady Hertford exercised over the portly gentleman which George had become? The Brighton mob could not imagine how so stern and unattractive a woman could influence an ageing rake. They had not heard of complexes. Lady Hertford did not hold her prey through the lures of the bedroom. His Royal Highness had lain with too many women. None could seduce him now. And though he loved only Maria Fitzherbert he feared losing power if associated with her at this crucial time. Lady Horatia had thought the Prince addled in his mind when he had called baby Minney 'his little governess'. But he loved being ordered about. He craved a tyrant and now one had appeared in a safe form—Protestant and Tory. The Whigs were out of luck. The Heir Apparent, about to attain power as Regent, deserted them because of his Governess Complex!

Nineteen

SOON Lady Hertford's arrogant demands that Mrs. Fitzherbert must accompany her to the Pavilion and then play second fiddle passed human bearing. So did a rude secretary. On December 18th, 1809, Mrs. Fitzherbert wrote bluntly:

'I trust Your Royal Highness will permit me to explain the reasons why I could not possibly accept the honour of your invitation to the Pavilion for yesterday and for this evening. The very great incivilities I have received these two years just because I obeyed your orders in going there was too visible to every one present, and too poignantly felt by me to admit of putting myself in a situation of again being treated with such indignity, for whatever may be thought of me by some individuals, it is well known Your Royal Highness four and twenty years ago placed me in a situation so nearly connected with your own that I have a claim on you for protection. I feel I owe it to myself not to be insulted under your roof with impunity. The influence you are now under and the conduct of one of your servants, I am sorry to say, has the appearance of your sanction and support, and renders my situation impossible any longer to submit to.'

She thought she had broken the fetters, but next day the Prince wrote back surprised and injured:

'In whatever time, my dear Maria, that you may be pleased to write to me or in whatever way you may at any time think proper to act by me, deeply as I may feel and lament it, yet that never can nor shall make me deviate from or forget those

147

affectionate feelings I have ever entertained for you. . . . With respect to the dear Child . . . she shall never under any circumstance experience any alteration from me . . . for as you may well recollect, I have told you how convinced I was and ever shall be of the innate excellence and sweetness of her dear little Heart, mind, nature and disposition.'

The Prince had at last raised his wife's allowance from £3,000 per annum to £6,000, but he had never paid her the annual £10,000 promised as a marriage settlement. When Maria wrote him that owing to *his* architect Porden outrunning the estimate for building her house she was in money difficulties she used terse phrases noting that 'as your wife I feel I have still a claim upon your protection'. She said she could not possibly pay Porden and that if arrested 'I shall feel no degradation in going to jail. It is no debt of extravagant folly, but a circumstance what will happen now and again--that of being deceived by those we place confidence in.'

Naturally the Prince did not show *this* letter to Lady Hertford. The debt to Porden was settled and perhaps to assuage his own discomfort of mind when he next ordered a diamond necklace for Lady Hertford he dispatched a duplicate to Mrs. Fitzherbert which she received with a wry face but did not return.

The Duke of Kent, who for twenty-seven years lived with Madame de St. Laurent, and the Duke of Clarence, still maintaining domestic bliss with Mrs. Jordan, both remained close friends of Mrs. Fitzherbert. They wrote her every few days, often giving details of the coughs, rheumatic colds and other fits which affected their chosen ladies whom the Royal Marriage Act kept to the status of 'unmarried wives'. So unhappy had been the results of their younger brother, the Duke of Sussex, taking the law into his own hands and marrying a lady of high estate without the King's consent that neither Clarence—who was to be King William IV—nor Kent dared attempt illegitimate Church services.

In 1792 the Duke of Sussex had married—as the Christian Church says a man must, of his own will and before witnesses— the Protestant Lady Augusta Murray, daughter of the fourth Earl of Dunmore. Later in the year they arranged a second marriage in St. George's, Hanover Square, and two children were born of this union. King George III perverted by unholy egotism which allowed him to contravene that clear dictum of his own religion, 'those God had joined together let no man put asunder', declared the marriage invalid and the children illegitimate. The senseless cruelty of this act ruined the life of the harmless Sussex, of his nobly-bred Scottish lady, and of their son and daughter who could not know what to call themselves. Ridiculously, the marriage was valid in Hanover and Ireland where the boy could be called 'Prince of the Blood Royal, grandson of the reigning King of England'. But despite every entreaty the inhuman old monarch refused to admit legitimacy in England to these two grandchildren, and the mortified Lady Augusta finally retired to seclusion in Scotland.[1]

Watching the trials and tribulations of the royal brothers and remaining in the confidence of them all, Mrs. Fitzherbert realized the desperate unhappiness bound to have fallen on any children she might have acknowledged bearing to the Prince of Wales. If they had come to her then she did wisely to maintain so rigidly the secret. And if she bore none, then she could count herself lucky. Little Minney had caused her torment enough as it was.

The Duke of York, who had been Heir Presumptive to the Heir Apparent, throughout the early difficult days maintained a steady and serious correspondence with Maria. He was her greatest friend for over twenty years, and it is unfortunate that all these letters, apparently ill-spelt but no less readable for that, should have been burned because they *were* interesting, while chests of harmless notes concerning Madame St. Laurent's cough and Mrs. Jordan's malaise from the other royal brothers remain. In 1809 the Duke of Clarence wrote his eldest son George from Portsmouth: 'The oftener you dine at Mrs. Fitzherbert's the better. Remember me to her in the kindest manner possible.'

Mrs. Jordan (whom the Duke referred to as 'your mother' when writing to his offspring) added wishes and advice. Young George forgot some of his father's letters in Mrs. Fitzherbert's house and they were swept into her papers:

'Your mother trusts you have gone down well to Brighton. I hope you called last night on Mrs. Fitzherbert. . . . I could

[1] Eventually the son became known as Sir Augustus d'Este. The daughter married Lord Truro.

not see the Prince as I was to dine with the Queen. The dinner was uncommonly pleasant and I had a very long and interesting conversation with the King. You must write frequently and believe that your mother and myself, whether present or absent, are attached to you in an unalterable manner, dear George. Your most affec. father.

William.'

George Fitzclarence showed, like his royal uncles, an inability to write proper English. The intensive education with eight hours a day of study punctuated by floggings organized by the old King had not produced even tolerable literacy in the Duke of York, so his nephew got nagged not to fall into the same category. Clarence writing to congratulate George on promotion in the Army added:

'You must pay attention to your spelling and get someone to correct your English. Show this letter to Colonel Quintin with my best compliments. . . . Write frequently either to your mother or to me. She is in town and plays tomorrow at the Opera House. My best wishes and compliments attend Mrs. Fitzherbert and give my love to Minney.'

Mrs. Jordan, an educated actress, better educated it seems than certain members of the royal family, implored him to take heed:

'Indeed, my dear George, this is of more consequence than you at present imagine. Only reflect how the Duke of York's letters and the spelling of the late Duke of Cumberland was ridiculed and is ever to this day.'

And again:

'You are to tell Mrs. Fitzherbert from your father that he wishes she would be so good as to introduce you to the Duchess of Bedford. It is reported that Lord Paget is killed in a duel by Henry Wellesley whose wife he ran away with last Monday. . . . Mrs. Fitzherbert speaks very handsomely and kindly of you. I see by your spelling that you do not make use of your Dictionary.'

George Fitzclarence was preparing to embark with his regiment for the Peninsular War and his sailor father sent him a farewell letter full of sensible advice:

'Dear George,
Your letter informing me your regiment is going abroad arrived yesterday. A soldier is always happy to obey, and I make no doubt you will do your duty as you ought, and I trust in God you will be as fortunate as you were on the last occasion. Give my best compliments to Col. Quintin and desire him to work you well in the riding house, & you must make the most of your time to become a good horseman. I hope for your sake Mrs. Fitzherbert will remain at Brighton till you march to embark. Thank her in my name for all her attention & goodness to you. . . . The less baggage you now know by experience the better. Only take what is useful & not ornamental. At the same time you must have what is ordered. Your mother goes on Saturday to Bath & Bristol, and will be absent between three & four weeks. She, Mrs. Sinclair . . . and your brothers & sisters write in love & best wishes, and I remain your affec. father,
William.'

In January 1809 Sir John Moore had been killed at Corunna in the heroic evacuation of his army. Years more of terrible warfare back and forth across the bleak Spanish mountains lay ahead, while a sanctimonious, criticizing home government failed to comprehend that Napoleon could be surely beaten by dragging out his line across a desolate country. The English soldier was in a bad way. He had lost his great General Moore in January, and in February he lost a reform-loving Commander-in-Chief in the Duke of York. Like all the royal dukes he could not keep out of trouble where ladies were concerned. After obediently marrying a German princess who proved childless, Frederick of York had proceeded to live openly with his mistress, the brazen, greedy Mary Anne Clarke. Not content with what remuneration she could squeeze out of her prince, this avaricious wanton organized a private trade in Army commissions. While serious-minded York (called by Lady Hester Stanhope 'the best friend a soldier ever had') had since 1795 struggled to reorganize Army training, administration and the appointment of officers, his mistress, unknown to him, dealt out commissions beneath the regulation price. The tragedy of Corunna was forgotten while a Grand Committee in the packed House of Commons questioned Mrs. Clarke whose impudent answers mesmerized all. She knew men. Six hundred members of Parliament were just six hundred possible victims. Although caught out in twenty-eight falsehoods she kept her head sufficiently to refuse answering a really difficult question on grounds of 'indelicacy', and before the trial ended a note had been thrust into her hand from an enterprising parliamentarian reading, '300 guineas & supper with me tonight'.

Everyone now understood the Duke. It was proved that her dishonest transactions took place behind his back, but nevertheless he had to resign as Commander-in-Chief at a time when he was sorely needed. Meanwhile the old Admiral Lord St. Vincent asked the House of Lords to give command in the field to one of the royal dukes—preferably Kent. He argued splendidly on methods of using royalty. 'They have made the science of war their study from childhood, if they are not to be employed, I am at a loss to conjecture for what purpose they were bred to arms.'

York and Kent during these uncomfortable debates called upon Mrs. Fitzherbert almost daily. Being well accustomed to gentlemen in trouble she had a soothing touch in moments of stress. Alas that all those letters to 'My ever dearest Mrs. Fitzherbert' except the trivial ones concerning their gout and 'the King's bilious eye' were burnt by her later.

The poor Duke of York felt the injustice of his fate bitterly. He had after all married as bidden. No one after a glance at his princess could possibly expect him *not* to keep a mistress. How could he have guessed what she would get up to?

Amidst these political storms young George Fitzclarence left England, feeling perhaps he had more to learn from his uncle York than the avoidance of spelling mistakes.

Twenty

Now came two years during which Mrs. Fitzherbert regarded the Prince's infrequent visits with cool politeness. She still received summons to the Pavilion and formally took her place there as his wife. But as the likelihood of being made Regent approached he grew nervous and evasive. There was talk of ministers asking the Prince to declare before he took his oaths for the Regency 'whether he was not married to a Papist'.

It is difficult to follow quite how that royal rubbery mind now worked. On January 31st, 1811, just a week before taking his oaths as ruler of the Three Kingdoms, the Prince sent for Mrs. Fitzherbert to drive from Brighton to see him in London. When she entered his presence he asked to which party he should, when Regent, confide administration of the country. Lord Grey the Whig leader was no friend of hers, but knowing how deeply the Prince had been involved with that party she thought it necessary to give old friends an interlude in office. 'Only retain them, Sir, six weeks in power. If you please, you may find some pretext to dismiss them at the end of that time.' He remonstrated. With immense effort he was trying to work himself up to overthrow his former friends, he wanted to hear Mrs. Fitzherbert speak Lady Hertford's words: 'Retain the Tories under Mr. Perceval.' For hours he kept Maria arguing. The Prince kept asking her opinion on the Whigs then tearing her answers to pieces.

At length seeing that her words availed little, Mrs. Fitzherbert asked leave to return to Brighton. His Royal Highness started and looked at her in his arrogant pathetic way. He saw his 'own dearest wife Maria', plump, fresh-skinned, still lovely at fifty-four grown smarter in self-defence than when he first knew her, but still carrying that calm he had never been able to destroy. This was the last time their eyes would meet, his shifting unhappily, hers serene. Once more he sensed that stability which he longed for and did not himself possess. Once more he wished he could return her cool, unflinching look. The Prince sighed with self-pity. Here lay his peace, but he might not take it. Happiness had all become so very complicated. He wanted the full power of Regent and Lady Hertford kept reminding him of the unpopularity of Catholic ties. He had to let her go.

Before she swept into her formal departing curtsy, Mrs. Fitzherbert remembered one matter which had long tormented her and she decided to make a statement wanted or unwanted.

'She then urged upon him, as strongly as she was able, the disadvantages which must accrue to his future happiness from treating his daughter, the Princess Charlotte, with so little kindness. "You now, Sir," she said, "may mould her at your pleasure, but soon it will not be so, and she may become, from mismanagement, a thorn in your side for life." "That is your opinion, Madam," was his only reply.'[1]

She drove back to Tilney Street exhausted. Next day in the street she met old Creevey who, alone among the Whigs, could not see why the Prince should not chuck his party if it had ceased to be useful to him.

On February 2nd he scribbled:

'I said all I thought to Sheridan in vindication of Prinney, but I presume I am wrong as I stand single in this opinion. I went however to Mrs. Fitzherbert at twelve today, an opportunity I made with her yesterday in the street, and she and I were agreed on this subject.'

She had fought as hard as she could for the Whig Party, but as the Regent was determined to abandon them she would not criticize his choice.

During the next few months Wellington's victories in Spain

[1] Lord Stourton's narrative.

kept England in jubilant mood. Until early summer Mrs. Fitzherbert must have remained in contact with the Prince Regent, for
the Duke of Kent—deep in financial troubles and much disliked
by his elder brother—after asking her to intercede for some
monetary request on his behalf, wrote to her.

May 31 1811
My ever dearest Mrs. Fitzherbert,
    As the House meets today . . . I fear I *must* put off the
pleasure of calling on you till Monday etc. . . . In the meantime
I must entreat your acceptance of my most warm and grateful
acknowledgments for your kind attention to my poor interest,
which but for you, I believe, would, in the midst of so much
more important arrangements have been altogether over-
looked and be the result of your affectionate negotiation for
me what it will, I shall ever bear in equally grateful recollection
the zeal with which you undertook it.'[1]

But in June came a final rudeness from the Prince. Perhaps
with a sense of relief that it was all over at last, Mrs. Fitzherbert
abandoned Brighton for several years and moved to Sherwood
Lodge, Battersea, which being near to London gave more educa-
tional amenities for Minney.

The conclusive break-up occurred over a magnificent dinner
celebrating the Regency to be given at Carlton House. The exiled
King Louis XVIII of France and his family were to be guests of
honour, as a slight perhaps to Napoleon whose marshals were
ranging their troops tiger-like for a last possible effort to wipe
out Wellington's Portuguese Army. Mrs. Fitzherbert received
her usual summons, but was hesitatingly informed by the Prince
Regent that a new seating arrangement would be made. Ever
since his marriage to a commoner the Prince had made it customary to sit at this table without regard to rank. Mrs. Fitzherbert
automatically took her place at the head of the table as his wife,
and when they went to other people's houses she had to be treated
as the highest lady in the room. This delicate, deliberate, carefully
observed etiquette had been insisted upon by the Prince for nearly
thirty years. Even Lady Hertford's nagging had not altered the

[1] Pierpont Morgan Library.

procedure, for he dreaded the day that Maria's door would be closed in his face for ever.

Now, intoxicated with that long-coveted power of being Regent, he decided to break his rule. He informed her that with a Bourbon King present the guests must sit according to rank. This meant that Mrs. Fitzherbert would be at the end of the table. Even had she been created a Duchess as he and Fox once wished, it could not have helped the situation as Maria Fitzherbert sat at the royal table *as the Prince's wife* or not at all. She underlined her refusal to accept future commands to Carlton House or the Pavilion in a letter of which she took a copy that survives tagged in her writing: 'Copy of letter written the Prince, June 7, 1811, when persuaded by Lady Hertford not to admit me to his table.'

'Sir,
        After the conversation Your Royal Highness held with me yesterday I am sure you will not be surprised that I have sent my excuses for not obeying your commands for Wednesday next. Much as it has ever been my wish during a period of near thirty years to save you from every embarrassment in my power yet there are situations when one ought not entirely to forget what is due to oneself. You, Sir, are not aware, in your anxiety to fill your table with persons only of the highest rank, that, by excluding her who now addresses you merely for want of those titles that others possess, you are excluding the person who is not unjustly suspected by the world of possessing in silence unassumed & unsustained a Rank given her by yourself above that of any other person present. Having never forfeited my title to Your Royal Highness's public as well as private consideration by any act of my life, to what could this etiquette be for the first time imputed: No one, my dear Sir, has proved themselves thro' life less solicitous than myself. But I cannot be indifferent to the fair, honourable appearance of consideration from you, which I have hitherto possessed & which I feel I deserve, & for which reason I can never submit to appear in your house in any place or situation but in that where you yourself first placed me many years ago.'

In this letter Mrs. Fitzherbert made her final curtsy to the

156

gentleman who had sworn before the heavenly hosts to love her into eternity, and packed her bags for Sherwood Lodge. She felt thankful she had purchased this retreat and soon the three elder royal dukes—who had begged her not to abandon their brother—were flocking to Battersea for sympathy and advice. The Duke of York avoiding all reference to the break-up wrote:

'I am rejoiced to learn that you are so well pleased with, and feel so comfortable at Sherwood Lodge. From what I could judge of the place, when I was with you there last year, I am certain it was capable of being made very pretty, and I shall be very anxious as soon as I return to town to see all your improvements.'

Gossip does not record what Louis XVIII thought of the splendid dinner at Carlton House. While Mrs. Fitzherbert had received a summons in the form of an insult, the Princess of Wales received no invitation at all. Generous of nature, she allowed her ladies-in-waiting to attend without her. However cruelly treated, Caroline of Brunswick never sought to spoil the enjoyment of others, and she considered this celebration 'well worth seeing'.

England commented caustically: 'Both wives have remained by their own firesides.'

Twenty-one

Now came a period of quiet content for Maria Fitzherbert. The strain was over. Nearly thirty years of moods, changeability, brain-storms and sulks had kept her nerves keyed taut. At last she could relax and enjoy life in her own way. There was no dearth of friends. The royal dukes hurried to her with each tidbit of news, and she found herself invited to the great houses of England and surrounded by genuinely devoted people. Apart from the sarcasm of lampoons and a few jealous women, not one derogatory remark is recorded concerning Mrs. Fitzherbert. In that age of slashing wit and infamous satire she passed almost unmolested. The English public, so ready to hate a Papist, acknowledged her dignity and tidy behaviour.

During the summer of 1811, soon after Mrs. Fitzherbert's separation from the Regent had become absolute, the Duke of Clarence decided to end his twenty-year liaison with Mrs. Jordan. His motives were mixed. He had lived cosily with her and the children at Bushey, and even allowed her to help support him with her earnings but, none the less, such a number of bastards proved a financial drag. He could never expect that his income of £20,500 per annum would be increased to the £40,000 usual for a married royal duke unless he shed the plump, hard-working, ever-devoted mother of his ten children. On the whole, William of Clarence had proved a kindly man, but now he began to worry about his proximity to the throne. Suddenly he felt sure he would outlive both Regent and the childless Duke of York. Then only Princess Charlotte stood between him and kingship. If *she* produced no children his progeny must inherit. He toyed with the idea of taking a legitimate bride, not immediately, of course, but sometime, somewhere. And the first step must be, of course, to assume the *appearance* of a bachelor. Not so easy with ten young Fitzclarences allowed to call him 'Father'. The first blow was delivered with blunt unkindness. England learnt that Mrs. Jordan had been given the sack in a pathetic manner.

To help eke out the Duke's insufficient income she was fulfilling a provisional engagement at Cheltenham and on the last night she played Nell in *The Devil to Pay*. The public loved their great comic actress and noticed nothing strange in her manner until she reached the laughing-drunk scene. Her audience then waited for that famous Jordan laugh, 'the most enlivening thing in nature equally beyond praise and description'. Instead they saw their star burst into tears.

By morning everyone knew the Duke of Clarence had written Mrs. Jordan to arrange a final separation. The newspapers angrily took it up. They knew she had borne him ten children and that he often lived on her earnings. If he thought he could fling her aside unnoticed he had made a mistake.

Mrs. Jordan, though heart-broken, did not scold. She could write a far more lucid letter than the royal brothers and one of these states quite simply:

'Could you believe or the world believe that we never had for twenty years the semblance of a quarrel. But this is so well known in our domestic circle that the astonishment is the greater. Money, money, my good friend, or the want of it, has I am convinced made HIM at the moment the most wretched of men, but having done wrong he does not like to retract. But with all his excellent qualities his *domestic virtues*, his love for his lovely children what must he not at this moment suffer?'

The Duke proved adamant. On the previous Christmas he had revelled in the joy of a family party in his apartments at St. James's decorated by Mrs. Jordan with blue and crimson hangings. George Fitzclarence had returned from the wars and she had written '. . . We shall have a full and merry house at Christmas. It is what the dear Duke delights in:—a happier set when altogether I believe never existed.'

But the set had been reunited for the last time. Mrs. Jordan's remaining five Christmases were to be spent in exile alone with her daughters, and harried by creditors. In 1816 she died at St. Cloud, of heart-break it seemed, because so many posts had come in without a kind letter from the Duke.

Mrs. Fitzherbert's case was, of course, less desperate. For one thing she was a lady and possessed a high place of her own in society. Her situation in the world appeared to be that of abandoned wife, not of cast-off mistress. After the rift became absolute Minney Seymour continued to receive every kindness from the Prince. The shadow of her elders' dispute never entered the schoolroom. After her fourteenth birthday, in the delicate hand developed by all those eager governesses she wrote the Regent:

'Brighton. Nov. 25 1812

My dear Prinney. How kind you were to remember my birthday and send me such a beautiful present! I have placed it in a very conspicuous situation and it is very much admired. Pray accept my most grateful thanks for it. I must not omit thanking you for the piece of paper I found inclosed in Colonel MacMahon's letter. It was very acceptable as sometimes I am rather an extravagant personage. I ride almost every day and Adonis is as great a favourite as ever. Dear little Sancho is rather neglected for I fancy myself almost too big to ride on him. I hope, my dear Prinney, that you enjoy good health & you will ever believe me to remain your most grateful & affec. Minney.'

To watch the flowering of this girl who had been the dearest love of her life atoned for Mrs. Fitzherbert's other tribulations. The Regent always kept her informed of his illnesses (perhaps he secretly believed in the efficacy of Maria's prayers), but she only corresponded with him henceforth about financial matters and rewards for various servants. On the few occasions they met in society she cut him in the grand manner. These haughtinesses were as avidly watched as their former sweet glances. Sir Henry Holland wrote: 'I witnessed once, when meeting the Prince Regent & Mrs. Fitzherbert in the same room at Bridgewater House, that rejection of every intercourse on *her* part which gave origin to so many anecdotes.' Professor Charles Webster in his Introduction to the *Letters of George IV* mentioning Mrs. Fitzherbert stated 'otherwise she only appears in connection with the *Prince's daughter*, Minney Seymour, a tie that still connected them when all others had been severed'. Experts, basing their opinion on George's own beliefs and his habit of signing letters to Minney as 'your father by adoption' decided that 'the conclusion is inescapable'. But a man who cannot speak the truth ceases to think the truth and the Prince's infatuation with the idea of being Minney's father is no proof at all. Mrs. Fitzherbert must have known the secret but she has left no clue. At the age of fifteen Minney wrote (in ever firmer script):

'November 27 1813
My dearest Prinney, For as you kindly commanded me always to call you so; you will I hope receive my most grateful thanks for the kind & affectionate letter, which you were so good as to write. It gave me additional pleasure, as it is some time since I have had the happiness of receiving a letter written by yourself. I must likewise thank you for the truly handsome & magnificent ornament which accompanied it; it is very beautiful and I shall have great pleasure in wearing it, as being your gift. I have not yet rode but intend doing so in a few days; the horses are very well and Adonis is as great a favourite as formerly. I ride dear little Sancho occasionally, but have almost outgrown the little fellow.'

Minney, kept happily occupied with her ponies and French lessons and music and dancing, was indeed growing up. And someone had fallen painfully in love with her. Poor George Fitzclarence, the eldest of the Duke of Clarence's ten children, returned at intervals from the bloodstained battles and perishing miseries of the Peninsula. As his father decreed, he visited Mrs. Fitzherbert frequently, but it was no longer for the sake of the old lady's kindness. Little pirouetting Minney, who was to drive many men to distraction, caught and thoughtlessly held his deeply sincere, intense, unhappy heart. With a terrible slow ache he realized that he had loved her since she was a girl of twelve. And was there hope for such as he, a royal bastard brought up and educated as if he were a legitimate son? He had seen his worthy father floundering in financial difficulties as an admiral on half-pay. He had seen his mother strong as a cart-horse worked to the bone on tours to provide for her extraordinary family. He himself had done bravely in the wars but he had no self-confidence, no proper name as yet and no sparkling wit. As far as Mrs. Fitzherbert was concerned he could never be considered a match for her darling ewe-lamb.

During his long campaigns in Spain, George sent frequent letters to the fourteen- or fifteen-year-old Minney whose tantalizing elf-shaped face never quite left his memory, and on August 4th, 1813, he wrote from Legaca:

'I cannot refrain from congratulating you, my dear Mrs. Fitzherbert, upon a most splendid victory we have gained over the enemy. We have fought some most desperate battles, & have always come off with victory. Horace is well, & what is not of so much consequence to a young lady in your house, so am I & my brother. Horace had his horse shot. Mine was grazed on the nose with a ball. Since the 25th ult. the French have lost 16,000 men, we 7,000. I refer you to the *Gazette* for leading facts, as I have not time to give an account of our most gallant exploits. Never has anything shown Lord Wellington to more advantage or the British soldiers' courage more than these operations. We have taken great part of the enemy's baggage & 4,000 prisoners. Captain Harding is slightly wounded. I have been in France. I sent you oak leaves I took from a tree to crown myself conqueror. I send Minney some box I wore in my hat during the whole of the action, as it was fought on the anniversary of Talavera.'

George was humble and afraid of showing feeling. On he went into France with Wellington's army, and his letters, always containing small hints and hopes that Minney might care about him, reflected the general excitement at Napoleon's abdication.

Early in 1815 Mrs. Fitzherbert travelled to Paris and was on February 12th received at the Tuileries by King Louis XVIII. Presumably the Regent's famous dinner-party could not have been among the topics discussed. She hurried back to England when Napoleon escaped from Elba and was at Brighton much waited on by her royal dukes when the news of Waterloo came through.

The famine price of wheat, the Corn Laws and the Nottingham riots, where starving workers battered themselves against the terrifying new advent of machinery, passed Mrs. Fitzherbert by, but she wrote imploringly to the Prince when any of his old servants were fallen on bad days and begged him for help or pensions that had escaped his secretaries' notice.

She travelled a great deal now between her houses in Tilney Street and Battersea and Brighton, and Minney could usually be seen in her carriage. Lady Verulam wrote:

'We met yesterday Mrs. Fitzherbert and her protégée. She was driving herself in one of the fashionable carriages. They have four wheels and one horse & go at a great rate. One could not help moralizing, as the road she was on was the very one on which the Princess of Wales was driven almost every day in her phaeton.'

Mrs. Fitzherbert's position in society remained the same as in former years, but there were curious incidents. A letter from Mrs. French at Cheltenham describes one:

'Mrs. Fitzherbert was judiciously invited to a fête by Colonel —— in honour of the Princess Charlotte's birthday. He first treated Mrs. Fitzherbert as Regentess by leading her into the supper room before all the women of rank, and then gave toasts & made orations upon the merits of the Prince & Princess and the lovely fruit of their union. Was ever such folly, inconsistency & want of feeling?'

When the Prince completely abandoned the cause of the Whigs, Ireland and the Catholics, Tom Moore wrote 'The Prince's Song' sung at the Duke of Devonshire's house in 1815:

'When first I met thee, warm & young,
There shone such truth about thee,
And on thy lip such promise hung,

163

I did not dare to doubt thee,
I saw thee changed, yet still relief,
Still clung with hope the fonder,
And thought, though false to all beside,
From me thou couldst not wander.'

But Moore had the wisdom to ask his publisher to date this poem '1789' to 'prevent the confusion of supposing it to be Mrs. Fitzherbert or some abandoned mistress instead of Ireland'.

In the spring of 1817 Minney, now a polished young lady of eighteen with a train of enamoured gentlemen in tow, was brought to London to 'come out'. As she had been giving small parties and balls for 'the young nobility' since she was ten this official début simply meant that she added her name to Mrs. Fitzherbert's visiting-cards. The power wielded by Miss Seymour at the Prince's Sunday receptions has been plainly recorded by John Gurwood, a penniless officer who had led the survivors into the breach at Ciudad Rodrigo and been presented by Wellington with the Governor's sword. The sword not being all the remuneration he desired, Gurwood was now seeking promotion and protection in Brighton. He exerted himself to please Mrs. Fitzherbert and

'Miss Seymour expressed her surprise that I had not received an invitation to the Pavilion, &, in the course of conversation, she asked me whether I am not desirous of going there. Both vanity & curiosity prompted me to confess that I certainly was desirous. . . . The Sunday following this conversation, I received a summons to attend. I judged, from Miss Seymour's manner that evening, & the Regent speaking to me when accompanied by her, that to her I was indebted for this wished for honour, which, if all went well, I intended to turn to my own advantage when a favourable opportunity presented itself.'

Gurwood always ostentatiously wore the Ciudad Rodrigo sword and eventually the Regent, seated between Lady Hertford and Lady Cholmondeley, asked him to relate the history of it.

'The opportunity I had so long desired now burst upon me. I was aware of its importance, & I never related the particulars of the forlorn hope of Rodrigo with greater deliberation, or with more effect. When I had finished, the Regent rose from his seat & striking me on the shoulder said, "By God! You are a damned fine fellow!" '

Eventually Gurwood obtained his promotion—and all because of Minney.

At about this time Mrs. Fitzherbert added in ink the name of Maryanne Smythe beneath that of Minney to her printed card. Maryanne, described as her niece, was the only daughter of the late Jack Smythe and had quietly joined the household. Here a mystery lies unravelled for the family records at Swynnerton state:

'If she was a daughter of John Smythe, she cannot have been legitimate, for John Smythe had no children by his wife, widow of Captain Strickland . . . many indications point with considerable probability to the conclusion that she was a daughter of Mrs. Fitzherbert by George IV.'

It seems possible that Maryanne could have been the Prince's daughter by Mrs. Fitzherbert just as it seems unlikely that Minney was his daughter by Lady Horatia. But neither contention can be proved or disproved. Only a few odd clues in letters lead one to feel that Maryanne may well have been Maria's own child. She was a quiet pretty girl with a face yet more pointed than Minney's and even bigger eyes, but she lacked the vivacity and irresistible fascination of the 'adopted daughter'. She seems to have been a little younger but no birth-date is on record. Mrs. Fitzherbert did not take her to France in August 1817 when she travelled to Namur with Minney. On the way back they were received by the royal family in Paris, and in October Mrs. Fitzherbert opened up her Brighton house for the winter. She had hardly launched her two girls into the social round when the death of Princess Charlotte in childbirth threw the Pavilion into mourning. Mrs. Fitzherbert's kind heart ached for the banished Princess of Wales, and she remembered a far-off day when 'she was much affected by the Princess Charlotte throwing her arms around her neck, and beseeching her to speak to her father, that he would receive her with greater marks of his affection; & she told me that she could not help weeping with this interesting child.'[1]

Now there was *no* heir to the throne. The six enormous portly royal dukes, who between them must have weighed as much as four carthorses, had not succeeded in producing a single, legitimate child. Promptly the Dukes of Clarence, Cambridge and Kent found themselves ordered to the continent to find suitable princesses and try respectably for a son. Before departing they came to Mrs. Fitzherbert for advice. Kent needed it in particular. For years he had written her every detail of his journeyings and financial straits and many of his eight or nine page letters survive. On his wanderings he had occasionally mentioned possible brides for his brothers and 'that odious Princess Amelia of Baden, whom I find the Papers have thought fit to give to me!' but dear Madame St. Laurent lived happily with him in Brussels as she had in Ealing and Knightsbridge and her health was ever in his thoughts and the subject of his pen. Now came a very difficult moment, for the papers were full of the necessity for the dukes to marry German princesses. After Princess Charlotte's death Kent had written Maria miserably:

'And when to that is added all that I foresee may happen, I might add *must* happen to myself in long consequence, you may imagine how deeply all these considerations must have affected me. Thank God, owing to my abstemious mode of living, and my availing myself of the opportunity of my own little Garden affords me of taking the air, I have preserved my health, but my heart is half-broke, and, when I look at my poor companion of four & twenty years, I think we may perhaps before long be imperatively forced by my duties to my family & my Country to part, it quite distresses me, and from morning till night I hardly ever have a dry eye. But I strive to think that an all-wise Providence will direct all eventually for the best, & to await the events that may be at hand with resignation & submission. . . . I hope I shall have the energy to do my duty, but the sacrifice of so much domestic comfort will be dreadful. Yet even that can only be thought of, if the means

[1] Lord Stourton's narrative.

166

are afforded me amply according to my feelings to provide for the honourable & comfortable independence for life of that individual who has been my sole comfort & companion during so many dreary years which I passed, one may say, almost beyond the Pale of Society. You see how openly I speak to you, but I know you will enter into all my feelings.'

Madame de St. Laurent after twenty-seven years as his accepted 'unmarried wife' retired into a convent and the Duke returned to England to be briefed on the German Courts he must visit. On May 6th, 1818, he wrote:

'My ever dearest Mrs. Fitzherbert,
    I called yesterday afternoon immediately on leaving the Queen's House, where I had gone straight from the Regent to appraise my Mother of all being settled as to my marriage with poor Prince Leopold's sister, to communicate this event to you as my oldest, dearest friend, but was unfortunate in missing you. I therefore now write to inform you of it, & to say that as my departure must be very near at hand I shall entreat your leave to look in on you this evening about 8, or a little after, when I can get away from the Queen's House, that I may not be deprived of the happiness of seeing you before I am off. And of course therefore if you don't send me word to the contrary before 5, I shall be with you. Till then, and ever, I remain, with the warmest & liveliest attachment, ever, my dearest Mrs. Fitzherbert,
                    Your most affectionate & devoted
                                            Edward.'

Within the month he married Princess Victoria of Saxe-Coburg, a plump little widow with two children by her former marriage. In June the Duke of Cambridge also found a German spouse and in July the Duke of Clarence followed suit. The three unlovely German princesses chosen by the three stout elderly dukes were put on their mettle to produce an heir for England.

The Duke of Clarence had, when he abandoned the gallant Mrs. Jordan, come to Mrs. Fitzherbert for comfort. He wanted Maria to feel sorry for him. Now, however, he was brave enough to make his own explanations to his horde of children. To George he wrote

'that both *public* and *private* duty conspired to make me see the absolute necessity of marrying a Princess: in addition to which I had the consolation to believe that, as Princes marry, I was fortunate indeed in having for my future wife the Princess Adelaide of Saxe-Meiningen.'

The Duke of Kent fussed over the predicament of Madame de St. Laurent but he was really sorrier for himself than for her. When he brought his Duchess to Kew for a second marriage service in the presence of Queen Charlotte he found time to visit Mrs. Fitzherbert and bewail his fate.

In a letter which refers unromantically to his honeymoon as 'the situation I have been placed in' he wrote:

'August 25 1818
Having at length the prospect (if you will admit me towards 7 & 8 oclock this Evening) of being able to pass half an hour with you, perhaps the only leisure moment I may have (as in fact it has been hitherto) before I leave England, I send this over by a messenger simply to say that I will take my chance & call at your door at all events. In the meanwhile pray do me the justice to believe that you never have been out of my thoughts & that nothing but the situation I have been placed in for the last seven weeks would have made me either abstain from writing or calling until now, as neither time or situation can alter the warmth or sincerity of my attachment for you. Remember me kindly to dear Miss Seymour & accept the assurance of all that unutterable, lively & friendly regard with which I shall remain to the latest hour of my existence, my ever dearest Mrs. Fitzherbert, your most affectionate & devoted.

Edward.'

That evening the unenthusiastic groom arrived at Tilney Street for a half-hour's gossip with his old friend. Maria seems to have cheered him up. At any rate nine months later to the day, on May 24th, 1819, the little Princess Victoria was born.

Twenty-two

AFTER Mrs. Fitzherbert reached the age of sixty her mind naturally centred on the romances of the new generation. By now she was far more interested in the flirtations of vivacious Minney and shy, gentle Maryanne than in her own finished 'affair'. And the 'daughters' took plenty of chaperoning! Mrs. Fitzherbert who had, after all, attained more experience of life than most women, sought to guide and advise them. She scolded naughty Miss Seymour for turning her back at dinner on her cousin, the ardent young Lord Beauchamp, and she prompted shy Miss Smythe. Both young ladies received a number of marriage proposals and although Mrs. Fitzherbert wrote of Minney: 'I confess however miserable I shall be to part with her, I am most anxious she should marry and I trust this Spring may produce something worthy of her', she secretly rejoiced that none suited. Who *could* be worthy of the exquisite, whimsical Miss Seymour, plum of the marriage market, with her royal dowry and romantic connections? After Minney had refused her hand to Lord Francis Leveson-Gower, Lord Arthur Hill and Lord Glengall, Mrs. Fitzherbert fussed because gossip linked her with a Mr. Bruce at Brighton. In a long letter to George Seymour she wrote:

'. . . there is not the smallest reason for the reports that have been so industriously circulated concerning her. She is certainly an object of attraction and particularly so in the confined circle and if a Man happens to speak to her or is seen to join her walking, it immediately sets people talking. . . . It is natural at her age to like being admired and I hope with her good sense as she grows older, that the love of flirtation will rebate.

169

Let me beg of you to contradict this absurd report which vexes me very much and certainly it is detrimental to her but really I don't know how it is to be avoided unless I lock her up in her room and never let her see a human being. I have, thank God, had my health so well this winter that I have never lost sight of her for a moment but the times she went to the Pavilion.'

For all her 'love of flirtation' Minney hated the hurt eyes of a rejected suitor. Wistfully, hopelessly, George Fitzclarence continued to call, hinting at his deep love. The Duke of Clarence seems to have favoured an alliance, but Minney remained firm and the Regent certainly disapproved. Clarence wrote his son warningly in 1819: 'Be prudent & cautious & don't irritate the Regent. I want to know in what manner he interfered respecting Miss Seymour for or against you. I am surprised at the conduct of Mrs. Fitzherbert which you did not deserve.'[1]

The Prince Regent, besotted with the idea that Minney was his daughter, wanted a spectacular marriage, and a worthy recipient for the £20,000 he had settled on her. Minney wanted a dashing hero.

George Fitzclarence fulfilled no one's requirements, he wasn't legitimate, he wasn't particularly rich and he could not scintillate. He might be brave, but *quietly* brave, a devoted officer adored by his men in the freezing miseries of the Peninsular War, and snubbed by young ladies in drawing-rooms. Minney relegated him to the shelf of dear dullards.

At the time gossip had it that the marriage was discouraged because of consanguinity—if the Regent was Minney's father as he said, then she and George were first cousins—but obviously the real answer lay in Minney's own feelings and perhaps in Mrs. Fitzherbert's terse assessment, 'One of the family is enough.'

After years of rebuff, George unhappily allowed his father to arrange a marriage for him. The Duke of Clarence chose Mary Wyndham, one of the six natural children of the 3rd Earl of Egremont. This gentleman, the owner of Petworth and one of the greatest picture collectors of the century, could be placed among

[1] Fitzclarence Papers.

170

the more awe-inspiring English eccentrics. Lord Egremont had inherited his enormous Sussex home at the age of twelve. He ruled for sixty-five years undisputed lord of his territories both outside and inside the magnificent façade of Petworth. The friend of Fox and Burke, an enterprising agriculturist and a patron of art in the grand manner, he delighted the distinguished men of his generation with lavish hospitality and abundant wit. He also managed to induce the lady who lived on the top storey of Petworth, carrying the courtesy title of Mrs. Wyndham, to bear him six children. Brought up as if legitimate the brood must have been slightly surprised when in 1801 their mother suddenly came downstairs, obtained marriage lines and became Countess of Egremont! The change proved disastrous. His Lordship could not abide the sight of a wife around, and probably she interfered with his friend Turner who was painting huge canvases there. By 1819 Egremont wished to marry off his daughters, no easy task with girls of noble blood and no title. A royal bastard seemed the perfect match.

Unfortunately Mary Wyndham and George Fitzclarence did not suit each other. Perhaps they had *too much* in common and were for ever capping each other's stories of how badly their mothers had been treated.

Minney was now twenty-one and Maryanne probably younger. Years of pleasant dalliance appeared to lie ahead. Not until a young lady reached twenty-seven did the bell toll—thereafter, in defiance of actuality, public opinion deemed 'a female incapable of the romantic passion'.

The Fitzherbert household moved chiefly between Tilney Street and Brighton where bracing winds kept society frisky whether or not the gout-ridden Prince inhabited his Pavilion. John Croker—the Regent's new toady who worked for him with the Press—wrote:

'One reason why Mrs. Fitzherbert may like this place is that she is treated as queen at least of Brighton. They don't *Highness* her in her domestic circle but they *Madam* her prodigiously, and stand up longer for her arrival than for ordinary folks, and in short, go as near to acknowledging her for *Princess* as they can, without actually giving her the title when she dines out she expects to be led out to dinner before Peeresses—mighty foolish all this!'

In fact Mrs. Fitzherbert had grown tired of her own story, and she knew how to live vividly and freshly in the present rather than in the past.

With slightly raised eyebrows she watched the Pavilion, in which a loving husband had once experimented with Chinese wallpapers to amuse her, grow into the most exotic architectural fantasy in Europe. Nash designed the new exterior in glorious Indian style with spires, minarets and pinnacles that prevented the immense dome of the stables from overweighting the effect. Maria refused to put foot across that threshold, but she listened fascinated to descriptions of the Chinese interior, of cyclamen pink wallpapers, and chandeliers, that glistened with writhing, roaring dragons. Minney reported the bold flaming colours and how the Regent marched friends through the vast new kitchen he was so proud of. The shimmering banqueting hall and music room were enough to reduce most of his guests to tongue-tied embarrassment or stuttering eulogy.

Maria, whose 'drawing room' the Pavilion had once been, felt she could not like that new Chinese interior—volcanic yet exquisite in inspiration, barbaric yet perfectly composed. Probably she was too conventional to appreciate such exuberance; her tastes belonged to the classical eighteenth century. She had loved the original well-proportioned farmhouse. On December 28th, 1819, she wrote old Creevey welcoming him back to Brighton:

'You would scarcely know Brighton. It is so enlarged since you were here, and is at this moment so full there is not a house to be had. I cannot boast of much society which formerly we abounded with at this season. When I tell you that 52 public coaches go from hence to London every day & bring people down for six shillings you will not be surprised at the sort of company we have besides which the Royal Palace attracts numbers who are puzzled to know what to make of the appearance of the building which it is impossible for me, or indeed anyone else to describe.

The Regent & all his household are here, but as he never

stirs out of his parlour, & no one sees him it makes no alteration in our proceedings. Minney desires me to assure you &
all her kind friends of her best wishes.'[1]

All this time Lady Hertford worked hard to keep the reins
tight on her naughty unstable Prince. Tierney wrote that Sir
John Leach might have been Chancellor, 'but that his name is now
in the black book of Hertford House and, of course, at the
Pavilion in consequence of his having dined with Mrs. Fitzherbert'.[2]

The royal personages who had framed and affected her life
started to die off. Queen Charlotte had gone to her grave in 1818,
the Duke of Kent died in 1820, leaving an eight-month-old
daughter, Victoria, and six days later the old King George III
passed to the deeper shades. Unhappy Caroline of Brunswick died
in 1821, a few months after the Coronation which she was not
allowed to attend. 'Prinney' was now King as he had so long
desired and, as far as English law went, a widower. There was no
question of remarriage however. As those nearest to him record,
'the wife of his youth' was ever in his thoughts and caused him
much pain. In fact he had taken the trouble to clearly announce
that in the event of the Princess of Wales's death no second
alliance would be considered.

Untruthful and changeable as George IV was, he never
showed stinginess. When he married Maria Fitzherbert he had
promised her £10,000 a year. Until 1801 he only managed to pay
her £3,000. He increased this to £4,000 when she returned to him.
As his financial troubles decreased the annuity grew to £6,000,
and finally in April 1820 to the long-promised £10,000.

Such figures had never been sufficient for a lady who had to
keep the style demanded of a Prince's wife and she had forever
been plagued by financial worries. The loyalty she bore had not
prevented a very angry wife penning stiff letters in the past. In
1813 she had written:

'The load of public business, which Your Royal Highness
must have had to occupy your time, has rendered me unwilling

[1] Creevey Papers.
[2] Glenbervie Diaries.

to press myself on your recollection: and the hope that I should find you remembering me without my having the pain of requesting you to do so, has withheld me from writing sooner; but now that business is considerably over, permit me to urge the promise, when you are still in Town, to recall to Your Royal Highness's recollection myself & my situation. Placed by you, Sir, when the memorable event of our Union took place in the year '85 under circumstances which rendered you the only person in this world, while life endured, that I could ever look up to for protection & support, bound by every tie that Honor or Religion could impose, & utterly precluded from forming any other connection for the future comfort, support or happiness of my life. You were at that period pleased to settle on me £10,000 per ann. as the income befitting the situation you placed me in. The act, Sir, was a voluntary one of your own etc. etc. . . . Permit me to receive henceforward the allowance you promised me twenty-eight years ago—an allowance which the times have not increased in value. The arrears may be inconvenient to Y.R.H. to grant, but with my best wishes for your welfare & happiness, I have the honour to subscribe myself respectfully,

Maria Fitzherbert.'

Respectfully, but sternly.

Apart from these businesslike epistles, she wrote the Regent a few appeals concerning his old servants, when they fell into distress. Obviously they still turned to her as the person most likely to evoke their royal master's pity, and as a rule her written, 'I only think the poor fellow from his good conduct deserves some reward', had the required effect.

Once or twice Maria and her husband met in public and cut each other in the grand manner. Corpulent as he had become, the Regent still possessed immense dignity—but he could not equal the dignity of Mrs. Fitzherbert. Watchers remarked that when they passed on the stairs however high he managed to carry his nose, hers appeared to be lifted yet higher.

Twenty-three

MRS. FITZHERBERT thought she could never be hurt again, but whoever loves remains vulnerable and she doted on her adopted daughters.

The inevitable happened. Each girl acted according to her character. Maryanne the obedient Catholic mouse took her cues from 'Mama' and only admired suitable gentlemen, while Protestant Minney the favourite, closely watched by the King, fell in love with quite the wrong man.

By modern standards he does not sound such a disaster. In fact one is now inclined to wonder what all the fuss was about. But those were the days when Miss Austen's heroines were discussing gentlemen's incomes, and the importance of title and fortune passes our imagination.

George Dawson[1] who was to cause Mrs. Fitzherbert five years of hysterics and Minney so many sleepless nights, was a fiery young cavalry officer who suffered the bad luck of being the *younger* son of an Irish earl. He had seen a bit of the world. Two horses were killed under him at Waterloo and he must have broadened his outlook when, attached to the British military mission to Russia, he witnessed the horrible scenes of Napoleon's retreat from Moscow. Mrs. Fitzherbert knew, however, that apart from distinguishing himself in battle, Captain Dawson's good looks and ready wit had already caused a number of ladies to fall, not very happily, in love. Such gentlemen must be kept fighting, not wooing.

There is a description of him, engaged in the former

[1] Later he and his brother, Lord Portarlington, added the name 'Damer' to please their aunt.

175

occupation. At the close of Waterloo, the Duke of Wellington sent him to order the Union Brigade to advance.

'When Dawson came up & said: "Now gentlemen, you are to advance with the rest of the Army," he said he should never forget the look Muter cast upon him. They all broke into a sort of canter & guided by Dawson came upon some French infantry who were still defending themselves. As Muter gave the order to charge, the French fired a volley & hit Dawson in the knee, who heard Muter grumble out in his Scotch: "I think you ha' it nu, sir." '[1]

The fact that he had courage as well as good looks impressed neither Mrs. Fitzherbert nor George IV who, watching the dowry he had granted increase to £20,000, had no wish to see it handed over to a penniless soldier, a mere leader of cavalry charges. Their precious Minney had been raised to make a spectacular marriage. No personal attributes could compensate for George Dawson's deficiency in having been born a *younger* son.

At first Mrs. Fitzherbert had found him charming, but when she realized that Minney was falling in love, she expressed horror at such a husband. Captain Dawson drank, but hardly more than his contemporaries, he gambled, but so did most of the aristocracy, he had a dreadful reputation with the ladies, and this Minney could well understand and presumed she could cure. Even worse, his elder brother would inherit title and property. There were floods of tears and endless beseechings because Minney could not bear to distress her beloved 'Mama' and yet she could not think of giving up George either.

The King and the Duke of York were called upon to devise methods of tactfully separating the young couple. George IV and Mrs. Fitzherbert had not spoken for ten years, but the awful prospect of Minney marrying Captain Dawson drew them together in plots and plans, which had the usual effect of throwing coals on a fire. Go-betweens hurried between the thwarted lovers until Mrs. Fitzherbert whisked Minney off to Paris. When George Dawson wanted to follow Minney warned him: 'Your proposal of meeting me abroad would but cause embarrassment to all

[1] *Reminiscences.* Colonel Gronar.

176

parties concerned and I am quite convinced could never lead to the consequence you anticipate.'

Nevertheless he appeared in Paris undaunted and wrote to his friend Lord Alvanley:

'When I first met Miss Seymour she seemed as if she wanted to avoid me: this & the repulsive manner of Mrs. Fitzherbert gave me but little hope & I resolved to stifle every feeling of my heart. . . . One day I had the good fortune to meet her alone & it was upon this occasion that I was made the happiest man in the world. I received the assurance that she was not indifferent to my attachment to her but at the same time she observed to me how insurmountable appeared the difficulties attending on eventual happiness! . . . she was bound by every event connected with her life to the King & to Mrs. Fitzherbert & she could not summon enough courage to propose to them what she knew would meet with their disapprobation! . . . Miss Seymour from every circumstance connected with herself has a right to look forward to making the most splendid marriage. . . . I know that I am nobody & have nothing. . . .'

Nothing but good looks and that most unfair gift of the gods —charm.

Meanwhile the good-natured Duke of York found himself promising George to put in a kind word for him, while at the same time assuring Mrs. Fitzherbert that he would do all in his power to disencourage the romance.

George quickly bethought him of a rich, childless, adoring aunt who had previously paid his debts after many a wild fling. The sister of Lord Dorchester, she had inherited two immense properties in Dorset, and Dorchester House in London. All her letters to George (preserved in the Portarlington Papers) are full of fun. When Queen Caroline bought a house near her, she sent her nephew 'a Prayer and I think a good one.

Gracious Queen we thee implore
Go away & sin no more,
But if that effort be too great
Go away at any rate.'

177

Now he turned to her and confided the whole story of his impossible love. To Minney he wrote:

'To one of my brothers Lady Caroline Damer made an allowance assuring him that she would provide for him at her death. I have no reason for supposing that she would not do as much for me. . . . And with this must be considered that the Duke of York was so kind as to promise that he would do something for me! I feel that from the intimate terms upon which he is with Mrs. Fitzherbert that nothing would do me so much good in her opinion as H.R.H. being so good as to express to her a desire to serve me. . . . I am the more anxious on this point from Mrs. Fitzherbert having authorised her friends here to say in her own & in Miss Seymour's name that I had behaved very ill to them, that I had repeatedly received from Miss Seymour an opinion of how indifferent I was to her, that I followed them from here & was constantly putting myself forward & annoying them!'

Society remained agog with excitement. Tom Moore in his diaries (March 24th, 1820), writes: 'George Dawson is gone off to England to try & Make interest with the Duke of York to get the King's consent to his marrying Miss Seymour.'

All through 1821, after she returned to Europe, Minney secretly sent long letters to her George describing with pain Mrs. Fitzherbert's miseries over 'the subject' and saying sadly: 'As for the King being spoken to by any of my brothers, I could hardly venture to wish them to undertake a commission I feel would be so ill-received.'

No one backed George except good old Lady Caroline who thought the blood of four Irish lords should suffice even if Miss Seymour *was* the King's daughter. She wrote her nephew a peremptory letter (May 17th, 1821):

'For my sake therefore as well as your own, I wish you to leave Paris & come to London immediately. Your Sisters wish it. Your friends wish it and most of all your —— wishes it. I think your coming would do good at present. Your enemies & rivals are busy spreading reports that you are too

178

happy at Paris with the Duchesse de Castris & your coming here would give the lie to them all & give you an opportunity of judging for yourself of the feelings of her you are interested in. My belief is that she feels inwardly as you & I wish her to feel & the contrary of what Mrs. Fitzherbert wishes but I think you ought to come now & rejoice her heart & refresh her memory with the sight of you. I pointed out your sister Lady Louisa to her the other night, at Lady Wortley's and she thanked me much for it & thought her like you. I am going to have a nice Party for the week of the Epsom Races & I wish you to be at it & I long to reassure you of the friendship & regard of your old Subscriber.'

Lady Caroline jovially signed herself thus because she had paid so many of his past debts.

In London the lovers could only meet by carefully contrived chance and each time Mrs. Fitzherbert heard about it she had to be given smelling-salts. At last Captain Dawson grew exasperated by these storms at his approach and dared to express himself 'in a strong manner about Mama'. For this he received a sound scolding from her loyal adopted daughter who would not allow one word against Mrs. Fitzherbert from anybody.

At the end of December 1821 she wrote from Brighton: 'I cannot make out one thing, which is an anxiety she has shewn she never before did of the King and myself having greater communication with another. She told me that the coldness which she has lately shewn me must originate from having those about him who misrepresent me to him.'

The Marchioness of Conyngham had replaced Lady Hertford in His Majesty's affections. Good natured, rapacious and nanny-like rather than governessy, she only bothered to run down Miss Seymour in order to increase the King's interest in her own girls. Minney wrote to George:

'However I wish I may soon see the King. I have only been out once since I have been here & that to Church on Christmas Day, when I met Lady Conyngham & family, who overpowered me with affection. I began to think she must be getting out of favour, but I believe this is not all the case. . . .

179

I think people are quite mistaken in thinking that the King's coldness to me was encouraged by Mama, as I am sure she herself was very annoyed by it & was very anxious for me to write which I was prevented doing by an invitation to the Pavilion the very day my letter was to have gone.'

She did prepare a letter however and left it with Mrs. Fitzherbert who relayed a description of its reception after Minney left for France:

'Sherwood Lodge. July 29 1822

Your letter, dearest Minney, gave me the greatest pleasure imaginable, for what I suffered all Wednesday it is impossible to describe. The wind was so high & the river so agitated that I did nothing but run from the house to watch the tide all day, and I worked myself up to a state of anxiety scarcely to be borne. . . .

Several people called on me that morning, among the rest the Duke of York. He took your letter & gave it to the King & stayed with him whilst he read it. The King was extremely delighted & pleased with it, and said to the Duke: "This is a very kind letter indeed." He asked him questions, how long you were to remain abroad & if, as he had been informed, I was going to join you & pass the winter in Paris: . . . I am very glad you wrote. I think it will make the Marchioness very angry & I trust it will convince the King that the stories told him respecting you were only her fabrication. . . .'

A month later Mrs. Fitzherbert unfortunately heard that Captain Dawson had told various friends that, perhaps reasonably, he would abandon the difficult chase were he not sure of Miss Seymour's affections. Mrs. Fitzherbert took this as bragging, and a fresh outburst reached George Seymour who was travelling to Dresden at the time with Minney in his charge:

'Sherwood Lodge. August 13 1822

It is so humiliating to her that I cannot bear it. I have not mentioned this to her in my letter because I know it would only irritate her. I hope to God she will fairly & truly give it up for if she does not I cannot conceive anything more deplorable to herself or to us all. As to *myself* I am perfectly unequal either in mind or body to support the misery I have endured any longer . . . etc.'

The elder Seymour sister, Racey, had married Mr. Morier, the British Minister there, and Minney hoped to enjoy the change of a small German Court. She wrote her lover: 'We are indeed much better separated when things are come to what they now are. . . . It is seven in the morning. I am still writing. . . .'
Through the next months after registering shock at the 'tragical end of Lord Londonderry' (Castlereagh's suicide), Mrs. Fitzherbert's lengthy letters are composed entirely of gossip concerning Minney's young friends and Maryanne's dance partners, their finances, their love affairs, and who is 'smitten' with whom. Minney's friend Harriet, daughter of Lord Glengall, is to marry Lord Belfast (later third Marquess of Donegal), and astutely the old lady observes: 'She is not in love, but I do not think knows anything about being so nor do I think she will ever be so with anyone.' Mrs. Fitzherbert knew what's what where the heart was concerned. A fortnight later the story grows more intriguing.

'As soon as they return from Ireland, my Lady & Harriet are to go to Paris, Belfast is to follow & they mean to be married there. Everyone is enraged at this proceeding after all the trouble there has been, but Lady Glengall told me in confidence that Harriet must & would go to Paris to get some corsets made which could not be done here, & her shape in every respect absolutely depended upon it. What a sad thing! I understand it is much worse than is perceptible. She now looks very graciously to Lord Belfast & we all agree that she now likes him extremely. Indeed he is very deserving.'

Whatever her health Mrs. Fitzherbert never ceased to give large dinner parties and the theme recurs: 'I only want you at the party to make it perfection' or 'When I am conversing with you, my dearest Minney, I never know when to leave off'.
A very different note is struck in the correspondence with brother George. They wrote to each other worried confidential

reports condemning Minney's frame of mind—was she recovering? Forgetting? Brooding? Minney's brother relayed:

'In the conversations I have had with her it is impossible for me not to see that the infatuation towards him still continues & therefore to dread the effect that his meeting her again may have. . . . She is persuaded that he will go out to the West Indies in October or November & is reasonable enough to acknowledge that absence will be likely to weaken the unfortunate impression he has made upon her mind which I trust circumstances & time & fresh impressions may remove particularly if she adheres to the resolution she now expresses to have no correspondence with him.'

Mrs. Fitzherbert and the King had pulled strings with the Duke of York, now reinstated as Commander-in-Chief. George was to be promoted and sent to the West Indies where perhaps he would conveniently get yellow-fever or marry some lovely Creole.

Minney had, perhaps understandably, become as sneaky with her brother as with Mrs. Fitzherbert. She never ceased to correspond with George Dawson. The long ardent letters of both lovers have been preserved. While she was travelling Minney's are naturally the most entertaining. At Aix-la-Chapelle the Duke of Devonshire tried to make the Seymours remain for a Ball 'but my *dansomanie* did not prevail nor were we anxious to be deprived of post horses the whole way up the Rhine'. The servants all ask to go to the execution of a woman who had murdered her husband in order to get her own head cut off, it seeming to her, 'the most desirable kind of death'. Walter Scott's son comes to dine, 'He appears the most pompous I ever saw'. They refuse to attend a Chasse where the Queen of Saxony and the rest of the royal family stood on a platform mowing down a herd of deer driven into an enclosed field. 'I never heard of a more inhuman proceeding'. Berlin she finds an exceeding dull garrison town but 'What pleased me the most was the Queen of Prussia's monument at Charlottenburg which I thought perfectly beautiful. . . .' Minney casually makes clear her own disbelief of the prevailing opinion concerning her parentage by describing:

'a *soirée* where . . . we met most of the society of Berlin & where the lady of the house thought proper to present every one person to me & I could not help remarking afterwards upon her carrying about a large picture which she was showing everybody & appearing to draw their attention upon me. I could not account for this till I was told someone had spread the unaccountably ridiculous report of my being the King of England's daughter & to improve the idea a Print of Princess Charlotte had been carried about to prove the likeness that was said to exist between us. I could not help laughing when all this was told me, though George for the honour of the family was inclined to take it *au serieux*. . . .'

Meanwhile Captain Dawson went off to visit Aunt Caroline in Dorsetshire who had not only stated that she would leave her smaller property Came to him, but had insisted that the King should *hear* how much he would inherit. He informed Minney:

'She wrote to Lord Bathurst that what she wished for me particularly was to be put about the dear King. Portarlington [George's brother] means to change our name to Damer. I don't think that signifies much though, there are too many grocers & butchers that bear the present one. The village near my brother's place in Ireland is inhabited by Dawsons who all swear they are related. God only knows! Perhaps they may!! . . . After writing last night I went to Lady Glengall's where I heard the lamentable details of Lord Londonderry's death. . . . Too intense occupation as in the case of Pitt, Fox, Whitbread & Romilly had destroyed the vigour of his mind. . . . I passed through St. James Square yesterday evening about 8 o'clock. There were a good number of persons of the Lower Classes assembled round the house & I am told that they loudly heaped every sort of imprecation upon him.'

From Dresden, Minney laughed at George's name-changing:

'You say you may be related probably to those of your name about your brother's place, so I am probably living in the house with one of your Cousins as the maître d'hôtel has the same appellation as yourself & Being the only English servant in the establishment I am always obliged to send for Mr. Dawson!'

How her light-hearted style changes when she pens a letter to His Majesty. There are a number of Minney's letters to George IV in the Windsor Archives and these beginning 'My dearest Sir' are all so formal and uninteresting that one obtains an insight into how difficult it is for royalty to know the fun of the world. The King loved Minney as much as he loved any creature alive, but a high wall lay between them. However, he was well pleased at the docility of her epistles at this time and Mrs. Fitzherbert approved of Minney's personal correspondence with His Majesty.

Thinking that she was winning, dearest Mama now announced that she could face a winter in Paris with Minney. George Dawson, approaching his last days in England, learnt:

'I think *Mama* more inclined to join me at Paris than she even was two days ago & I should think it would be almost the moment of your departure for the West Indies. She has always dwelt so much upon the misery she went through when last abroad by your having followed us to Paris that I am sure a renewal of it would make her more irritated than ever. . . .'

But before Mrs. Fitzherbert would actually leave England and join her adopted daughter in Paris she wrote a long ultimatum which ended:

'You must be well aware of the misery we both have suffered for the last three or four years on a subject most painful to me and to all those who are attached & interested about you. It has quite destroyed the entire comfort & happiness of both our lives. It has so completely destroyed mine that neither my health or spirits can bear it any longer. What am I to think when scarcely three weeks ago you voluntarily declared to me that *this sad affair* was quite at an end & in less than a week afterwards the whole business was begun over again. The purport of my writing to you is to implore you to come to a final decision upon this business. You must decide

184

& that decision must be done immediately. I beg your answer may be a written one to avoid all unpleasant conversation upon a subject so heart-rending to one whose whole life has been dedicated to you & whose affection to you none can surpass.'

George Dawson lost his temper outright when he heard of this 'impolitic, weak & ridiculous act'. He accused 'Mama' of not fighting fair and quoted in fury a recent incident when he had intended to accompany the Duke of York from Brighton to London, but Sir Derek Keppel warned him, 'I am not sure you will be *bien venu.*' The Duke's A.D.C., a certain Cooke, had told him

'the Duke was very much irritated against you, had said that you behaved very ill to Miss Seymour & Mrs. Fitzherbert, that you had told stories & bragged of circumstances which had never taken place, that he the Duke of York, had had an interview with Miss Seymour before she set out etc. etc.'

George's friend, Lord Alvanley, had replied he did not believe any of this story, whereupon Cooke

'offered to bet him fifty guineas that it was true & further that we should never be married. Cooke is a cautious man about money, however mischievous he may be from being a gossiping & fawning toady & you may therefore judge what Mrs. Fitzherbert must have told the Duke!'

In November, 1822, Lt.-Colonel Dawson sailed for the West Indies. Well he knew that Mrs. Fitzherbert hoped he would never reappear and in a final diatribe he let fly:

'What do you think of Gurwood going to my brother, who is at Paris, & saying that he knew our friendship was at an end & that you no longer cared for me. . . . There is nothing so abject as a fawning flatterer who will sacrifice any old friend to furnish matter for gossip for their Protectors. Gurwood I have no doubt writes in the same manner to his idol Beauchamp. [George was jealous of this rival, who being Lord Hertford's eldest son, an art expert, and Minney's cousin received encouragement from Mrs. Fitzherbert.] . . . Goodnight my dearest love. The officers of a Frigate just paid off are dining in the next room & are beginning to get drunk & noisy & I shall go to bed. . . .

At this moment . . . I feel that if I am not doomed to return, the only injuries I have received which I shall not be able to forgive will be that Mrs. Fitzherbert has been guilty of to me. For her sake I hope that God will be more merciful to her than I know she deserves and, if my life is sacrificed, may not feel the pangs of Conscience at her latter end, which she richly deserves for having caused & prolonged my misery.'

Then the canvas of his ship swelled and there came a long silence. George Dawson had been swept away in the Trade Winds.

Twenty-four

D URING her lifetime Mrs. Fitzherbert never used a postage stamp. Her numerous letters and most of Minney's went by courier. So many notes survive that, reflecting that her entire correspondences with the Duke of York and several other people were destroyed, one is forced to the conclusion that these ladies spent several hours each day scratching away at their writing desks.

During the winter of 1822-3 Mrs. Fitzherbert and Minney both seemed to find social life flat. George might be out of the way but dearest Mama still fussed. She knew Minney was thinking of him, waiting for the rare posts from the West Indies, secretly reading his letters in her room and writing back every detail of their life:

'. . . I have never begun upon the subject to Mama but contented myself with desiring my brother to tell her I heard from you before you sailed & that I was ready to speak upon the subject, if she would afford me any opening to it, but this she has never done. . . .

At Stuttgart there was nothing worth remaining for, but the old Queen of Württemberg, eldest sister of George IV, hearing from the Minister of our arrival despatched a messenger to desire we would dine with her the following day. I had never seen the old lady before, but was not reminded of this being our first acquaintance. I was rather amused by finding my *nom de guerre* familiar with her & hearing myself addressed as "Minney" by one who had never seen me & who had left England thirty years before, eleven of which she told me she had passed without receiving a single letter from her own family & Bonaparte had afforded her the first opportunity of transmitting one to the old King during the War. She kept me a long time in her Cabinet, asking me all sort of questions about the King, although she appeared to be as much *au courant* of London gossip as I could possibly have made her. . . .

Count Orloff committed a dreadful *gaffe* the other day with Lady Downshire, who happening to tell him we had arrived at Paris, he asked her if I had not lately refused *un* Lord Arthur Hill, who had for some years been *a mes pieds* & it was not till she changed countenance he recollected he was speaking of her son. . . .

I hear very bad accounts of the King's health. He is said to have been more haunted by the Blue Devils than I could have supposed when I imagined myself to have been surrounded by the entire set. He is said to have the gout, but I fear this is not really the case & that his mind is affected.'

Perhaps unwisely for his own tranquillity George had asked Minney to recount her flirtations. With humour she did so.

'Paris. March 3 1823
    I believe you made me promise to give you a list of *péchés d'habitude* I was likely to commit here. They would have contented themselves by occasionally raising the report about Beauchamp & myself, which ceasing upon his & Major Gurwood's departure from Paris has been followed by the discovery of a *passion malheureuse* entertained for me by Prince Jules de Polignac [newly appointed French Ambassador to London].

    I am at this moment causing to be employed 500 agents of the Police in consequence of my écrin having been robbed of everything but my last few diamonds. Fifteen of my best bracelets are gone & among them your beautiful blue one & the King's picture. I have almost been amused at how much *au tragique* French people take things of this sort.'

Lady Gwydir wrote on April 9th, 1823:

'Miss Seymour, I begin to hope, will not marry Prince Jules de Polignac, though it looked like it at one time. Mrs. Fitzherbert was in great danger; gout in the stomach. Miss Seymour has not recovered her trinkets including the King's picture, notwithstanding the reward she offered.'

A man's letter, dated August 1st, 1823 preserved in the Fitzherbert Papers shows how much interest Minney's love affairs aroused:

'The Royal Squadron is moored at Cowes but no prospect is held out of His Majesty repairing thither for that purpose. He is held at Council today to receive Mons. de Polignac, who delivers his credentials from His Most Christian Majesty. There is no doubt of Mons. de Polignac having offered marriage to Miss Seymour but it was done *sub rosa* & with all due finesse & diplomatic tact so that *son amour propre n'est pas blessé*, *Monsieur* & the mortification of a refusal to a proposal only informally made has been spared to His Excellency. The impudence & the selfishness of these Frenchmen is really intolerable.'

On February 1st, 1824, Minney's brother Frederick wrote her from Geneva and referred in curious fashion to Mrs. Fitzherbert and Maryanne:

'I have not heard any accounts of you for a length of time but perceive by a Pavilion Concert list that you are in Brighton & that you there appeared among the Nobility, thanks to be rendered I suppose for such an honour to the most gracious lady who has always been so active in promoting your interests with the Sovereign, even to the prejudice *of her own daughter. . . .*'

Evidently the Seymours, who were always eager to refuse suggestions of Minney's royal blood, took it for granted that Maryanne was the King's daughter.

When George Dawson returned from the West Indies in 1824

he intended to force Mrs. Fitzherbert to enumerate his villainies or else stop treating him like an outcast. In a long supplicating letter he told her his debts were all paid off but: 'Miss Seymour has informed me that she never will agree to marry me unless you can consent to her marriage, having restored to me the good opinion you once entertained of me.'

This plea with Mrs. Fitzherbert's brief cold reply survives in the Portarlington Papers. Still refusing to consent to the couple meeting under her roof, she suggested that as Minney's elder sister was in Town that 'would be the properest place for you to see her'. Nor was she prepared to state exactly what she had against the Colonel. 'My feelings have been so harrassed upon this *sad subject* & I have been made so completely miserable & unhappy that I must beg your permission to decline entering into the details contained in your letter.'

Poor Minney, who had been kept under stress for over four years, now wrote to her beloved from Brighton (April 9th, 1824): 'I am being reduced to the alternative of making one of the two beings most interested about me wretched.'

At this point the Duke of York, kind, blustering, portly Frederick, the Heir to the Throne and dearest of the King's brothers, made it his business to put in a good word for Dawson both to Mrs. Fitzherbert and to George IV.

By July 13th, 1825, the couple had announced their engagement and Minney was penning one of her anxious epistles to 'My dearest Sir':

'It would be disingenuous in me to attempt to conceal from Your Majesty that time has not reconciled Mama or my brothers to the step, upon which my future happiness depends. . . . I dare not entreat that Your Majesty should so far condescend as to add so important a favour to the innumerable ones you have already lavished upon me, by affording that sanction & support on a subject (which with all my decided opinions upon) I know that Your Majesty must condemn . . . etc.'[1]

On the day after he received Minney's letter, George IV dis-

Windsor Archives.

cussed the marriage with the Duke of York. His Majesty considered it hopeless to thwart true love further—and who could have known it better? He took the precaution, however, of cutting George Dawson out of Minney's settlement. Next day the King wrote his brother what he considered to be 'the best *palliative* or *justification* in some degree for her sad imprudence'. In those days a wife's fortune automatically became her husband's property, but Minney's fortune was to be '*placed in trustee's hands & settled entirely, solely & only upon her & upon any children she may probably have hereafter*. When she has done this, she will completely exonerate Mr. Dawson from every possible imputation of having been activated upon by any principle or motive of *self-interest*'. The King then desired his brother to read the whole contents of this letter '*in extenso*, both to Mrs. Fitzherbert, as well as to Minney Seymour, the *first moment* you can obtain an interview with them'.[1]

Comatose the King might appear but he remained level-headed in this emergency. Drawing up marriage settlements was after all his forte.

The Duke called at Tilney Street three days later, although Minney wrote crossly to George that she supposed 'his own *affaires de cœur* interfere with the interest he may shew in those of his friends'. His Royal Highness reported his visit to George IV thus:

'Both ladies appeared most affected by the extreme kindness of your letter, and after Miss Seymour, who was so nervous as to be hardly able to speak, had retired, Mrs. Fitzherbert expressed herself in most feeling terms of acknowledgement of your goodness.'[1]

George Dawson found the Marriage Settlement as drawn up by the King himself, 'unusual, degrading & clearly betraying a want of confidence in me'. It was the snub he minded, not the fact he could not touch his wife's money. He was struggling to be materially worthy of her and to give her all he possessed in the world.

[1] Windsor Archives.

Minney's brother, George Seymour, wrote a note of peace saying he could not expect kind feelings after so violently opposing the marriage, but that now he wished them both happiness. Only the vanquished Mrs. Fitzherbert could not bear to meet the bridegroom.

On August 12th a radiantly happy Minney visited Cowes. She wrote one last soothing letter to the man who for nearly five years had fought so hard for her hand.

'. . . as for your not understanding my feelings as to the cutting remarks of His Majesty I cannot attempt to explain what you naturally cannot enter into. I am neither apprehensive of his reminding you of your not being a Duke or of actual absence of fortune. . . .'

After all the disputes it was impossible for Minney to be married from Tilney Street so she had moved to her brother's house. Mrs. Fitzherbert kissed her fondly as she left, but she could not face the ordeal of attending the ceremony and disappeared to the country, ostensibly to bow her head in grief.

On August 20th, 1825, the couple were married quietly at St. George's, Hanover Square. Both families signed the Register, George Seymour and the Moriers witnessing for Minney, Lord Portarlington and Lady Louisa Dawson for George, and Mr. Forster, the King's Solicitor, for His Majesty.

George IV thought tenderly on this day of his pretty, wilful ward. With a letter asking her to be kind to his 'poor old friend Mrs. Fitzherbert' he gave a splendid wedding present.

The couple departed for their honeymoon to an apartment lent them in Hampton Court Palace. As their carriage moved through the summer haze Minney lifted shining eyes to George. She was his at last. The King had sent a fine jewel. And no one had reminded him that he was not a duke.

Twenty-five

MRS. FITZHERBERT recovered from her defeat with remarkable resiliency. The threatened miserable retirement turned into a round of country house visits with Maryanne.

Boxes of her affectionate letters to Minney survive. On the very day after the wedding, August 21st, 1825, she wrote:

'No mother I am certain ever loved her *own child* more dearly than I have loved you. I pray to God from morning to night that your happiness may be as complete as I wish and as you deserve. Mr. Dawson will, I trust, do all in his power to render you happy.

I have had kind invitations from the Cholmondeleys and also from the Seftons but as I had written the Duke of Devonshire to fix being at Chatsworth on the 8th I was under the necessity of sending my excuses. . . . The other day I went to Lord Grosvenor, who gave us a fine lunch. The house is the most magnificent thing I ever saw. . . . I am expecting to hear every day of you from Paris where I hope you will not be tempted to make a long stay.'

What a relief to be able to write light-heartedly:

'Dearest Minney,
    Pray accept the enclosed to buy Hats and Bonnets at Paris. I wish I was able to make it thousands instead of hundreds.'

'Chatsworth. October 17 1825
    I cannot tell you, dearest Minney, the delight I felt when

the Duke gave me a letter from you dated Nantes. . . . He said it was addressed in your handwriting and he knew it would make me happy. . . . The Duke seemed very pleased at your having bought so many French hats etc. He is greatly occupied with ladies' dresses. He says you dress remarkably well, and that at one of his parties, you desired him to admire a gown you had on. He said it was certainly very pretty but that it was an old one. He had seen you in it before. He expects everybody to be dressed here as if going to a Ball and looks rather shy if you have not a fresh gown for every day. This is rather a bore for me, for I hate the trouble of dressing up and in this particular I am afraid I don't stand very high in his estimation. . . .'

'Tilney Street. November 7 1825
I arrived here the day before yesterday, rather glad to get to my fireside before the very bad weather sets in. . . . After I left Chatsworth I went to the Fitzherberts and then to Trentham where I met the whole family. Lady Stafford was constantly lamenting you were not her daughter-in-law.'

Indeed many lamented for Minney. Neither Lord Beauchamp nor Lord Arthur Hill who had been at her feet for so long ever married. Nor did Mrs. Fitzherbert's own particular choice the Duke of Devonshire, only son of the unforgettable Georgina. George Fitzclarence continued to hint his devotion until his tragic death.

When Minney reached Rome in January 1826 she confided glad news to Mrs. Fitzherbert who needed a new fuss. When she heard that precious Minney expected a baby and had not even a house in which to nest, it gave the old lady good grounds for exertion. She wrote off to Naples:

'I have been enquiring all over London to get a house for you, for I cannot bear the idea of your not having a Home somewhere and since I have had your last letter I am more anxious than ever.
All your old lovers are now providing for themselves in a great hurry. Wortley [Lord Wharncliffe] is married and the day before yesterday I got a letter from Lord Clare to inform

194

me of his marriage. . . . Pray do write to Louise [Mrs. Wat Smythe, widow of Mrs. Fitzherbert's brother]. Her extreme jealousy of me is owing to my visit to Hooton where I was treated with great affection and kindness and her hatred of Maryanne she makes no secret of, as she has taken into her head people take more notice of her than of her girls.'

Mrs. Fitzherbert, always fond of these Smythe nieces, hints that Mrs. Wat has taken to the bottle, 'the only possible explanation of her resentments unless she is not right in her mind'. She adds:

'Pray do write to Louise who is in such an uncomfortable state with everybody and I am sure if you don't write she will think I have prevented you. . . .

I have determined to take no notice and shew her and the girls every kindness and attention in my power, for really I have a very sincere affection for her and would do everything on earth I could both for her and her children.'

Mrs. Wat's two pretty daughters were poor but Protestant, so it should have been far easier to find a selection of suitable husbands for them than for Maryanne. Eventually with Minney's help they married well.

Towards the end of February 1827 when the Dawson-Damers, as they now were, planned to leave Naples Mrs. Fitz wrote:

'You may depend upon finding on your arrival a comfortable house, and everything you can want. Therefore make your mind easy upon that score, only if, my dear Minney, if taking so long a journey in your situation will not be detrimental to you, for Gods sake don't hesitate but set out immediately. You can make another tour of Italy whenever you like. . . .'

When the young couple arrived back in London they took up residence in Tilney Street with Mrs. Fitzherbert, who now found, perhaps to her own surprise, that George was the most fascinating of men.

At the request of Lord and Lady Glengall he hurried off to

195

stand for Tipperary in the June election. Sir Henry Halford, the King's physician, came to inquire about Minney's confinement, while Mama wrote daily soothings to the prospective father. On June 13th a little daughter arrived. George IV immediately sent his best wishes and Mrs. Fitzherbert dispatched hourly bulletins to Tipperary:

'June 16 1826
I have the best possible news to send you. Our dear Minney has had a very good night and Doctor Herbert says she is quite well and has ordered her chicken for dinner. She desires a thousand loves to you and bids me tell you the baby is in a very flourishing state. . . .'

For twenty-four hours after Minney's accouchement Mrs. Fitzherbert's hand trembles so she can hardly write but she then informs George that the Duke of York approved of his standing for Parliament in Ireland.

A few days later both she and Minney were furious to learn that Lord Glengall's mother had written to Lady Caroline Damer requesting her to send £2,000 'to carry on the Election' which might 'irritate and make the Old Lady very cross and out of humour'. Mrs. Fitzherbert wrote it was: 'I really think very meddling and interfering with what she has nothing to do with.'

On June 19th Minney disobediently took up a pen to write her husband:

'Mama took care to recount to Sir Henry Halford all your Parliamentary intentions which she does in a manner directly opposite to what Lady Glengall's story would be. This is for the sake of being repeated at Windsor, and *elle s'excuse* to talk of your ideas to anyone as if Tipperary was on its knees to have you for its member.'

Lady Glengall had impeded George IV's Irish tour in 1821 by wearing mourning for Queen Caroline and saying His Majesty had landed dead drunk. The King had an elephant's memory for slights.

There is something disarming about the happy end of Mrs.

196

Fitzherbert's relationship with Colonel Dawson as she still calls him. Now she is scheming for his sake with King and Duke of York and writes him: 'your sisters are very anxious for your return in which all the inhabitants of this House most lovingly join'.

On July 1st Minney wrote to her husband:

'Supposing you are successful, do not let your manifestations of gratitude be prolonged to an extent that will reduce you to hear of me suspended to the bedpost. . . . I cut the enclosed out of the Paper yesterday. It looks as if your wish of being put on full pay was complied with but the Duke [of York] whom Mama saw yesterday never mentioned it and I had not, when she went to Brompton, found it in the Paper. She found the Duke very low and his legs terribly swelled. He spoke of your Election, of your certainty of success next Parliament. . . .'

On July 13th the baby daughter was christened Georgina, His Majesty King George the Fourth having condescended to be godfather.[1]

Mrs. Fitzherbert hung tenderly over the first little creature born in her house, savouring as nearly as possible the joys of grandmotherhood.

[1] This baby, the first flower of the Seymour romance, grew up to suffer the fate of many unfortunate Victorian females. She married Earl Fortescue, an insufferable tyrant who forced her to bear fourteen children. She died worn out at the age of forty. The several sons who survived into the 1920s still remembered with fear and dislike that father who fifty years before had stood in front of the fire warming his coat-tails, roaring furiously at his cowering family and fading wife.

Twenty-six

IN JANUARY 1827 the Duke of York died. He wrote to 'dearest Mrs. Fitzherbert' to the very end assuring her he was much better and in good spirits. They had both agreed to destroy each other's letters, and it was with relief that she received back her own correspondence which she spent two years perusing and burning. She told Lord Stourton that with these papers she could have given the best private and public history of all the transactions of the country from the close of the American War down to the death of the Duke of York, either from her communications with the Duke, or her own connections with the opposite party, through the Prince and his friends.

Minney wrote His Majesty a letter of condolence, describing his little god-daughter and adding sincere wishes 'from the person in whose house I am now living'.

Mrs. Fitzherbert's letter-file contained hundreds of letters from various members of the royal family. She went over them constantly herself, destroying any which might lead to trouble. Minney's daughter would in time carry on this work with Victorian scissors. George Dawson-Damer and George Seymour occasionally scribbled a note on their own which they left among family papers and many of these survived. George Seymour coldly recorded that the Duke of Clarence told him: 'he knew George IV had paid £95,000 to Lady Conyngham to buy Bifrons' [the estate to which she eventually retired]. Lady Conyngham had never been able to abide Brighton where Mrs. Fitzherbert's house was forever catching His Majesty's eye evoking memories which he smothered with elephantine sighs. In March 1827 she persuaded him to leave the Pavilion for ever and incarcerate himself

with her in Windsor Castle. Incarceration is the only word to describe the King's fate now; he could not escape from the burden of
his 350 lb. of wine-sodden flesh. He who loved beauty and grace
and had cared so much for his personal appearance now suffered
a loathing of his own body and wished no one to see it. And his
mind also felt imprisoned. He kept pretending he had been a
different person. Sometimes he pretended he had led a charge at
Waterloo, or that he had fought with his fists and beaten a stout
Brighton butcher. Or he told himself how he had been loved and
seduced by the upright Lady Horatia Seymour. Lying alone in
growing pain he remembered only how splendidly he had always
acted and how brave and truthful his friends should think him.
Fox, Burke, Sheridan—they would attest his prowess, were they
here. But the cold eye of the Duke of Wellington froze these
fantasies unpleasantly, and only too often now George of England
felt like heaving his huge body round and lying with his face to
the wall, sick of the world, sick of all he had missed.

The King wept easily nowadays, not merely if he were contradicted, for Lady Conyngham seldom allowed that, but no sooner
did he start to talk about himself at all than tears would begin to
pour down his fat cheeks.

No one had understood him, no one except . . . The locket
containing her picture still hung around his neck. Lady Conyngham had never attempted to get it off him. She did not really care
whose face haunted him and being corpulent herself avoided
physical manœuvre.

Mrs. Fitzherbert wrote often that she also shed tears, but they
were always tears of happiness over her two daughters. Surrounded by young people who adored her, she was enjoying her
seventies.

A letter to Minney from Brighton says:

'I cannot let the post go out this Evening without thanking
you a thousand times for the very useful & delightful present
you sent me. . . . On seeing your writing I immediately called
out for my spectacles. Judge then of my surprise when I found
what the contents of the little box contained. I have worn
them ever since & think them quite perfect. What a sly person
you was to have concealed the Glass which I tormented every-

199

body about for a length of time. . . . Old Sally says she does not mind all the trouble she had to look for it, as it was such a *pretty* thought and attention of Mrs. Dawson.'

She goes on to scold Minney for her surprisingly modern habit of banting. How often in the last thirty years have daughters not heard their mamas use like words:

'Harriet tells me you are dreadfully thin & that you eat nothing but starve yourself. I am very sorry to hear it for I know your passion for growing thin. Depend upon it, it is not becoming to you & everybody I see is of the same opinion.'

Other letters from Brighton ramble on:

'There has not been for years so deep a snow as there is here. It would kill poor dear Baby to take her out in this sad weather. . . .'

'I have just received a letter from Eude, the poor Duke of York's cook, to offer me to purchase some lamps I gave the Duke some years ago. It would make me quite unhappy to have them back again, and would bring all sorts of uncomfortable facts to my recollections. . . .'

'I hear nothing but your gay parties in town. I have had a very kind letter from Sir Henry [the King's physician]. I understand he recommends strongly to you a change with respect to hours etc. I hope, my dear Minney, you will follow his directions & get a little more embonpoint which is certainly necessary both for your health as well as your looks. . . . We are all very angry at your having had the baby's head shaved!'

To George Dawson-Damer, who had little political ambition, she wrote, April 24th, 1827, 'I suppose there will be no small difficulty in arranging the new Ministry if it can be managed at all. I wish in the scramble you might get some of the good things. *But*, but will it last? . . .'

Later from Bath she hoped the change of air would help Mary-anne to recover from an illness: 'Our lodgings are very good & our living most perfect having one of the best cooks I ever met with. . . .' She who had supped for twenty years at the Prince of Wales's table should have been a fair judge.

As well as looking after Maryanne, Mrs. Fitzherbert kept Mrs. Wat Smythe and her daughters during the winter months at Brighton.

Prince Puckler-Muskau, an outrageous German looking for an English heiress, gave a foreigner's version of life there. He often went to Mrs. Fitzherbert's to 'play "écarté" and whist with the men, or loo with the young ladies. These small circles are much more agreeable than the great parties of the metropolis. There, every art is understood but the art of society.'

On February 24th, 1827, he wrote:

'I spent this evening at Mrs. F.'s a very dignified & delightful woman, formerly as it is affirmed, married to the King. She is now without influence in that region, but still universally beloved & respected—"d'un excellent ton et sans pretention".

In this house one sees only "beau monde". Indeed there is not much of the very emptiest in the exclusive society here; or they live completely retired, that they may not come into collision with the persons they call "Nobodies", whom they shun with greater horror than Brahmins shun Parias. Though my station & connections allow me to enter the sanctuary, I do not on that account disdain the worth without.'

Mrs. Fitzherbert may have been fussy in selecting her company, but she saw that the girls all enjoyed themselves while prudently pursuing rich husbands. In June she was at Richmond when news of old uncle Errington's death came through, and Maria Fitzherbert remembered with a throb that far-off night when he had introduced her to the Prince on the Opera steps. Both the witnesses to her marriage had now died, and a new generation had arisen bent on their own romances and chafing to get to a glamorous garden party near by. Heartless little Louisa Smythe wrote in her journal:

'Saturday. June 30 1827. . . . It certainly was not an unexpected event and it is only to be wondered at that he arrived
to such an advanced age, but however unexpected the event I
could not help wishing it had not happened today, as it
agitated dear Mama very much. We did not get to Richmond
Hill till after four, when we found Aunt Fitz very cross & the
rest of the party rather in a fuss; however we all arrived quite
safely at Boyle Farm, where we proceeded down a little
winding path till we reached the house where Lord Castlereagh & Ld. Chesterfield met us in the most graceful manner
with bouquets.'[1]

The Lords Castlereagh and Chesterfield, hosts at this glamorous breakfast, were about the most eligible young men in London.
The weather remained perfect, the guests dined in tents to the
sound of village bells and there was dancing, fireworks and supper
till three in the morning.

Only Aunt Fitz (who was engineering her Smythe nieces'
début in smart society) had been cross—cross and sad, for one who
stood gallantly by her in the past. Kind great-uncle Errington had
in fact left the Smythes some money, but the ungrateful youngsters resented having to wear black at the smart expensive Al-
mack's balls. On July 4th Louisa lamented: 'We went to Tilney
Street, and drove all over the Town to get black beads. Mama did
not go to Almacks, therefore Mary & I went with Minney. We
went *en noir*, but did not look so triste as our costumes bespoke
us. . . .'

Great-uncles should not die in the middle of a gay social
season.

That winter Mrs. Fitzherbert wrote to Minney who was
approaching her twenty-ninth birthday:

'Tilney Street. November 20 1827
   I imagine, dearest Minney, that you will receive this on the
23rd. I wish I were with you to express to you in person all
I feel upon the occasion, and how sincerely and from the
bottom of my heart, I wish you, my dear Child, many happy
returns of the day, with everything you wish for or desire.

[1] *The Prettiest Girl in England*. Richard Buckle. 1958.

You talk of old age, think what I am! I assure you I should be very sorry to have to pass my youthful days over again. It is a great consolation, at my advanced age, to have those I love the most (yourself and Mary, my two children) both well & happy, and to receive from them kindness & affection and to end my days in peace & quietness.'

Ten days later she moved to Brighton where society still 'ma'am'ed' her and stood up when she entered the room as for royalty.

'November 29 1827.
   Here I am with all England at Brighton! There never were so many people of Fashion here before, & my house has been like a Fair all day yesterday & today. But I shall not be comfortable, my dearest Minney, until I get you & George here. It is the only thing I have to look forward to with pleasure. The day before I left town I was with Princess Sophia [sister of King George IV] for an hour & an half. She said she was quite sure Lady Conyngham had done what she told them all she intended to do, and that the King said he was very happy at it. Henry Halford assured me that he was now quite well. He had been ill with the gout and had lost a great deal of his size by Halford's making him live very abstemiously but he was the better for it.'

At the end of December Mrs. Fitzherbert wrote much perturbed over the early death of George Dawson's sister, Lady Harriet Erskine:

'It must have been a great comfort to Dawson his having been to visit her. I hope Lady Caroline will continue her pension. . . . I am now, thank God, got well again, & have exerted myself to the utmost to make my inhabitants gay & happy. I have longed for you, dearest, to assist me for I am not able to do much. My mind is youthful but my body is very old.'

On January 1st, 1828, Minney wrote to the King pleading for Lady Harriet's family:

'My dearest Sir,
    It becomes once again my most welcome duty to congratu-
late Your Majesty upon the arrival of the New Year etc. etc.
    I have had to bear for the last ten days the melancholy in-
telligence of the very sudden death of my sister-in-law, poor
Lady Harriet Erskine without a day's previous illness &
leaving her husband, Your Majesty may know as a son of the
late Lord [Chancellor] with eight children two younger than
Your Majesty's little god-daughter & with her death nothing
remaining to them but his small living, as the allowance Lady
Caroline Damer made for her has I fear ceased with her.

His Majesty always listened to his Minney. The destitute papa
was made Dean of Ripon.
    A final letter from Paris to Mrs. Fitzherbert described the
social life there:

'Hotel Bristol
    You really would have laughed to have seen my levee to-
day. Lady Granville called & said the file of carriages went
round the *Place Vendome*. Lady Anglesey & Lady Mary
Stanley and the Bear [Chairman of the Hudson Bay Fur Co.]
are in this Hotel, the latter very particular in his enquiries
after you. He says *you* are the only person who can talk openly
to the King & give him good advice & that you must get
the Garter for Louis Philippe. Tomorrow we dine with old
Tallyrand but Paris is & he very dull they say. Everybody has
been to see me but Yarmouth [Lord Hertford's son also called
Beauchamp] & I mean to go and see him on Sunday when he
again starts in the Balloon.'

Would that we heard more about Talleyrand and early
Ballooning and less about dear Baby and the price of hats.
    To George Dawson Mrs. Fitzherbert wrote often:

'Brighton. January 7 1828
    Though scarce able to hold my pen from another attack
of gout in my right hand, I will not let this post go without
thanking you for the kind letter I have received from you.

It cheers me very much by the good accounts you sent me of dear Minney & the Baby. By your accounts you are not near so gay at Paris as we are here. There never was anything so delightful as the girls in this house. We have now a very good Society & a great many Beaux from Town but I suppose they will all soon take their departure to hunt after the Loaves & Fishes [political and court appointments] and fine confusion we shall have at the meetings of Parliament.'

In her journal Louisa Smythe recorded the daily round at Aunt Fitz's house from January 1st when she had a dinner for twelve people to January 25th when she gave a ball at Steyne House.

'We all dined at three & by halfpast-ten we were dressed & in the drawing-room. Our costumes were exceedingly admired. . . . The Ball was universally considered charming. Aunt F looked à merveille, & everybody seemed in high force.'

Next day the girls did not come down till after two when their beaux arrived to talk it over. Young and tireless they were slightly indignant at being sent to bed at eleven, 'sacrificed to the Treasures' as they called Mrs. Fitzherbert's servants.

Meanwhile the old lady refused to join the Dawson-Damers in Paris though Minney wrote: 'The weather here is heavenly. We can hardly believe a word of the snow you complain of. We suspect it a little excuse for your not telling us when you will come here, you dear naughty woman! We can lodge you so charmingly close to us next door. . . .' She did not intend to cease watching Maryanne's courtship by a certain gentleman although this meek little mouse would not have dreamt of riding her own line.

It was not so easy to find a handsome Catholic husband, and although this suitor was a younger son Mrs. Fitzherbert liked him.

On April 1st, 1828, after returning to London, she wrote a hard-headed assessment of the match:

'I have little hopes of the event I announced taking place. Everything we could wish for or desire except that odious commodity money, which on the part of the young man is very deficient. The person's name & connections are most desirable in every point of view & the father & mother have connected with them & have written such kind & affectionate letters upon the subject that we are both charmed & so would you if you knew all. Mary is not able to write to you herself which she had intended doing to tell these particulars which for the present we beg & implore of you not to mention or to give an idea of to any soul breathing. The young man is Edward Jerningham, second son of Lord Stafford, very amiable, good-looking and gentlemanlike. His brother I believe is now in Paris. Therefore for Heaven's sake don't say anything about it to a human being. There are unfortunately ten younger children, their fortune five thousand each, which is so very trifling that though I shall give Mary at present twenty thousand added to this, they could not exist without a further addition. I have written to beg they will endeavour to do something more. If this is not acceded to, the marriage cannot take place. However I do not as yet quite despair. Fortunately Mary has not seen enough of him to be much attached & feels the smallness of his fortune would be a great drawback to their mutual comfort, for it really would not enable them to have the common necessaries & comforts of life & if they should have children they would absolutely be beggars.'

How many young couples must have lived on tenterhooks in those days, when if sufficient fortune could not be produced a marriage had to be broken off. There was never any question of the suitor *earning* money. Indeed there seems to have been no method of stepping down into the new world of industry or banking. If devoid of inherited wealth a gentleman had only one method of making himself a fortune, and that was to become captain of a ship in the Royal Navy and earn prize-money in action at sea.

Maryanne's romance was not frustrated however. Lord Stafford, particularly anxious for the match, probably stinted the ten younger children to procure this pretty little bit of Catholic fluff for his second son and the wedding took place.

On June 16th, 1828, Mrs. Fitzherbert gave 'a fine breakfast in Tilney Street, where Maryanne remained till four o'clock'.

206

Next day she wrote to the bride a very perfect description of the aftermath of many such festivities:

'June 17 1828

Though half dead with fatigue I will not let the post go without scribbling a few lines to you, dearest Mary. I long to hear you got safe to Tunbridge & that you found your new habitation comfortable. I never passed a more melancholy day than I did yesterday. After you left me I really felt quite alone in the world. Minney came to me about seven o'clock & we went to Lady Stanley's [her niece] a little after ten. My servants were very anxious to get me out of the house that they might begin their amusements. They were all in high spirits & kept up the Ball till near six this morning. I went to bed about twelve & shutting all the doors it did not annoy me, in the least. Mrs. Wat brought me home from Lady Stanley's & her new footman was so extremely in liquor that we were obliged to get one of Sir Thomas' servants to hold him behind the carriage to keep him from breaking his neck. Her carriage wheel broke down as she left this house in the morning. There never was anything so unlucky as she is with her Establishment. . . . Say a thousand kind things from me to my son-in-law & believe me ever most affectionately.'

Why does she call Jerningham her son-in-law when she never refers thus to Colonel Dawson? Why did she expect a Duke for Minney & yet gladly acquiesce to a second son for Maryanne? There is no clue in this mystery. Mrs. Fitzherbert must have known what blood ran in the veins of both girls, but if she left a hint it has not survived the scissors of Minney's daughters. We only know that when Lord Stourton counselled her to leave some evidence in her own handwriting that no children had been born 'she smilingly objected on the score of delicacy'.

When an American Catholic called James Ord who had been educated by the Jesuits in Georgetown College wrote to Mrs. Fitzherbert asking 'discreetly & in guarded language' if he was not her son born the year after her marriage to the Prince, he received no reply.

207

Twenty-seven

DULL one might call her life now with its grandmotherly fusses and tenderness, but after so much turbulence and drama is the ultimate achievement of happiness, contentment and love really dull?

While the King groaned and swelled, his Maria remained radiant through her seventies. There is nothing senile in Mrs. Fitzherbert's affection to her adopted daughters. She and Minney were unusually congenial beings. To Maryanne visiting her new in-laws she writes more maternally:

'July 21 1828

Your welcome letter has given me the greatest pleasure and delight to hear my little girl has been received in the manner you mention. It really affected me so much that I have shed abundance of tears. I should have behaved very ill, had I been present, for kindness and joy such as you have received is very affecting. . . . You would laugh at me if at this moment you could witness the large drops that trickle down my cheeks. . . . Minney quite well. I am going to her and shall show her your letter and I shall do the same thing in Cumberland Place. [Mrs. Smythe's house.] I shall enjoy seeing their faces when they read all the great and grand doings and the delightful welcome you have received from all both high and low. You are a fortunate little girl. . . .'

Apparently the Smythe girls suffered from jealousy of Maryanne and Minney. Nevertheless, that winter Mrs. Fitzherbert again had them to stay at Brighton and on January 12th, 1829, she gave a Fancy Dress Ball. The *Brighton Gazette* published an exuberant account:

'Mrs. Fitzherbert's grand Fancy Dress Ball was not only the most splendid party given during the present season, but the most splendid probably ever seen in Brighton. There were more than two hundred present, including all the Fashionables now residing in the town. No magnificence can be conceived greater than that displayed in the various dresses, which were exceedingly rich. . . . The fine rooms of the noble mansion, thus lighted up, presented a most brilliant and dazzling appearance & on the supper table every delicacy was seen in profusion. . . . We do hope that Mrs. Fitzherbert may long enjoy health to promote the prosperity of the town. . . . Mrs. Fitzherbert, who we are happy to say, looked in excellent health and spirits, wore a rich dress of white satin; the Hon. Mrs. Dawson-Damer a handsome black fancy dress, head-dress of diamonds; Hon. Mrs. Jerningham a black velvet dress, with richly ornamented stomacher. . . . Miss Smythe, a beautiful Turkish dress, with handsome turban of scarlet and gold and a profusion of diamonds; Miss G. Smythe looked most lovely in a simple white fancy dress, with a veil confined with a chaplet of white roses. . . .'

Louisa Smythe's chief suitor, Sir Frederick Hervey-Bathurst, reappeared unexpectedly for this ball. Mrs. Fitzherbert discouraged him as being 'a bore', but what did Louisa think of Maryanne's choice?:

'Oh! how I should get bored with such a life, & such an aimiable, good natured, stupid husband. *Mais qui se ressemble s'assemble.*'

And when criticized by a certain gentleman for being a flirt, Louisa confided in her journal that she feared 'that the generality of the world give me credit for following Mrs. Dawson's example & walking in her footsteps'.

Brighton was certainly gayer than Windsor these days. Ireland had reached the brink of civil war because the King reputedly refused to allow Catholic emancipation. George III had gone off his head each time this subject was broached, and now his son announced that his views were those of his 'revered & sainted father'. In March 1829 George IV said he would dismiss his Ministry rather than consent to the Bill and sent for his Cabinet. The ministers travelled to Windsor in trepidation. There is a perfect description of the scene:

> 'He spoke to them for nearly six hours fortifying himself with repeated sips of brandy & water. Threats to retire to Hanover, tears, and even kisses, were all tried to shake the ministers' attachment to the Bill, but all in vain, & the King boldly dismissed them from office! He was found after the interview by Lady Conyngham & Kingston lying on a sofa, utterly exhausted.'[1]

They explained to him that the Bill's opponents were too few to form a government for him. He had got to obey Wellington. Furiously, the King gave in. Oh, to be so badly treated! His 'sainted father' had in the past been anti-Catholic and so was he. Hadn't Lady Hertford made him give up Maria because she was a Catholic? And now he was asked to grant them emancipation!

Peacefully from Tilney Street Mrs. Fitzherbert wrote Minney:

> 'October 19 1829
>
> I will not bore you with a repetition of our goings on at Brighton, as you must have read it in the newspapers. I must say I was very sorry to leave that place as I never passed my time more pleasantly. I suppose you have heard that the Duke of Wellington went to Brighton to visit Lady Jersey [daughter-in-law of the ancient enemy]? He dined with her & went away at night. What will Mrs. Arbuthnot [Wellington's lady-love] say to this? . . . I must bid you adieu, my dearest, with kind love to Dawson. Pray tell him not to call me Madame. It is so formal. Lady Conyngham is not well. The thought of Brighton I believe has made her sick. You'll see by the Papers His Majesty does not intend honouring us with his presence.'

[1] *George IV*, Roger Fulford.

Mrs. Fitzherbert spent November redecorating Steyne House. To Minney: 'Think of me, dearest, in this house quite alone, and unless I have you or the Jerninghams I am content to be so.' To Maryanne: 'I have quite finished my drawingrooms, but I don't like them half so well as I did the old red & white.'

Her letters to George Dawson-Damer who was hunting up in Lancashire are many pages long. An 'odious' paragraph appeared in the newspapers intimating the King meant to slight the Dawsons by not inviting them to an imaginary party at Windsor. Mrs. Fitzherbert sent the proper channels buzzing and could write George:

'The King read it & has behaved beautifully upon the occasion (violent outrageous to the greatest degree) & wishing very much to find out who could have been the author of so diabolical & malicious an invention, he put himself into a violent passion & declared that he had always had the greatest affection & always should have for Minney & that he had done everything to prove it to her & that if he had given any party she & Colonel Dawson, would have been the first he should have invited. . . .'

Five years after losing her battle with the determined Colonel she is able to end her missive: 'God bless you dear George.'

In December she was worried over a horrid hunting accident which befell Minney's nephew, the eldest son of George Seymour. It was the day of frantic doctoring and no anaesthetics. George had to hold his son during a fifteen-minute operation which the patient bore with resolution but: 'Poor George was very nearly dead of it.' She had spared Minney this news 'as I know she was rather uneasy that you might meet with some accident'. She goes on to hope the 'dear children are getting over the Chicken-pox', to say the Duke of Devonshire 'raved about you & Minney & said after you left Chatsworth all was dull & stupid'; to hope the Duke of Wellington will 'come off triumphant' in the political confusion.

Apart from the chaperoning, and not very successful snubbing of her nieces' beaux, Mrs. Fitzherbert's life continued to overflow with family interests. She lived her girls' lives with them. Her references to servants are always kind. 'The Treasures' included one decrepit old Daykin, easy to visualize: 'I would not think of taking a Butler whilst poor Daykin is able to crawl about the house. It would kill him to have anyone put in his place.'

Human beings arouse interest and compassion in Maria to the very end, be they ancient butlers or asthmatic royal dukes. When poor Maryanne lost a baby Sussex hastened to condole:

'Kensington Palace

It was only last night I was aware of the sad misfortune with which poor Mrs. Jerningham had been visited. As I always must feel interested in what concerns you & knowing how much you have your niece's interest at heart I cannot refuse myself the melancholy satisfaction of expressing to you my concern on the occasion & likewise to inquire after the poor little lady. Believe me, dear Mrs. Fitzherbert, with great sincerity

Augustus Frederick.'

During 1830 George IV became very ill and Mrs. Fitzherbert retreated to Brighton:

'The constant histories respecting the King & people's curiosity to find out what I think & what I do, would annoy me so much that, dull as it is here, I am spared many uncomfortable occurrences that would annoy me. . . . I have this day got your letter, dearest Minney. George's account the day before of what the Duke of Wellington reported had made me hope that the King wasn't so ill as rumour said, & that the Drawing Room etc. being put an end to, would relieve his mind. I remembered the King always liked to make himself out worse than he was to excite compassion, & that he always wished everyone to think him dangerously ill, when little was the matter with him. This I had hoped was the case at present, but alas I fear it is not so from your account. . . .'

When His Majesty rallied she wrote: 'I never thought the case so desperate as many did because I knew *the Man.*'

Minney had already informed Mrs. Fitzherbert that Lady

Conyngham had consulted two bishops 'as to the propriety or rather impropriety of her remaining with the King & that they had given it in favor of morality, her remaining where she was, from the chance it afforded of making the King look out for & create fresh scandal'. The King's doctor, Sir Henry Halford, wrote that he had passed Minney's sympathetic inquiries to His Majesty, 'who desired me to be sure to give you His very affectionate love'.

That was all.

He did not want Minney or Mrs. Fitzherbert by his bedside. Hardly able to breathe and forced to sleep sitting up the King did not wish to be seen by those who had once loved him. Watched by his physicians, with Lady Conyngham and the Duke of Wellington coldly eyeing each other in the background, he awaited the end in pain.

Sir Henry, his exhausted physician, wrote Mrs. Fitzherbert a description:

'Windsor. June 3 1830
    My dear Kind Madam. . . . The King has been, & continues excessively ill, with embarrassment & difficulty of breathing. The worst circumstances under which I ever witnessed the Dukes of Clarence & of Sussex under their attacks of spasmodic asthma, hardly come up to His Majesty's distress at times. What result I can hardly venture to say with confidence. His Majesty's constitution is a gigantic one & his elasticity under the most severe pressure exceeds what I have ever witnessed in thirty-eight years' experience. I think I can say with much more certainty what must be *my own fate* unless a speedy amendment or fatal issue arrives soon. . . .'

At the end of June, hearing that the King's gigantic constitution was failing at last, Mrs. Fitzherbert drove to Tilney Street. Through Sir Henry Halford she sent a letter to her dying husband who seized it gladly, read it with emotion and placed it under his pillow. Dear Maria, he could rely on her thoughts and her prayers, he knew she suffered for him. But he was beyond sending an answer. The King's wife awaited her summons in vain.

Just before dawn on the morning of June 26th George IV

213

broke an internal blood-vessel. In agitation he sent for the sleeping Sir Henry who arrived to see the King take his other physician's hand, look up into his face and say: 'My boy, this is death.'

An express messenger galloped off to inform the Duke of Clarence he was King.

The great bell of St. Paul's gave the news to London. A friend of Mrs. Fitzherbert's heard the tolling and hurried to Tilney Street to tell her that for the third time she was a widow.

According to the *Grenville Memoirs* Clarence on becoming William IV immediately 'sent the Duke of Sussex to Mrs. Fitzherbert to put her servants into mourning'.

Within a week the new King returned nine of her portraits but there was one still missing, a miniature by Cosway set with diamonds. Maria fretted to know what had become of this small, exquisite locket, for she knew that George IV had kept it to the end.

The Duke of Wellington divulged to Minney that George IV had always worn this miniature and wished to be buried with it around his neck. Minney felt shy of telling her for some time and when she did: 'Mrs. Fitzherbert made no observation but soon large tears fell from her eyes.'

Maria then knew that she had never left his mind. All through the long years of mutual coldness, all through the ugly end, she had been able to serve him. He died with the picture of her around his neck and the thought of her in his heart.

Twenty-eight

THE House of Hanover produced better brothers-in-law than husbands. William IV treated Mrs. Fitzherbert with love and respect. At first she worried over finances but she held a charge on the Pavilion for £6,000 a year and the new King amicably settled this. In return she signed a release on any claim to the property of George IV. Creevey heard the Duke of Sussex say to a lady: 'You'll be glad to hear, Ma'am that the King has continued to Mrs. Fitzherbert the same pension she had before— I am very glad of it, Sir, it does His Majesty great honour—Oh, Ma'am, the whole family made a point of it.'

On July 26th, her seventy-fifth birthday, she wrote Minney in a rare mood of despondency:

'I was so worried with all the *tracasseries* of yesterday that I could not sleep, & therefore I got up early & went to ten o'clock church. I am just returned when I found your dear little note & the beautiful fan. . . . Dont wish me happy returns of the day. I do not desire them for myself. I often regret (though I am told it is wrong) that I ever was born, but I wont touch upon this subject, as I dont wish to hurt your feelings, & because I hope & believe you have an affection for me.'

Later on she felt: 'I am getting every day better & I think I owe it chiefly to having declined all torment with lawyers.'

The Duke of Wellington, cold, straight and unsentimental, inspired confidence in the old lady. When as George IV's executor he paid business visits she felt herself on firm ground.

That was more than Mrs. Dawson-Damer was feeling then.

She had insisted on marrying an attractive lady-killer. Always the spoilt darling of her own brilliant little set, Minney could not realize that handsome gentlemen with an eye for the fair sex remain true to form after marriage. Now Louisa Smythe exulted: 'Minney was there. I never was more struck by anything than the change in her appearance, anxiety & jealousy have aged her to a degree which I should not have thought possible.'

For once Minney could not turn to Mrs. Fitzherbert for sympathy for dear Mama now adored that 'most fascinating of men'.

George Dawson-Damer was the only person present when, soon after his accession, William IV called at Steyne House. It must have been a curious moment. Mrs. Fitzherbert showed for the first time her marriage certificate and the King's eyes filled with tears. With what fortitude she had kept that secret proof![1]

His Majesty inquired if he could make amends for his brother's treatment. According to a note left by Minney's youngest daughter Constance, he begged her 'to wear the Royal Liveries and accept the Title of Duchess. Mrs. Fitzherbert replied that as she had never forfeited her good name as Mrs. Fitzherbert she would not change it; *my father* then with her told us this.' She merely put her servants in mourning and herself wore widow's weeds.

A few days later Mrs. Fitzherbert lunched at the Pavilion. His Majesty handed her out of her carriage and the Queen received her with a kiss. It must have been a strange sensation, to hobble back through those portals. To Minney she wrote:

'September 10 1830
    My reception was most flattering. I was overwhelmed with kisses from males & females. The Princess Augusta [one of George III's unmarried daughters] was particularly gracious. I felt rather nervous, never having been in the Pavilion since I was drove away by Lady Hertford. I cannot tell you my astonishment at the magnificence, & the total change since my first acquaintance in that house. They live a very quiet life. His family are the only inhabitants. I think I counted today eight Fitzclarences. George comes next week. You never saw people appear so happy as they all do.'

[1] She also showed him 'another interesting & most affecting paper'. What was this? Why did King William weep? He had long known of her marriage.

216

In this strange household it took a person of Mrs. Fitzherbert's calibre to comfort Queen Adelaide on failing to produce a legal heir while smoothing the disputes of ten royal bastards. Colonel George Fitzclarence became Earl of Munster on which *The Times* remarked 'that the relationship of this gentleman to the fountain of honour united to his high attainments, moral worth and professional reputation entitle him to a mark of paternal regard', but this one title seemed insufficient to the remainder of the brood who, merely given the rank of Marquis's children, began to sulk and bicker with each other. They wanted crosses and grand orders and all kinds of fancy decorations.

On October 1st Mrs. Fitzherbert wrote from Brighton:

'I am going today to dine at the Pavilion, & tomorrow with Lady Aldborough who keeps open house & has very good parties, but is sadly mortified at having her Company often taken from her to dine with the Royalties, & never once being invited herself. I think it is very hard upon her, particularly as she has taken a house here & furnished it with her fine things from Paris, & means to make Brighton her home. I never saw this place so full in my life. You can scarcely get along the streets for the number of carriages, very smart, & the owners dressed out as if going to some entertainment, but not a face you ever saw before.'

The year came to its end with Mrs. Fitzherbert reinstated as a member of the royal family, her servants wearing the royal livery of scarlet and blue. King William continually visited her both at Tilney Street and Brighton while Queen Adelaide sent little notes.

Minney with her children reached Steyne House late on December 31st and scribbled to her husband:

'I write one little line to tell you that instead of the road being bad & requiring four horses we arrived here at seven after remaining an hour at dinner at Crawley. The Ducks are quite well & Maryanne & I have the house to ourselves very comfortably as Mama is dining at the Pavilion where she is particularly desired to remain to see the New Year in, so I suppose she will wait to be kissed & I shall not see her to-night.'

Mrs. Fitzherbert, a rheumaticky old lady, was again being kissed by a Sovereign.

On February 8th, 1831, Mary Frampton wrote in her diary:

'The magnificence of the parties given by the King & Queen at the Pavilion are spoken of as realising the ideas of entertainments described in the Arabian Nights. The King consults Mrs. Fitzherbert much as an old friend in matters relating to the fêtes.'

Mrs. Fitzherbert now talked openly of her marriage to George IV and the new Court accepted her as his widow.

Minney's brother, Sir George Seymour, joined the party at Steyne House and kept a detailed diary. He and the Dawson-Damers were frequently dining at the Pavilion. So was the Duke of Wellington, and when the King complimented him in an after-dinner speech the Duke sat in respectful silence which Seymour thought showed his good taste. 'A subject should receive a compliment from his Sovereign as a son from his father.'

More endearing, we read that on January 26th 'Mrs. Fitzherbert had a very nice children's Ball when little Blanche [Minney's three-year-old daughter][1] made her début'.

George Seymour paid long visits to Steyne House; he spent the days riding on the Downs with the harriers and evenings playing whist with his dear old hostess. They talked over past and present, material assets which had once mattered seriously seemed less important now and there did not really seem much to worry about. Mrs. Fitzherbert had paid £13,000 for a London house which she gave to the Dawson-Damers and old Lady Caroline had died leaving them Came, a splendid Dorsetshire property.

In May 1831 George Dawson-Damer departed for Tipperary to contest his seat while England quivered over Lord Grey's First Reform Bill.

[1] As Lady Blanche Haygarth, she died in 1916, the last person who remembered seeing Mrs. Fitzherbert.

Minney wrote humorously to her husband of Mrs. Fitz-herbert's partiality for him (May 17th, 1831).

'I cannot help being amused at Mama's little vanity about it. She talks so big of your success & arranges the whole thing *à sa manière tort et à travers*. However her auditors do not know better. She is so gay . . . she is bent on going to the Opera to see Taglioni & has engaged a box with Lady Guildford. Last night I chaperoned Melle d'Este [the Duke of Sussex's daughter, sometimes called "Princess Emma"] at Devonshire House Concert which was much less good than Leopold's as Walesky [Napoleon's son by Marie Waleska] described: *l'impression vous restait d'avoir causé longtemps avec un ennuyeux.* . . . I am told Prince Leopold is much annoyed at the King giving the new Earl [Munster] the Royal Livery.'

There was much bad feeling over the d'Estes; legitimate but illegal children of Sussex, who received no titles while the King's outright bastards collected a variety.

'May 23 1831
Yesterday I dined in Tilney St. where I met the Jerning-hams, Smythes, Mrs. Bruce & Mr. Weld. His reforming ideas do not suit Mama, who though she had no opinion, is I see in her heart very anti-Reformist. . . . Poor d'Este is gone abroad very ill. I think he must feel pretty hurt that Lord Grey, the Duke of Sussex's friend, should not have done something for him, when he has been making Lords & Ladies of the Fitz-clarences.'

'May 25 1831
Minney [aged five] was at the Ball. I saw nothing of His Majesty but the Queen was very amiable & introduced me to her sister who recollected little Minney's animation and figure. . . . At last I lost her & found that for want of a more commodious seat she had popped herself under the railings & seated herself on the Throne, where by-the-by she would look very well, for I think her much more *distinguée* looking than little Victoria.

Mama got quite *tête montée* about your getting in yesterday.
. . . Only think of my dissipation last night at Devonshire
House & there we stayed till three-thirty as the Duke would
make me dance the *Cotillon* with him. . . . There was a variety
of opinions about Fitzclarence's Peerage generally unfavour-
able but however he is gazetted as Earl of Munster, Baron
Tewkesbury, which latter title he chose from merely the circumstance of our having suggested it.'

'June 3 1831
I have done nought except spending the evening in
Tilney St, where Mama is looking as well as possible. . . . I
had a letter from Fitzclarence today from Windsor to give me
an account of the party which he states is heavy: that Lady
Grey looks bored, that the King was much better received
yesterday and that when Lord Grey was cheered & recog-
nised, he with great good taste withdrew from the popular
demonstration & that the Jerseys dined there yesterday. What
an awkward party though, the King is right if he wishes to
make no distinctions. Lord Worcester described the King
speechifying & drinking Lord Grey's health but that the King
did not waken from table till near one o'clock.'

Mrs. Fitzherbert worried about Munster. Although his letters
to Minney had all been full of fun and humour, the old lady wrote:
'I fear you will find him in a state of great excitement which I
regret very much. I hope you may be able to quiet his mind for he
makes himself quite ill with it & I fear & dread the consequences
to him.'
That summer she remained in London. Although Minney
pronounced her un-Reformist, she watched with interest the
efforts of Lord Grey to alter the whole political fabric of England.

'August 21 1831
The town is quiet but at the smallest signal from Lord Grey
is ready to rise. We are in a sad state. God knows what is to
happen. Munster tells me he writes to you every other day
what passes. He is violently unhappy & really has a great
reason to be so. His father is in great good spirits. He does

everything Lord Grey wishes & I am sorry to say is only occupied with dinners & balls. It is quite melancholy! Talleyrand & Montrond appear much more active than any of our people. Talleyrand is certainly the cleverest person in existence.'

Minney toured Ireland with her husband during the remainder of the summer and so missed King William's Coronation. Staying with the Duke of Leinster at Carton, the largest house in Ireland, she wrote:

'August 23 1831

You will perceive from the date we are still here. It is so pleasant & their kindness is beyond anything. . . . Last Saturday they discovered to be our wedding-day so they prepared a little surprise in the shape *of a fête champêtre* & to my not agreeable surprise the Duke & the boys fired a salute under our windows. . . . Only think of our being married six years. Time passes dreadfully quick. One always dreads the future not being as happy as the past & I want no change nor could it be for the better.'

Mrs. Fitzherbert wrote thanking them for the grapes, melon and peaches which reached her from Came and fussed a little:

'Have you read the account of another steam-vessel having been lost near Beaumaris: Promise me, my dearest Minney, that you will not return, either yourself, George or your children by any other than the regular way from Dublin to Holyhead. The number of people that have lost their lives is quite shocking to think of.'

On September 8th the Coronation of William IV took place and next morning both Mrs. Fitzherbert and George Munster wrote to Minney. From Tilney Street came the usual personal gossip:

'Munster came two days before the Coronation. He certainly has the govt flying about him . . . nothing could persuade Her Ladyship to go there. . . . People are quite outrageous

221

with the Duchess of Kent for refusing to come to the Coronation. She has got some bad advisers about her & this refusal
will do her much mischief with the public. . . . I saw nothing
for I had got cold at Chiswick, though we fortunately had a
beautiful day. . . . I have had three dinner invitations from the
Palace & have been obliged to send excuses. You will see an
extraordinary list of Peers. I understand there are to be fifteen
more made to get the majority in the House of Lords. Several
have refused accepting this dignity & several that ought not
from birth or situation are very anxious to be appointed. This
is lowering the Peerage sadly.'

William IV created peers galore to push through the Reform
Bill but still omitted his nephew d'Este.

George Fitzclarence, Earl of Munster, watched his father
crowned and wrote Minney an amusing account:

'September 9 1831
Thank heaven the Coronation is over & for your consolation I can assure you it was an exact repetition of the last, only
the music was feeble, if not bad, & the King's robes only cost
(to George's cost) £1,400 instead of £20,000! I only arrived in
town on Monday & found the Palace & its inmates in a
glorious bustle. But for the rain, a most ridiculous rehearsal
had been ordered for Wednesday. The wall separating the
Kings Mews from Buckingham House garden was pulled
down, & the King was to stand in the garden, & see all the
coaches & horses & footmen in their state-liveries go through
this absurd & childish rehearsal! Fortunately it rained; or so
they tell me, if the State Coach which weighs seven ton, had
once got on the wet turf or gravel, it would have so sunk that
no power under an eighty-horse steamer could have drawn it
back into the stable. The King, however, went over the Abbey
to see the locale, and in so doing caught a cold which showed
itself in a swelled face. As it was his left cheek, no doubt it was
intended providentially in order to offer a larger surface to his
liege lords when they did homage.
All London was on the move at six o'clock & the arrangements for arriving at the Abbey excellent, & no trouble or

222

difficulty arose throughout the day. Lady Munster was ill & could not go, hoping to save herself to dine with the King who had a party of 100 covers. I did not leave my house till half-past nine, trusting to my crimson & gold liveries, which looked magnificent, to make all barriers fly open before me.

The arrangements of the Interior were the same as the last, only there was a second chair—for the Queen, on a stage a step lower than the King's. About 150 Peers & 70 or 80 Peeresses were present & the seats of the latter looked very well, like a parterre of tulips—only the Duchess of St. Albans in the front looked like a full blown peony; the young Duchess of Richmond was next to her, making the contrast still more remarkable. Lady Clanricarde in front looked well & was seated next to Lady Salisbury. All the Peeresses, who had received their Coronets to make honest women of them, were present and it was amusing to see the virtuous women indignant at their neighbourhood. Lady Rosebery was, I hear, seated between two whose past life might be, not questioned, but with truth commented on. Lady Waldegrave, your fair cousin was present.

When the Peers did homage the Duke of Wellington was loudly & spontaneously cheered, which was all very well, as the great Captain of the Age, though contrary to etiquette. But the silly Whigs made it political by cheering Lord Grey and then some fools cheered Brougham & it became ridiculous from the attorney's clerks & sheriffs' officers who had got smuggled into the galleries applauding the Law Lords!

I had not embraced (I find that is the correct expression) the King since my birthday, when ten years old, on which occasion he told me that I was no longer a boy, & that he did not like kissing (I beg pardon) men. He told me he was not at all tired. The sermon of the Bishop of London was good & impressive and had the advantage of only lasting seventeen or eighteen minutes, whereas if you recollect, on the former occasion it detained us near an hour.

The scramble for medals was highly indecorous, very like schoolboys quarrelling at chuck-farthing & fighting for half-pence. Portarlington was on the bench before me. I had my cocked hat in the King's dressing-room & giving my Coronet & Robes to one of his pages, I jumped on my horse and saw the whole Procession on its return. It was a fine sight, but one coach-and-six is so like another coach-and-six that it is after all but a tame affair. Tens of thousands of loyal alias Reforming spectators all very vehement of course. Frederick [his brother] who, I think foolishly had the head of the Procession arranged it well but in his anxiety to be as fine as possible was nearly killed. He had put a Persian bridle on his horse, so heavy with silver that it absolutely dropped off, and he went along Pall Mall & Charing Cross like Johnny Gilpin, till fortunately stopped without accident.

What do you think of his sending Erroll [Lord Erroll had married His Majesty's third daughter] the night before to the King, passing over all his brothers and without saying a word to any of us . . . and asking for the Grand Cross of the Guelph and which the King gave him! and this after I had spontaneously gone to Taylor [Private Secretary] & saying that to prevent difficulties & in order Justice might be done my Brothers they ought only to accept the Grand Cross! Adolphus is very angry. I shall have nothing but the Bath [second most noble British order]. We had a dinner of 100 at the Palace which went off well only the King made some unwise speeches.'

Minney received this & numerous other accounts of Williams's coronation as she journeyed with her husband through Cork and Kerry where they visited the great houses and enjoyed the fair autumn weather. 'I wish you were not so afraid of the sea for I am sure you would be delighted with Killarney & altogether amused by Ireland which seems to me now the quiet part of the world.'

All the letters of this year are crammed with political gossip. Minney is most indignant that Lady Shrewsbury 'who means to cut a great figure' has spread the untrue rumour that Maryanne's Jerningham diamonds are borrowed plumes lent by Mrs. Fitzherbert for Court occasions. 'Is not this truly Cattish?'

Minney kept the entertaining letters she received weekly from Lord Clanricarde and his wife Harriet describing the Reform Bill dramas:

224

'October 10 1831

Harriet being too indolent or tired to write herself has desired me to tell some of the details of the late debate & of the reports that are rife through the Town. Harriet may be excused when you hear that she began at ½ to 3 or 4 every day & sat or stood through the whole of the five nights debate excepting the last two hours of Saturday's morning when she missed the most eloquent (save one) speech that I ever heard, I mean Lord Grey's. There was a delightful re-union below our Bar, from 70 to 90 ladies each night. These were attended by amorous M.P.s and Heirs apparent and were as thick as a Birthday Squeeze. . . .'

'Oct 11

Edward Lord Rokeby is in fine spirits . . . behind the Woolsack he greatly admired the quantity of Port wine (3 bottles) that Brougham drank in the course of his great speech.'

Lady Clanricarde continued the saga of '*les grandes crises*' with descriptions of the speeches:

'Peel's I am told was also excellent but I cannot make a comparison between them for there was something in the kindling enthusiasm of Stanley's manner quite beyond description & which I think proceed from a more generous heart & less cool head than I have ever suspected Peel of possessing. . . . We dined yesterday at Holland House. What odd questions Lady Holland asks. She asked me yesterday before John Ponsonby "whether I had anything on when I went into the Shower Baths?" From an indefinable sense of decency I told a lie and said: oh, yes a great deal. I am glad Mrs. Fitzherbert liked the Bravura.'

Actually Mrs. Fitzherbert was growing tired of the new industrial slum problems.

'I wish that odious Reform Bill was over one way or another. Everybody is worn out with it and it makes Society dreadfully dull. The Town is still very full but no parties, dinners or anything going on. After three excuses to the Palace for not being well, I felt bound not to send a fourth & I dined there on Sunday & really had a very pleasant party. The King is in high form & all the rest in high good humour. Many enquiries after Minney for none of them call you by any other name. I wish I could send you a comfortable account of Munster, who I am sorry to say is huffed with everybody & is exactly in the same state he was in last winter. He tells me his father takes no notice of him. The Queen is jealous . . . etc. Frederick [the King's second son] has hope for the Guelph Order after having, as you know, refused it with great impertinence and contempt. This is another grievance. I feel very angry with Munster at the same time I pity him, for he makes himself quite miserable. The King desires him to go to the Palace whenever he likes, & he did so for some time. Now he says he will not go without an invitation. *Entre nous* I think he is a little wrong in the upper storey.'

'October 21 1831
The King is so entirely at Lord Grey's orders that he has no will of his own. . . . I met the whole family at the Palace the other day. They . . . made many enquiries about you. I was rather disappointed with the Grand Duchess [Helena of Russia], I had heard so much of her beauty. She is certainly pretty & pleasing, & covered with the finest diamonds I ever saw, far superior to our Queen's.

Much as I like Brighton, I feel uncomfortable with respect to the Royalties. That happy family last year at the Pavilion is very different now to what it was then. . . . I am engaged to dine there every Sunday during their stay at Brighton which they told me was not to prevent my dining there the other days of the week. They are all very kind & I feel grateful but you know what it generally is.'

Yes, Minney knew as well as Maria Fitzherbert that life in Hanoverian royal circles tended to become rather a bore.

Twenty-nine

THE last six years of Mrs. Fitzherbert's life flow evenly. There is no twilight. To the end she remains a busy old lady giving parties and arranging visits for the Damers, Jerninghams, Seymours and Smythes. William IV and his Queen Adelaide continued to inundate her with invitations, but the squabbles of His Majesty's sons and sons-in-law put the whole royal family 'in a sad state of confusion' so that she frequently made excuses and then felt guilty. Mrs. Fitzherbert was not one to show ingratitude, especially at a time when the monarchy had become so unpopular and poor King William had to face the Reform Bill.

The country's disturbed state is echoed in Mrs. Fitzherbert's letters which record amazement at the Riots, and complain of endless Reform discussions which spoil general conversation. She had been brought up in the distant eighteenth century to ignore the barbarous lower classes, and though her own servants adored (and indeed bullied) her, the idea of granting power to the uneducated shocked her. Yet she must have felt admiration as well as agitation after the fall of Wellington when Lord Grey, Fox's true successor, formed a Whig Ministry and for fifteen months stood up to the hysterical masses, the furious Tories and outraged Lords. Would that Georgina Devonshire might have risen from the shades to watch her erstwhile lover, now a fearless old man, forcing through the Bill which was to alter England! Mrs. Fitzherbert never moved out of her own eighteenth century and when the people grew unruly she thought the end of the world had come. Indeed, the gentle, brocade-clad old lady proclaimed herself hard hit when Brighton forbade fireworks! 'The horrid Radicals in Brighton would not allow fireworks or illuminations for the King's arrival which has always been done. I am grieved beyond words at the place. Being one of the oldest inhabitants, I cannot bear to see it in the state it is in now.'

King William, portly yet lacking in majesty, certainly had to undergo a trying time. Even his relations grew disrespectful. When he was finally cornered and forced to sign the Bill his vapid cousin the Duke of Gloucester, Minney's half-uncle, transferred his own nickname impertinently asking, 'Who is Silly Billy now?'

Minney, who had always enjoyed the company of George IV, wrote uncharitably to her husband after the heated election of 1832:

'I dined at the Pavilion on Friday. The King (Old Goose in high spirits) did not know who stood for Sussex. . . .

I was cruelly disappointed at finding you did not arrive till New Year's Day & I thought Mama so unkind to be hurt by your delay that I have represented you gouty, so remember & keep up to my assertions. Poor dear Mama is terribly languid . . . the King coming made her feel we would have so little time to ourselves, *mais n'importe* . . . I talked of your gout till I expect to see you lame!'

When cholera flickered through England, Mrs. Fitzherbert moved to Brighton but bade Minney have no fear. The Austrian and Russian ambassadors had both assured her 'this disease confines itself to the lower & dirty poor class of people'.

On November 21st, 1831, Mrs. Fitzherbert casually mentioned that she had heard of the death of Mrs. Jack Smythe—widow of Maryanne's presumed father. Now, however, the Hon. Mrs. Jerningham seemed to have forgotten she had been launched in society as Jack's daughter and she did not turn aside from a hunting trip to attend the funeral. This absolute disregard of her technical mother's death coupled with Mrs. Fitzherbert's reference to Jerningham as a son-in-law—Minney's husband never received this appellation—are the only real pointers to any likelihood that Maryanne might be her own daughter.

The fascinating Journals of the Smythe girls recently discovered and published by a great-great-grandson reveal mingled fondness and irritation for the old aunt in whose house they spent each winter. Louisa Smythe finally accepted a rich suitor, Sir Frederick Hervey-Bathurst, and Aunt Fitz, who had been against the match, reversed her opinion.

Numerous family arrangements were being made by the old lady of Tilney Street to the very end. A Smythe nephew wanted to become a midshipman; she pointed out the 'disagreeable side' but asked George Seymour to place him. Colonel Dawson-Damer contemplated giving up his seat in Parliament to become an equerry—she let the King know; Maryanne's third baby seemed to be dying—she wrote: 'If it please God to take the dear Baby to himself, you, my dearest must exert all your fortitude & submit to his Will.'

The younger generation turned to her in trouble and her thoughts were so occupied by them that often she forgot her own past. It was better so. On March 3rd, 1833, she wrote from Brighton:

'Many thanks, dear Minney, for your letter this morning. The account you give of your conversations with the Duke of Wellington makes me rather nervous. I am not very well, & anything upon *the* subject always annoys me very much. . . .

The exchange of letters is not yet done but I am permitted everything to be settled by Thursday. On Friday I am to see the King, & then I hope I shall be at liberty to depart. The Duke of Wellington & Lord Albemarle are to come to me at twelve o'clock tomorrow morning. I am frightened to death for fear of setting my house on fire, I shall be heartily glad when this business is finished.'

And next day when free to journey to Aix-la-Chapelle to sip the waters she wrote: 'Thank God my mind is relieved by having all the papers except some particular ones committed to the flames.'

From this moment on Mrs. Fitzherbert dismissed the past and her letters are studded with the dramas of 'dear Baby's ninth tooth'. Minney and Maryanne both proved prolific and baby after baby produces tooth after tooth.

In May 1833, while the parents travelled, the old lady took Minney's year-old son to stay at Petworth where Lord Egremont's

229

illegitimate daughter, now Countess of Munster, 'odious as usual', plagued her unhappy husband. Mrs. Fitzherbert informed the Dawson-Damers:

'I arrived in town last night from Petworth & your dear child is quite well. There never was anything behaved so well. He was the admiration of the whole House. I never saw so intelligent a little animal as it is. He walked about the whole House & took such notice of all the fine pictures & statues that you would have been astonished, had you seen him, Lord Egremont took him several times into his own room & swears he must be two or three years old as he never saw anything like him.'

If Mrs. Fitzherbert's maternal instincts had been thwarted in the past now she made up for it, playing the rôle of doting Granny to whole packs of little Dawsons and Jerninghams. To Maryanne she wrote in this her seventy-seventh summer: 'How dull & stupid the house is without you all, particularly little Augustus, who kept us all alive & though I scolded him for the noise of his drums, yet I would give anything to hear them again.'

Minney scorned Baden:

'The French Society here is good but the English what one meets with at Cheltenham, of which the whole place puts me in mind. I am afraid you will find Minney looking very ugly. She has lost her front teeth but Blanche is looking in beauty & very angry she cannot speak German.'

Mrs. Fitzherbert cheers Maryanne with the news that the Brisbanes could

'talk of nothing but their admiration of your little Augustus & laughed heartily at his telling them I had a *Roman Catholic nose*. . . . My house has been quite like a Fair. So many people called yesterday & today that I was quite worn out. We went to a party at the Pavilion last night, two hundred &

fifty people. . . . The King as usual singled me out & stuck by
me all night. The poor Queen so ill with a cold she could
hardly speak. . . .'

That winter she crossed to France and took once again her
apartment in the Hôtel Bristol. Paris appeared gayer than Brighton
these days but even there an unusually dull pair occupied the
throne. As soon as Mrs. Fitzherbert arrived Louis Philippe and
Queen Amélie desired her to go to them:

'Nothing could exceed the kindness of their reception of
me: they are both old acquaintances of mine. I have declined
all their fêtes, and they have given me a general invitation to
go there every evening whenever I like it, in a quiet family
way, which suits me very much. I really think I never saw a
more amiable family; so happy & united. The King seems
worn to death with business all day & all night, but he
assured me that things were going on much better, though
there were a great many people trying to make mischief.
I told him I was afraid he had sent many of them to make
disturbances in our country. He is very much attached to
England & hopes we shall always be friends.'

Minney spent most of the winter with dear Mama and parts of
her letters to George describe the balls and operas they attend together. Dinner at the Tuileries is always 'very dull'. Mrs. Fitzherbert suffered from gout but she could still entertain a younger
generation. Minney wrote:

'December 17 1833
There never was such a constitution! I sat with her in the
dark bedroom, for she had not got out of her bed for 48 hours.
She was very amusing about her younger days & told me it
was the 48th anniversary of her marriage with the King,
December 15, 1785. She says she is not at home & will not
allow she is ill to those who call. . . . There is a ridiculous report that has reached Mama's ears of the King's intention to
prove to the world his respect & feelings towards Mama, that
as she never would accept a Title, to make me for her sake a

231

Baroness in her own right to descend to my son, & this because Mama had no male relation & that I was in consequence nearest to her as the adopted child of the late King, & herself. . . .'

Mrs. Fitzherbert need not have worried about titles for her favourites. By chance Minney's son was to become 4th Earl of Portarlington, George Seymour's son 5th Marquess of Hertford and Maryanne's sons would be the 10th and 11th Lord Staffords.

In the late summer of 1834 she decided to return to England permanently and wrote Minney: 'I should have much pleasure in joining you anywhere you & George might propose but alas! *mes beaux jours sont passés*, & I must make up my mind to my armchair & my fireside. I am not fit for anything else!'

From then on Mrs. Fitzherbert contented herself with travelling around England staying with favourite relations.

On October 12th, 1835, Mrs. Fitzherbert wrote to Minney from Hooton, the country home of her niece Lady Stanley:

'Sir Thomas Stanley braves all wind & weather, which he never allows to stop him from hunting & shooting every day. . . . I had set my mind upon going to see the famous railroad at Liverpool, which is only about seven miles from this place, for although we planned going every day we have never on account of the weather been able to succeed in our wishes.'

Maria Fitzherbert never rode in a train but she actually saw a track! One of her last surviving letters written about seven months before she died, to Maryanne, shows what an eager mind she retained:

'I never was at Baden but at all the other places you mention. I know well & should like to go over them again. You will be delighted with Switzerland. I have been there four times & know every inch of the country. Zurich is charming. . . . I am sure you will be glad to hear dear Minney is quite recovered her confinement. I sincerely hope it will be the last. Four girls & one little boy is quite sufficient.'[1]

[1] It was the last and this baby Constance survived until 1925 when she gave the author a faint impression of that distant lovely lady called Mrs. Fitzherbert.

Meanwhile George Seymour relayed disapproval of the young Princess Victoria. His doctor 'has no opinion of the Duchess of Kent's abilities or of her daughter's . . . the latter never sees those of her own associates & is educated as if her capacity was as remarkable as her own station'. And Munster's behaviour grew more worrying: 'His manner contradicted his intention of behaving better to the King.' Yet he was kind when Mrs. Fitzherbert wanted help for an illegitimate relative. She wrote on October 2nd, 1836:

'I am sure you will be glad to hear I have at last persuaded Henry Smythe to accept a most excellent situation with a Salary of £200 per ann. He seems delighted with it, as the fair Lady he wanted to marry has consistently refused his offers. He has been nearly four years trying what *his beautiful appearance* would do & has unfortunately found no one so in love with him as he is with himself. I hope however he will do well. It is a situation many have been anxious to obtain. Lord Munster has been kind enough to get it to me.'

Princess Augusta, George III's second daughter and now a spinster in her sixties, remained one of Mrs. Fitzherbert's most affectionate old acquaintances. When in London the Princess frequently asked her sister-in-law to dine 'in my comfortable pretty little Den', in St. James's Palace. They had shared four decades of royal rows. Now their gossip sometimes pertained to the turmoils of industrial England, but more often they enjoyed the scandals and witticisms of the live world relayed by Minney and George. Mrs. Fitzherbert's feelings towards her old enemy Fox had mellowed. She could laugh when the Damers recounted a conversation between Talleyrand and Lord Brougham. Talleyrand thought that among other activities Fox had enjoyed a love affair with the great actress Mrs. Siddons. Brougham shook his head: 'That would resemble a love affair with the Ocean.'

Mrs. Fitzherbert spent the winter of 1836 at Steyne House. Along the roads where she had once nimbly handled a single fast horse now a large barouche drew her out for air, and Brightonians proudly saluted her footmen in royal livery. As always she visited the Church of St. John the Baptist once a week for confession. At her hour the church was closed to all except a young charwoman whom the priest instructed to drop a deep curtsy to the mysterious veiled lady 'for maybe it was the Queen of England & maybe not'.[1]

Mrs. Fitzherbert knew the time had come to settle mundane affairs. She sent George an inventory of her plate which he was to distribute after selecting the pieces he and Minney desired. She made a sensible detailed Will providing for her servants. To Minney and Maryanne went all her jewellery. In Minney's hands she placed a miniature of the Duke of Kent, given her by old Queen Charlotte, and a bundle of Kent's letters. These she requested Minney to give to his daughter Victoria. (The old lady never realized how strongly the young Princess hated the Fitzherbert story with its rumours of children born in wedlock.)

Mrs. Fitzherbert spent her last Christmas at Brighton. In March 1837 she arranged to visit the Dawson-Damers in Dorset and they were planning a gay Easter at Came when news arrived that the woman who had been the mainspring of their lives for so many years had collapsed. Minney and George drove hurriedly across England and Maryanne set out from Norfolk. Mrs. Fitzherbert died on Easter Monday fortified by the last rites of her Church. Though she had often suggested that eighty-one years is too long on earth those she left wept bitterly as if a young person had departed from their midst. Minney's heartbroken letters reiterate the beauty of her face in death.

Maria Fitzherbert, who never broke her word, lies buried in her Catholic church in Brighton with three wedding rings carved on the stone finger of her effigy.

The charwoman survived until 1900 when she related this to the parish priest.

Envoi

None of the younger people whom Mrs. Fitzherbert loved so dearly lived into old age. George Dawson-Damer died in 1856 before inheriting his brother's earldom. Minney died even earlier, in 1847, at the age of forty-nine. Yet this gave her time to impress on her twelve-year-old daughter Constance how charming a person Mrs. Fitzherbert must have been. And in her turn Constance, who lived to be nearly ninety, could transmit something of that far-off human story to her great-grandchildren. Maryanne died in 1848.

George Fitzclarence, Earl of Munster, shot himself in March 1842. He worshipped Minney to the end, and before committing suicide he ordered a clock specially made for her in Paris. Her name and her birth-date are engraved on the face to represent the hours, around the clock itself coils the serpent of eternity, while rosemary for remembrance surmounted by enamel forget-me-nots states firmly what he never dared to say right out.

This clock, his last gift, he arranged should be delivered to her on her birthday, November 23rd, eight months after his death.

It looks down on me as I write these last pages, so perfectly fashioned, so wistfully devised—a reminder of almost forgotten loves and griefs.

Bibliography

1806   The Patriots Review of Mr. Jeffrey's Pamphlet reflecting the conduct of the Prince of Wales.

1831   *Memoirs of George the Fourth.* Robert Huish.

1856   *Memoirs of Mrs. Fitzherbert* with an account of her marriage with H.R.H. The Prince of Wales, by the Hon. Charles Langdale.

1903   *The Creevey Papers* (1768-1838), edited by Sir Herbert Maxwell, Bt. (John Murray).

1905   *Mrs. Fitzherbert and George IV.* W. H. Wilkins (Longmans Green).

1930   *Queen Caroline.* Sir Edward Parry (Ernest Benn).

1933   *Royal Dukes.* Roger Fulford (Duckworth).

1935   *Brighton.* Sir Osbert Sitwell and Margaret Barton (Faber & Faber).

1939   *Mrs. Fitzherbert,* A Life chiefly from unpublished sources. Shane Leslie (Burns, Oates & Washbourne).

1940   *Letters of Mrs. Fitzherbert,* edited by Shane Leslie (Burns, Oates & Washbourne).

1955   *Georgina, Duchess of Devonshire.* Earl of Bessborough (John Murray).

1958   *The Prettiest Girl in England.* The Love Story of Mrs. Fitzherbert's niece, from journals edited by Richard Buckle (John Murray).

Brighton Gazette.

Sussex Advertiser.

Morning Post.

Index

237

238